THE STAUFFER SYMPOSIUM ON APPLIED PSYCHOLOGY AT THE CLAREMONT COLLEGES

This series of volumes highlight important new developments on the leading edge of applied psychology. Each volume focuses on one area in which psychological knowledge is being applied to the resolution of social problems. Within that area, a distinguished group of authorities present chapters summarizing recent theoretical views or empirical findings, including the results of their own research and applied activities. An introductory chapter frames the material, pointing out common themes and varied areas of practical applications. Thus, each volume brings together trenchant new ideas, research results, and fruitful applications bearing on an area of current social interest. The volumes will be of value not only to practitioners and researchers, but also to students and lay people interested in this vital and expanding area of psychology.

Series books published by Lawrence Erlbaum Associates:

- *Reducing Prejudice and Discrimination*, edited by Stuart Oskamp (2000).

- *Mass Media and Drug Prevention: Classic and Contemporary Theories and Research*, edited by William D. Crano and Michael Burgoon (2002).

- *Evaluating Social Programs and Problems: Visions for the New Millennium*, edited by Stewart I. Donaldson and Michael Scriven (2002).

Evaluating Social Programs and Problems
Visions for the New Millennium

Edited by

Stewart I. Donaldson
Michael Scriven
Claremont Graduate University

The Stauffer Symposium on
Applied Psychology at the Claremont Colleges

LEA LAWRENCE ERLBAUM ASSOCIATES, PUBLISHERS
2003   Mahwah, New Jersey   London

Lawrence Erlbaum Associates, Inc., Publishers
10 Industrial Avenue
Mahwah, NJ 07430

Cover design by Kathryn Houghtaling Lacey

Library of Congress Cataloging-in-Publication Data

Evaluating Social Programs and Problems: Visions for the New Millennium;
edited by Stewart I. Donaldson and Michael Scriven

Includes bibliographical references and index.

ISBN 0-8058-4184-9 (cloth : alk. paper); ISBN 0-8058-4185-7 (pbk. : alk. paper)

Copyright information for this volume can be obtained by contacting the Library of Congress.

Printed in the United States of America
10 9 8 7 6 5 4 3 2 1

Dedication

To Michelle and Mary Anne for all your love
and support, and for understanding our tireless
pursuit of ghosts and dragons in exotic domains

A special thanks to the contributors and many
other colleagues, and students at home in
Claremont Graduate University and abroad,
for support that made the impossible possible

CONTENTS

Preface

Evaluation appears to be in a second major boom period in its rather short history. For example, in 1990 there were about five major evaluation professional associations, whereas today there are nearly 40 worldwide. It is clear that the most important work of evaluators in the 21st century will be to evaluate social programs designed to prevent and ameliorate social problems that threaten the well being of children, adolescents, substantial portions of the world's adult populations, and the elderly. This work will inevitably be carried out in a wide range of settings, including schools, communities, and non-profit and for-profit organizations of many shapes and sizes.

This volume intends to provide some visions and agenda items for this undertaking. Drawing on the knowledge and experience of some of the most well-traveled and well-known evaluators in the world today, it incorporates "bleeding-edge" perspectives on evaluation as a transdiscipline, results-oriented management, empowerment evaluation, fourth-generation evaluation, inclusive evaluation, theory-driven evaluation, cultural competency in evaluation, and frameworks for integrating diverse visions for evaluation. We hope this book will be of value to practicing evaluators grappling with the challenges of providing valid and useful evaluations in an increasingly complex, diverse, high-tech, and global landscape, as well as evaluators-in-training, scholars, teachers of evaluation and research methods, and other professionals interested in how to improve social problem-solving efforts in the new millennium.

The editors of this volume would first like to express abundant gratitude to the Stauffer Symposium Coordinator, Katrina Bledsoe, and her team of Claremont Graduate University graduate students—Thomas Andry, Heather Campbell, Susie Cervantez, Kelly Fischbein, Cindy Gilbert, Marycarmen Kunicki, Stuart Jordan, and Theodore Joseph—for organizing and managing a top-rate symposium. Special thanks to Stuart

Oskamp for developing the Claremont Symposium series and running many successful predecessors.

We appreciate the encouragement and support of Mark Costanzo, Claremont McKenna College, Dale Berger, and President Steadman Upham of Claremont Graduate University. Thanks to Christy Ballweber for all her efforts to make this volume camera-ready for Lawrence Erlbaum Associates, and to Mary Anne Craft for outstanding copyediting support. Finally, the size and scope of this symposium would not have been possible without the generous gift provided by the John Stauffer Charitable Trust to the School of Behavioral and Organizational Sciences, Claremont Graduate University, use of the facilities and a grant from Claremont McKenna College, and the additional support we received from our associate sponsors including Harvey Mudd College, Pitzer College, Pomona College, and Scripps College. A hearty "thank you" to our primary and associate sponsors for supporting this effort to improve social problem-solving and to inspire a brighter future in the new millennium!

Stewart I. Donaldson
Michael Scriven
Claremont, California

I

INTRODUCTION

1

Diverse Visions for Evaluation in the New Millennium: Should We Integrate or Embrace Diversity?

Stewart I. Donaldson
Michael Scriven
Claremont Graduate University

INTRODUCTION

On February 24th, 2001, the earth stopped spinning and time stood still. At least it seemed that way to some of the more than 300 participants of the Stauffer Symposium on Applied Psychology at the Claremont Colleges in southern California. They came from near and far to hear world-renowned evaluators articulate their visions of how we should evaluate social programs and solve social problems in the 21st century. The format was highly interactive and included six visions for the new millennium, five reactions talks in response to the vision presentations, brief responses by the visionaries to the reactors, and a facilitated discussion with the large and vocal audience. Footprints from this rich, dynamic, vibrant, and sometimes contentious discourse appear in some detail in this volume.

Why did so many venture to the Claremont Colleges on that wet winter day? After all, it was Saturday, considered a "holy day" on the academic calendar, and at least some of the participants must have had a life outside of work. As we peered into the full auditorium, and then at the large monitor that showed an overflow of participants seated in the teleconference classroom next door, we found ourselves asking what it was about this gathering that had brought us all together. What was our common ground?

Let us begin by sharing a few thoughts on our responses to these questions. The previous summer an author of this chapter traveled to the

International Conference on Evaluation for Practice, in Huddersfield, England. It was a stimulating and successful conference, and the return trip included a visit to one of London's newest attractions at the time, the Millennium Dome. The Dome is a museum of the future with thought-provoking exhibits focusing on:

- The Body
- The Mind
- Communication
- Transportation
- Our Home Planet
- Shared Ground—Neighborhoods and Communities
- Learning
- Money
- Leisure
- Work and Worklife in the New Millennium

One striking statistic appropriately adorning a clock was, "The average person works 100,000 hours in her or his lifetime." We assume that most of the symposium participants probably register quite a bit above average on this statistic.

This leads to the question of what these many hours of a human lifetime consist of. A cursory occupational analysis suggests that for most Americans, it is the pursuit of profit for a corporation, organization, or small enterprise. That is, the majority of these working hours involve applying one's education, skills, intellectual and physical energy toward ultimately making a profit—most often for someone else.

In contrast, the presenters at this symposium and we expect, most of the participants in the audience, spent much of their time helping to prevent and alleviate social problems that stunted the development of our children, troubled our adolescents, and compromised the quality of life of working adults and the elderly. This focus on the betterment of human lives and society was what we believed to be our common ground.

The vision presenters and reaction panel members devoted, and will continue to devote, much of their careers—their 100,000+ working hours, their advanced education and intellectual talents—not in selling products or corporate profit seeking, but in helping the less fortunate members of our society through research and implementation of social programs that targeted such issues as:

- Inequality—removing barriers to educational, occupational, and economic achievement.
- Reducing prejudice and discrimination.
- Terror, crime, and violence prevention.
- Curbing child and domestic abuse.
- Alcohol and drug abuse treatment and prevention.
- HIV prevention.
- Creating access to health care for the underserved.
- Improving mental health services.
- Preventing and reducing homelessness.
- Positive welfare reform.
- Reducing under and unemployment.

Unfortunately, the list of social problems we could face in the 21st century could expand in unpredictable directions.

There were no exhibits on social problems and programs at the Millennium Dome in London--a bit too heavy an issue for a family attraction, perhaps. In Claremont, California, however, on that chilly Saturday, we created content for such an exhibit. Much of what follows in this volume adds flesh to the "template for a better future" that emerged from our deliberations.

VISIONS FOR THE NEW MILLENNIUM

Rather than following a conventional format of assembling experts for the symposium with similar and complementary views that would reinforce an easily digestible and coherent vision or theme, we deliberately invited evaluators from diverse, sometimes rival, backgrounds, and from a range of primary disciplines, across a wide expanse of social program and evaluation settings. Although, as predicted, there appeared to be a reasonable amount of agreement about what we needed to strive for in the new millennium (i.e., more effective social programs), there were clearly fundamental differences expressed about how to get there. The open expression and lively debates about these different views and visions was what seemed to make this symposium unique and special.

It is our hope that we have captured enough of this lively discourse and passion for solving social problems, that the symposium and this book will become known and remembered for its contributions, and possibly as one of the treasures in the history of social program evaluation. So please sit back, fasten your seat belt, and enjoy the ride—however bumpy it may become, as you read about diverse visions for how we should (not how we might) evaluate social programs and problems in the new millennium.

Evaluation as a Transdiscipline

Michael Scriven opened the morning session by articulating his imagined and hoped-for future for the "discipline of evaluation." He hoped to see a profound transformation of the social sciences in the next millennium. Part of this paradigm shift involved the universal recognition of evaluation as a discipline with clear definition, subject matter, logical structure, and multiple fields of application (e.g., program, personnel, and product evaluation). More specifically, he wanted evaluation to become recognized as one of the elite group of disciplines that he called *transdisciplines*. These were unique in that they supplied essential tools for other disciplines, while retaining an autonomous structure and research effort of their own.

In chapter 2, Scriven argues that the transdisciplinary view of evaluation would revolutionize the application of social sciences to social problems. He believes that the new millennium schools of social science will divide themselves into progressive, evaluation-enriched schools, and into conservative, evaluation-impaired schools. This caveat signals Deans, Chairs, Faculty, and other leaders in the social sciences that if they continue to follow the conventional applied social science track, they will gradually *wither on the vine, with their aging adherents exchanging stories about the good old days*. However, those who move now toward becoming evaluation-enriched, will become the winners of nearly all bids for separating solutions from nonsolutions of social problems. Scriven goes on to outline what is needed to realize his vision, and provides us with a list of the missing elements in the conventional applied social science repertoire (i.e., "The Something More List").

Results-Oriented Management

Joseph S. Wholey focused his remarks on how to use evaluation to improve performance and accountability in public and nonprofit organizations. He pointed out that throughout the world social programs often fell short of their goals, failed to meet public needs and to earn public support, and that some programs were even harmful. He argued persuasively that results-oriented management was a new approach that promised to reform social programming in the public and not-for-profit sectors.

In chapter 3 of this volume, the reader will find Wholey's vision of how to implement results-oriented management. He presents a three-step process that includes (a) developing agreement among key stakeholders on goals and strategies; (b) measuring and evaluating performance outcomes on a regular basis, and; (c) using performance information to improve program effectiveness and strengthen accountability to key stakeholders and the public. This approach dictates that evaluators should interact with stakeholders as part of the strategic planning process, the processes of developing performance measurement systems and reporting on performance, and in using performance measurement and evaluation information. In general, we might describe this vision as advocating a participatory evaluation approach, which focuses primarily on internal evaluation but also identifies places for external evaluation. Wholey concludes the chapter by discussing the increasing demand for program evaluation skills, the mutually reinforcing roles for performance measurement, evaluation, as well as progress, problems and the next steps for his vision of how we should evaluate social programs in the new millennium.

Empowerment Evaluation

David Fetterman's vision offered a simple, logical, and systematic approach to facilitating self-evaluation. His brand of evaluation was designed to help people help themselves. He argued that we should use evaluation concepts, techniques, and findings to foster improvement and self-determination and help stakeholders improve their own programs using a form of self-evaluation and critical reflection. The role of the evaluator in the new millennium should be that of a facilitator, coach, critical friend, and knowledgeable colleague with evaluation expertise, rather than simply a judge. Fetterman advocated using innovative and traditional quantitative and qualitative social science research methods. His view differed from that of others in that he puts these tools in the hands of program sponsors, staff members, and participants, and uses the assistance and guidance of professional evaluators. Finally, he warned against methodological overkill, and recommended using the simplest methods needed for the task at hand.

Fetterman's empowerment evaluation vision and approach is described in some detail in chapter 4. For example, he outlines three steps involved in helping others learn to evaluate their own programs: (a) developing a mission, vision, or unifying purpose; (b) taking stock or determining where the program stands, including strengths and weaknesses; and (c) planning for the future by establishing goals and helping participants determine their own strategies to accomplish program goals and objectives. He argues that the entire process creates an implicit logic model or program theory, and demonstrates how there is nothing as practical as a good theory of action, especially one grounded in participants' own experiences. He underscores that empowerment evaluation is a collaborative group activity, not an individual pursuit. "An evaluator does not and cannot empower anyone; people empower themselves, often with assistance and coaching." Finally, he concludes by identifying one defining characteristic of empowerment evaluation that sets it apart from many other forms of evaluation, namely that the empowerment evaluator "passes the baton to the stakeholders or the orchestra."

Fourth Generation Evaluation

Yvonna Lincoln presented a vision that argued for the value of fourth-generation evaluation as described by Guba and Lincoln (1989), in contrast to views promoted by untutored critics. She argued persuasively that fourth-generation evaluation was the approach to take in the new millennium and is based on the understanding that what is commonly called *scientific truth* only represents ideological claims, advanced within political regimes of power within the academy and in evaluation practice. Grounded in relativist ontology, monist (subjectivist) epistemology, and interpretive anthropology, fourth-generation evaluation strives to redress power imbalances and expands the repertoire of legitimate data-gathering and analytic methods for evaluation practice. Contrary to common belief, Lincoln argued that fourth-generation evaluation has never rejected conventional methods of knowing, and has always advocated using quantitative methods as well as naturalistic inquiry.

In chapter 5, Lincoln connects five powerful social forces to the use of fourth-generation evaluation. She argues that postmodernism, the interpretive turn, identity politics, globalization, and the postcolonial critique are powerful historical movements which will not go away. She warns that our only hope as evaluation practitioners is to "choose models-or adapt those which exist-which exhibit contemporary mindsets, and practice them with integrity and cultural and political respect." Finally, she explains why fourth-generation evaluation, and the closely related inclusive evaluation vision (Mertens, chapter 6 this volume) contain the evaluation models that should be used, or adapted, to improve the evaluation of social programs in the new millennium.

Inclusive Evaluation

Donna Mertens presented a vision that included those community members who would be affected in the methodological decisions governing the conduct of the evaluation. She advocated emphasizing deliberate inclusiveness of groups that have historically experienced oppression and discrimination on the basis of gender, culture, economic levels, ethnicities/races, sexual orientation, and disabilities, with a conscious effort to build a link between the results of the evaluation and social action. To this end, the inclusive evaluator attempts to redress power imbalances in society by including all relevant stakeholders in a way that was authentic and that accurately represented the stakeholders' viewpoints. Furthermore, she argued that inclusive evaluators must be cognizant of issues of social justice that are operating in society and impact the definition of social problems. For example, they must be wary of the deficit models that place the blame for social problems in the individual or culture, rather than in the societal response to the individual or cultural group.

In chapter 6, Mertens explores the territory between the need for inclusion in response to the pressures for pluralism, and the role of the evaluator in creating social change. She argues that the growing need to represent multiple perspectives within the political context has and will continue to pave the way for an inclusive approach to evaluation. She carefully describes the transformative-emancipatory paradigm, which provides the foundation for inclusive evaluation, and assumes that all knowledge reflects power and social relationships within society. That is, Mertens and other transformative scholars reject the position that knowledge is neutral and untainted by human interests.

Mertens then goes on to illustrate how this theoretical foundation has implications for every step in evaluation practice (e.g., problem definition, study design, selection of indicators for success, sampling and data collection decisions, addressing power differentials, and setting standards). In her vision, the role of the evaluator is to proactively rectify the factors that support social injustice. This is accomplished by explicitly challenging the status quo in terms of the seeming intransigence of social problems, by raising questions about the inferred inadequacy of social interventions, and by adopting a stance that is conducive to uncovering the variables that contribute to these social problems and to their solutions.

Theory-Driven Program Evaluation

Stewart Donaldson gave the final vision presentation of the morning. Reflecting on analyses and interpretations of the data and lessons learned from the past three decades of social programming, Donaldson identified five key problems currently limiting social problem solving through social intervention: (a) inadequate program conceptualization, (b) poor program implementation, (c) insensitive program evaluation, (d) poor stakeholder evaluator relations, and (e) barriers that prevented cumulative knowledge and wisdom. He argued theory-driven program evaluation, a contingency perspective of evaluation matching evaluation approaches and methods with situational demands and practical constraints, was well-positioned to help overcome these problems and improve social problem solving in the new millennium.

After presenting a brief overview of the theory-driven evaluation process and several recent examples from the literature, he illustrated how to conduct theory-driven evaluation so that it was flexible and feasible across evaluation settings, empowered stakeholders, offered inclusiveness, maximized design sensitivity, enhanced the validity of evaluation conclusions, improved social programs, and contributed to the cumulative knowledge base about social problem solving.

In chapter 7, Donaldson shows how theory-driven program evaluation promises to close the gap between the current state of affairs in social programming, and his vision of a more desirable state where most social programs are (a) well-designed and based on sound theory and research, (b) implemented with high fidelity, (c) evaluated in a manner that minimizes the chances of design sensitivity and validity errors, (d) evaluated in a way that empowers stakeholder to use the findings to continuously improve their efforts, and (e) evaluated so that cumulative knowledge and wisdom about social programming is advanced.

Because this approach acknowledges that some evaluation approaches and methods work well under some circumstances but fail miserably under others, a key role for the theory-driven evaluator is to develop a thorough understanding of the social problem, program, and implementation context (i.e., develop program theory), before deciding, in collaboration with stakeholders, which evaluation questions to answer and which methods to use to answer those questions. Finally, Donaldson provides evidence that theory-driven evaluation has gained considerable momentum in recent years, and is, or is quickly becoming, considered the "state-of-the art" approach in many social program domains.

REACTIONS AND ALTERNATIVE VISIONS

After lunch, a new panel of evaluators assembled on stage to share their reactions to the morning vision presentations. Some panelists also chose to provide alternative visions for how social programs and problems should be evaluated in the new millennium. The morning vision presenters were subsequently given an opportunity to respond to comments and critiques of their positions. Finally, the morning vision presenters and those serving in the reactor role sat on stage together fielding audience questions and discussing similarities and differences between the various perspectives. A brief summary of panelists reactions and a preview of their corresponding reaction chapter is provided below.

Social Experimentation

Thomas D. Cook opened the afternoon session by admitting that he was going to cheat a little and give his vision for evaluation rather than respond directly to the six visions presented in the morning. However, he told the audience that he hoped they would detect in one part of his talk, a critical analysis of what was said earlier. Although the vision presenters were not hit on the head, they were critiqued slyly and elusively.

As an evaluation scholar and practitioner, Cook began by describing, "the planet on which he lives as an evaluator." After discussing in some detail three large federally funded social experiments in which he is currently engaged (e.g., the Moving to Opportunity project, the analysis of Head Start data), he implied that the visions presented earlier did not resonate with his views and experiences as an evaluator. Our interpretation of his message was that experimental and quasi-experimental designs are still the approach of choice for determining the impact of social programs.

Cook and others (Cook & Campbell, 1979; Crano, this chapter 8 this volume; Lipsey & Cordray, 2000; Shadish, Cook, & Campbell, 2001) continue to argue that the experimental paradigm is superior to rival alternatives for providing scientifically credible evidence about the effects of social programs. Some of the lessons he presented from his evaluation projects suggested that random assignment and social experiments were feasible and ethical despite common criticisms to the contrary. Further, he seemed to believe that random experiments were still the best way to rule out threats to validity and were therefore superior to known alternatives for evaluating social programs.

Unfortunately, we encountered technical difficulties while recording Cook's talk which prevented our providing him a written transcript as we had promised. Consequently, there is no corresponding chapter to his oral presentation in this volume as there is for the other panelists' presentations. We sincerely regret this omission.

Theory-Driven Evaluation and Construct Validity

William Crano opened his remarks by acknowledging the short history of social program evaluation and two of the most powerful voices since its inception, Michael Scriven and Donald Campbell. He noted that while Campbell was not there in body, his reaction to the morning presentations would demonstrate that he was there in spirit. Crano noted that aspects of the theory-driven evaluation approach, whether described that way or not by the presenters, seemed to cut across many of the morning vision presentations. Therefore, he chose to focus his reaction on what he called the "theory-driven movement in evaluation research."

In chapter 8, Crano describes why he is both happy and distracted when he reads about theory-driven evaluation. On the up side, he believes the field is finally on track and he is impressed with the tie-in to some of the best methodological work for field settings. However, he reports that he is distracted because he believes that users of this approach could do more, and act more quickly, to adopt the methods that have been established over the past century for developing and enhancing construct validity. Crano closes the chapter by making us aware that there is a wealth of methodological work, particularly on construct validity, that could dramatically help evaluators to improve how they evaluate social programs and problems in the new millennium.

Diverse Evaluators for Diverse Communities

Edith P. Thomas reacted directly to most of the morning presentations, noting what she thought were virtues and challenges for the various visions. She also shared her strong feelings about the need for evaluators to assist communities and individuals to improve their quality of life. Thomas argued that many of the underlying shortcomings of past efforts were not methodological but substantive issues related to issues of racial and ethnic diversity that were often the cause of failures in social program evaluation.

In chapter 9, Thomas summarizes her thoughts about most of the morning vision presentations. In addition, she shares her views about what is needed to improve the competencies of evaluators in the new millennium. For example, she said that the press for evaluators of color, for feminists, and for those competent to serve racially, culturally, and linguistically diverse communities will substantially increase as these communities assume a population majority in the ensuing years.

Thomas stated that in order to deal with increasing diversity and the redistribution of power in changing communities, evaluators with multiple perspectives on evaluation with a transformative and empowerment agenda would likely thrive. In closing, she acknowledges that the creative tension between qualitative and quantitative approaches in evaluation will continue to be fertile ground for intellectual exchange in the 21st century and beyond.

Culturally Competent Evaluation

After providing some brief remarks about the morning vision presentations, Bianca Guzman focused her reaction on the issue of how to conduct culturally competent evaluations of social programs. Guzman pointed out societal trends that suggest the need for increased cultural sensitivity in the increasingly multicultural and multiethnic society of the new millennium. She concluded by suggesting promising directions for training evaluators how to be culturally competent in their efforts to evaluate social programs and problems.

Guzman provides a framework in chapter 10 intended to help evaluators of social programs establish cultural competency in their work. Consistent with the views of Lincoln (chapter 5, this volume), Mertens (chapter 6, this volume), and Thomas (chapter 9, this volume), she argues that evaluation should serve a social justice function, and that the evaluation process has the potential for being a social justice agent. She observes that traditional training causes evaluators to believe evaluation is about thinking or discovering, but not feeling.

Guzman discusses how the emotions of participants and evaluators must be acknowledged and become part of the culturally competent evaluation process. Although in her experience, there is no universal definition of culture, she holds to four characteristics shared by existing definitions, which are: (1) culture is an abstract, human-made idea; (2) culture is a context or setting within which behavior occurs, is shaped, and transformed; (3) culture is containing of values, beliefs, attitudes and languages that have emerged as adaptations; and (4) culture is important enough to be passed on to other generations. Finally, she discusses how these four characteristics are relevant to cultural competency and how evaluators should develop protocols that ensure culturally competent evaluation of social programs and problems in the new millennium.

Toward an Integrative View

Melvin Mark was the designated clean-up hitter. As the last presenter of the day, he offered some selected observations about many of the diverse visions that had been expressed throughout the proceedings. A main theme in his remarks was a concern that most visions seemed to give a central place to one evaluation approach in the new millennium. He discussed some possible explanations for this apparent over-advocacy, and offered his own vision of how to integrate the diverse visions for the future of evaluating social programs and programs.

In chapter 11, Mark tries to sort out thoughtful portrayals of a desired future from some of the more nightmarish possibilities. After critiquing each vision, he asks how big a place the vision or approach deserves in the toolkit of evaluation, and under what conditions it is most appropriate. He observes some general themes across the visions that suggest whatever peace has been achieved in the so-called paradigm wars, is an uneasy peace. For example, stakeholder inclusion is an issue that remains hot in the debate about appropriate evaluation practice.

Advocating the integration of diverse approaches, he finds it ironic that "evaluators who espouse inclusion, empowerment, and participation would like to exclude and disempower, and see no participation by evaluators who hold different views." Finally, he discusses how to develop, use, and refine a higher order framework to guide decisions about which approach to use contingent upon the particular evaluation context.

IMPROVING EVALUATION THEORY: INTEGRATION OR EMBRACING DIVERSITY?

We believe the highly interactive format of symposium was a success. It seemed to push the presenters as well as the audience to new heights in terms of understanding where the field is going, the similarities and differences among some of the more popular evaluation approaches, and to provide new ideas and visions about improving the evaluation of social programs and problems in the new millennium.

It seems natural and has been common in the short history of program evaluation for those interested in evaluation theory to seek closure. Frustrations over diverse and sometimes inconsistent approaches seem to motivate the pursuit of higher order frameworks or integrative theories. Mark (chapter 11, this volume) argues persuasively the value of this approach for improving evaluation theory in the new millennium.

Another approach that might be considered to achieve peace and a productive future for the field of evaluation, is to recognize and embrace the differences or diversity of evaluators and evaluation approaches. There is a smorgasbord of options in evaluation, some containing fundamental differences that cannot be reconciled or integrated, and choosing one approach can preclude the use of another.

Similarly, evaluator characteristics may inspire or constrain one's ability to practice any particular approach. As suggested by Donaldson (chapter 7, this volume) and Lincoln (chapter 5, this volume), there can be great value in learning an approach from those who have practiced it extensively, in contrast to critics of the approach (who are usually advocates for another approach) or those who try to integrate the approach into a higher order framework without having close familiarity with the nuances of practice.

Perhaps the strongest argument for embracing diversity over integration is that integrators and their colleagues and followers, and scholars and teachers of evaluation who are not heavily involved in practice, typically are the ones most likely to accept the new integrative framework. That is, most attempts to integrate diverse visions into higher order frameworks create winners and losers (e.g., Shadish, Cook, & Levition, 1991; Stufflebeam, 2001), and many of the original evaluation theorists and practicing evaluators may come to view the integration as self-serving or biased. For example, many of the visions presented in this volume and previous attempts to integrate evaluation approaches (e.g., Rossi, Freeman, & Lipsey, 1999; Shadish, Cook, & Levition, 1991) suggest the value of program theory and theory-driven evaluation. In contrast, Stufflebeam (2001) dismisses it as a viable model or evaluation approach in his recent attempt at integrating evaluation models. Furthermore, we think it is safe to say that the diverse visionaries at this conference would come up with very different integrative frameworks if they were asked to perform this task.

Finally, it would be a real loss if the impact of this volume was limited to evaluation theory. Although sometimes implicit, the chapters that follow also have important implications for practice and training in the new millennium. As you read the visions presented, in this volume, we urge you to think about what it would take to become well trained to effectively practice a particular approach. More broadly, you might consider if and how graduate programs in evaluation would be structured differently if they adopted one (or two) of the visions, an integrative view, an embracing diversity perspective, or some other broad perspective on the field of evaluating social programs and problems.

CONCLUSION

This symposium and volume aspired to facilitate the expression of some of the most innovative, sound, and state-of-the-art thinking about how to evaluate social programs and problems. As you will discover in the following chapters, we appear to have created an environment and process that has allowed diverse voices in evaluation to feel safe and comfortable while freely discussing their visions. We are hopeful that this effort will serve as a model for future interactions between those with different views about evaluation, and that the content in the chapters that follow will substantially improve our chances of preventing and solving the social problems confronting us in the new millennium.

REFERENCES

Cook, T. D., & Campbell, D. T. (1979). *Quasi-experimentation: Design and analysis issues for field settings*. Skokie, IL: Rand MaNally.

Guba, E. G., & Lincoln, Y. S. (1989). *Fourth generation evaluation*. Thousand Oaks, CA: Sage.

Lipsey, M. W., & Cordray, D. S. (2000). Evaluation methods for social intervention. *Annual Review of Psychology, 51*, 345-375.

Rossi, P. H., Freeman, H. E., & Lipsey, M. W. (1999). *Evaluation: A systematic approach* (6th Ed.). Thousand Oaks, CA: Sage.

Shadish, W. R., Cook, T. D., & Campbell, D. T. (2001). *Experimental and quasi-experimental designs for generalized causal inference*. Boston: Houghton-Mifflin.

Stufflebeam, D. L. (Ed.) (2001). *Evaluation models* (New Directions for Evaluation, No. 89). San Francisco: Jossey-Bass.

II

VISIONS FOR EVALUATING SOCIAL
PROGRAMS AND PROBLEMS

2
Evaluation in the New Millennium: The Transdisciplinary Vision

Michael Scriven

Claremont Graduate University

A vision in the sense here is an imagined and hoped-for future—an aspiration—not a hard-money prediction of what will actually occur. My vision for the future of evaluation has several components, some of which coincide with my expectations but many of which do not. On this occasion, we're allowed to dream, and hence perhaps by dreaming to nudge the future a little nearer to our dreams. I shall first talk about the discipline of evaluation, by contrast with the practice of evaluation, as we distinguish the discipline of jurisprudence or medicine or pedagogy by contrast with the common practice of it.

1. First, I hope—and, in this case, expect—that the essential nature of evaluation itself will crystallize in our minds into a clear and essentially universal recognition of it as a discipline, a discipline with a clear definition, subject matter, logical structure, and multiple fields of application. In particular, it will, I think, become recognized as one of that elite group of disciplines which I call *transdisciplines* (using this term in a slightly different but related way to that employed by President Upham in his welcoming remarks). These disciplines are notable because they supply essential tools for other disciplines, while retaining an autonomous structure and research effort of their own. More on this 'service function' in a moment.

2. Second, I hope to see a gradual but profound transformation of the social sciences under the influence of evaluation in the following three ways.

2.1 Applied social science will divide into the progressive, evaluation-enriched, school, and the conservative, evaluation-impaired school. The evaluation-enriched group—continuing to be led, we hope, by the School of Behavioral & Organizational Sciences at Claremont Graduate University—will become the winner in nearly all bids for contracts aimed at separating solutions from non-solutions of social/educational problems. The evaluation-impaired branch, following in the tracks of typical applied social science departments today, will gradually wither on the vine, with its aging adherents exchanging stories about the good old days.

Now, we should not forget that they *were* good old days, from at least the point of view of psychological science. Experiments were run in those days, before the notion of informed consent had become a constraint, that we could never get away with today, and we learned some very interesting things about human behavior from them. We learned that following instructions is more important than causing extreme pain to innocent victims, even for those brought up in our own relatively democratic society; we learned, from Hartshorne and May, amongst others, that our standard conceptualizations of behavior often rest firmly on completely unfounded assumptions about stereotypes; and we learned from Meehl and Dawes that experienced clinicians can't match the predictions of inexperienced statisticians armed with a longitudinal database. But none of this learning solved social problems, although it helped head off some popular non-solutions. When it comes down to determining whether specific solutions work for specific problems such as reducing crime, controlling the abuse of alcohol, assisting refugees from the dot.coms to find another job, then we need serious social program evaluators. Anything less lets in the snake-oil salesmen, like those peddling the DARE program—who, in a move that is most auspicious for our millennial vision, although two years or more overdue with the attendant costs—finally got their comeuppance a week ago when the program's supporters capitulated.

A key point in the war against snake-oil is that it can't be won by those who just have a PhD in what is now generally thought of as the applied social sciences. Contrary to popular belief amongst faculty in the more traditional programs of that genre, that's not always enough to make you competent to reliably distinguish worthless from competent programs. It's a great start, but in many a race, it stops well short of the stretch. Later in this chapter, you'll find a list of some of the missing elements from the conventional applied psych PhD's repertoire—it's called the Something More List. Mind you, that's only a list of the curriculum component of what's missing: the application skills must also be acquired.

So, academic social science training will be radically different, from course content to internship experiences: it will include large components of evaluation, both the logic and the application practice. That's the first of the big changes in the social sciences that evaluation will, I am certain, eventually produce.

2.2 Second, I expect to see a change in the metaview of social science from that of the last century. The metaview is the view of the nature of the subject itself—the conception of the proper paradigm for it—held by the educated citizenry, not just by the social scientists whose activities it fuels. The last century was dominated by the value-free paradigm of the social sciences; this century will, I hope, be dominated by the paradigm of what I'll call the "evaluative social sciences." The social sciences will be seen as the proper home of the scientific study of evaluative questions. This not only includes the *descriptive* study of values and those who hold them—a role they have always had without dispute—but as the home range of *normative* evaluative inquiry, meaning inquiry whose conclusions are directly evaluative, directly about good and bad solutions to social problems, directly about right and wrong approaches, directly about better and worse problems.

Consequent upon the change in the metaview of social science by social scientists, I expect to see a major change in the public view of the social sciences. This will be an acutely bivalent change, with the conservative forces arguing that the new evaluative social science is a devil that has escaped from its proper confinement, and the more enlightened group realizing that the confinement had been a confidence trick that took them in, and whose destruction liberates them to attack the great social problems in a scientific and comprehensive way.

Of course, I am not suggesting that the social sciences should relinquish any part of their traditional role in analyzing the configuration and causation of social and behavioral phenomena; but rather that they must add an extra dimension to that, in order to take on the extra topic of true evaluative research. An extreme example of the results of this change in the ideology of, and conception of, the social sciences is discussed in more detail below. Under the present heading however, I want to give an illustration of the present thesis by reminding you of what happened in the analogous case of measurement, where S.S. Stevens added a whole new dimension to courses in social science methods by extending the repertoire of useful tools for tackling problems. In my vision of the future of methods courses, evaluation will do the same by adding coverage of the evaluative family of concepts, and then plunging into the methodology of evaluation, which has its own substantial territory, including some areas that merely extend existing techniques (e.g., of cost analysis), and others that introduce new techniques (e.g., of values critique and weighting). It is this change that will revolutionize the application of the social sciences to social problems.

2.3 Third, we come to the question, naturally arising from reading the brochure for this symposium, of the relation between evaluating social problems and solving them. The conventional stance in evaluation has been "You cook 'em, and we'll taste 'em" but I'm going to argue that the division of labor is neither optimal nor realistic. For those of us who have long worked as professional evaluators, the traditional distinction has turned out to be not only blurred in practice but one that often misses the best path to a solution. It may be time to reconsider it completely, perhaps by reflecting on the following options. I think that evaluation in the future will be seen as legitimately including a limited range of problem-solving activities that include some of these options.

There are at least two paths that practicing evaluators of proposed solutions to social problems quite often follow, thereby turning into co-solution providers, a phenomenon that is analogous to the way that great editors are often nearer to coauthors than the conventional wisdom supposes. The first of these cases is the one that leads so often to the evaluator's lament that "I could have done so much more if only they had brought me in earlier." This connects with the practice of evaluability critique, whose distinguished originator, Joe Wholey, is with us today. If we are in at the planning stage, as is most appropriate for evaluability analysis, we can often bring focus to a fuzzy plan by asking exactly how anyone will be able to tell whether the plan has succeeded or not (by contrast with the spurious substitute often proposed, namely, how do we tell whether the plan was implemented as promised, or not). Sometimes more appropriately, we may ask whether or how it represents a new approach at all. Used too crudely, these 'shaping questions'—legitimate formative evaluation commentary on a plan—run the risk of becoming what is often rightly condemned as 'the evaluation driving the program.' But used well, what in fact often happens is that a good evaluator, like the good editor, sees and suggests a way to modify, rather than merely clarify, the original concept in ways that make it more valuable and more distinctive.

The second main way in which this happens involves the enlightened use of theory-driven evaluation. By 'enlightened' I mean an approach that is clear from the beginning about the tripartite role of program theories. Nearly always, one needs to distinguish between:

A. The *alleged* program theory (this is usually what is meant by the term *program logic*) according to which the program is *believed* to operate by the major stakeholders; the one behind the commitment of the program designer and other active stakeholders, usually including the program's funders. Sometimes good to start with this, just as it's sometimes good to start by identifying the program goals; but sometimes better not to be cued that much (Cf. goal-free evaluation).

B. The *real* logic of the program, that is, the machinery map according to which the program *in fact* operates, as it runs in the field. This is usually but not always different from A, and is sometimes well known to the field staff of the program, even if not the top administrators: but sometimes has to be discovered by the evaluator. Often, in the field, it becomes clear that one of the cogs in the alleged engine doesn't work but can be bypassed; and sometimes it just needs more grease than the design specifies. The real program logic may or may not be superior to the alleged program logic (i.e., more effective or more efficient). The evaluator has to decide whether to take on the task of answering that question, which requires some time (if it's possible at all) and is not strictly speaking part of the primary evaluation task, namely, to find out how well the actual program performs. Evaluators are so often imbued with the search for explanations by their training in the social sciences that they can't shake off the feeling that explaining what's happening is part of their job, whereas in fact it's often the grave of the evaluation or at least of its budget. Of course, other things being equal, it's nice to find the explanations but we all know how often other things are equal.

C. The *optimal* program theory—the account of how the program *should* operate, in order to achieve optimal effectiveness from available resources. Is this different from theories A and B? That's something that the evaluator may decide she or he needs to discover: sometimes it's obvious that there's a better way to organize subsystems at least, for example, the information flow, or the supply ordering, and the evaluator makes a suggestion that actually provides the winning margin for the operation. And sometimes there are more radical contributions to be made. Consider a hypothetical program of the newly fashionable "broken window" variety, aimed at the reduction of urban crime. According to the academic originators of this approach, controlling apparently minor events in a crime-ridden neighborhood (the eponymous broken windows) can eventually lead to substantial reduction of major crimes. The Type A program theory is that the presence and toleration of the broken windows legitimates the perpetration of more of the same crimes, and eventually more serious infringements. This theory has gotten the program we are evaluating rolling in our hypothetical community of study, as it has in several cities across this country.

In the schools in our community of study, the program field staff is the school administrators and counselors, who of course have been run through the usual kind of training seminars on Program Theory A. Their interpretation of it, in many sites, has turned out to be the so-called "zero tolerance" policy about a range of behaviors including those related to carrying any kind of weapons; this is Theory B. The step from Theory A to Theory B is a big one and the evaluator often needs to point this out under the heading of implementation, when doing formative or summative process evaluation. In an incident last month about which you may have read, a child was suspended for pointing a chicken bone from his lunch box at the teacher and saying "Bang! Bang!" This has caused considerable controversy, which should be laid at the door of Theory B, not Theory A. But it has brought the whole approach, that is, the broken windows approach, into disrepute, especially but not only at this site.

Enter the evaluator, who can adopt a reactive or a proactive stance to the situation. In the traditional reactive mode, he or she points out the above interpretation of the events, thereby doing something to salvage Theory A. But it is not uncommon for the evaluator, and in my view often defensible, to go one step further and propose a way to interpret Theory A that will avoid the bad results of Theory B1, the one we've so far mentioned. One such proposal would be to have the borderline cases (e.g., the chicken bone) adjudicated by a panel of 4, comprising—for example—a retired school superintendent who knows and is known to this community, a senior police officer, the president of the PTA, and an ACLU attorney, operating under the rules that (a) it takes three votes to expel, and (b) any case of expulsion will be converted immediately into a refinement of the public policy that will simplify future decisions.

The idea that this would lead to a net improvement over Theory B, by reducing serious bad side-effects, would be Theory C. For a proactive evaluator like myself, it's a much more attractive alternative than an academic rethinking of Theory A, something which is, by the way, going on at a great rate at the moment and should also continue; or merely recording the deep trouble that the whole project is in because Theory B has run into trouble, although in fact Theory A has not been shown to be faulty by the probable failure of B.

There are other ways in which the evaluator becomes a problem-solver and not just a solution-assessor, but time prevents elaboration on them with one exception that illustrates a qualitatively different approach. This example focuses on the usually critical necessity for an evaluator to provide a comparative perspective for the (evaluator's) client, whether doing formative or summative evaluation. In making the critically important choice of entities with which to make the comparison, of course amongst those with closely comparable resource requirements, a crucial question is whether one should only compare with *existing* alternatives. In my view, a good evaluator should not so restrict the field of comparison; there are times when an evaluator can see how a better alternative could be *constructed* from available components. An evaluator might, for example, suggest that the limited success of a so-called "faith-based" Christian or Muslim church approach to teen pregnancy reduction might be bettered (by increasing its reach) by a program using a "female sports-hero role-model" approach, now that female sports hero(ine) are beginning to achieve very high recognition levels amongst young women. Thus the 'editor' becomes "coauthor of a prospective best-seller," and we see another way in which the evaluator can, and I think sometimes should, contribute more than certification to the solution of social problems.

These comments are meant to bear on the way in which evaluation should have a different and more powerful role in social problem solving in the 21st century. We now turn to the fourth and last—and most radical—of the arguments for that aspect of the vision I am outlining, the aspect that would most profoundly change the way the social sciences connect to evaluation.

2.4 The following is an Emperor's New Clothes argument. It is now many years since it became obvious that the social sciences contained all the ingredients for *generating normative ethics*. In other words, the suggestion here is that ethics is a legitimate although massively underdeveloped field of the social sciences. The simple-minded versions of utilitarianism that originally tried for this title of scientific ethics are long gone, but more sophisticated accounts of ethics (roughly speaking, a combination of the "good reasons" approach with Rawls) have provided a workable framework, immune to the powerful objections that brought down the Benthamesque version of utilitarianism. Of course, for those brought up to believe in the doctrine of value-free social science, this is a deeply blasphemous suggestion, but consider two facts. One, the American Psychological Association has worked out a detailed although highly focused normative ethics in the Testing Standards document, and there's no apparent reason this *approach* can't be expanded, at least in principle and with the help of specialized knowledge from others, to cover the usual field of ethics. Once one sees that it is possible to generate a field of ethics from scientific considerations plus a single ethical premise such as the doctrine of prima facie equal rights for humans, the rest is made feasible. Two, if one looks at the tools provided by game theory, welfare economics, cost analysis, decision theory, sociobiology, and implicit function theory from social anthropology, one finds more than enough hardware to get the job done, which includes justifying the premise about equal rights.

Only the dying hand of an old positivist doctrine, perhaps combined with the implicit threat of an attack by organized religion, prevents us from full recognition of this situation. So, the last brick in the edifice of this part of the vision is that a particular field of evaluation, ethics itself, should come to be a stand-alone component in the totality of studies that makes up the social sciences. Not that it will wrestle this subject away from philosophy, but rather that it will lend its own invaluable resources to objectify and precisify ethical theory and judgment.

3. Now we come to the third major part of this vision. It refers to the vast domains of evaluation that lie outside the social sciences. These domains are not of direct relevance to the traditional subject matter of this series of symposia, but they are of great importance in talking about the future of evaluation. And they are of considerable importance in correcting the narrow-mindedness of some of those social scientists who have grasped part of the general expansionist thesis with which we have been principally concerned so far, the thesis that evaluation has a key role to play in the social sciences. The best-selling text in evaluation, Rossi, Freeman, and Lipsey's book entitled *Evaluation: A Systematic Approach*, now in its sixth edition, has the effrontery to define evaluation as the application of social science methods to the solution of social problems. But evaluation, in systematic and explicit form, existed long before the social sciences existed and continues to exist in many areas without resting on any work or methods from the social sciences. For example, the work of the courts largely comprises the evaluation of legal arguments and conclusions, precedents and analogies, done for the most part in a highly skilled and highly trained way and with a high degree of reliability and validity. When and if it appeals to the findings of social science, it is for data not for methodology.

Engineering is another example of a massively evaluative subject, one whose evaluations of bridges and buildings and highways are so important that our lives depend on them every day: a subject with more than two millennia of explicit doctrine and skilled practice behind it. A third is provided by medicine, of which the same might equally well be said. Logic provides us with a fourth evaluative subject, largely concerned with the evaluation of arguments and inferences, evidence and presentations, a subject whose axioms are wholly independent of the content of the social sciences. A fifth example is consumer product evaluation, with a history of professional applications going back to the middle ages in Japan. These branches of evaluation exhibit precisely the same logic as program evaluation or personnel evaluation, and achieve essentially similar levels of credibility and validity without any significant reliance on social science data or methods. Perhaps more interestingly, they come into program evaluation quite often, and the time is long past for acting as if there are waterproof or even practically useful barriers between the fields of evaluation. It is unsatisfactory to find no mention in Rossi, Freeman, and Lipsey of personnel evaluation, although programs are just persons in action and fixes are often just personnel fixes, let alone no mention of legal constraints, or product evaluation or, for that matter, substantive ethics (by contrast with professional ethics, not much help when deciding whether and how to evaluate an abortion clinic).

Perhaps more important than all these other areas of evaluation that are independent of social science methodology, and perhaps the one with the most promise for future benefits in this vision of evaluation, is what I have called *intradisciplinary evaluation*. The skeleton that holds any discipline together, that makes it a discipline at all, is evaluation; without evaluation there is nothing to distinguish a discipline from charlatanry. No historian or physicist who was incompetent at distinguishing good practice or good theories from bad could be competent in their discipline. Every faculty member in the sciences earns their keep by doing evaluation as the basis for their research and their teaching. It is a kind of sick joke that most of them were co-conspirators in the plot to exclude evaluation from the pantheon of respectability, when their own careers were doubly dependent on it. Of course, this kind of evaluation was often done very well, and it was not using anything from the social sciences in its logic. Of course, too, these skills in intradisciplinary evaluation do not generalize or transfer any significant distance—see below. That does not in the least alter the fact that these evaluation skills are a definitional part of competence in and hence of the essence of science.

An interesting question remains: does the highly trained general purpose evaluator have anything at all to contribute to the quality of intradisciplinary evaluation? We know that skilled disciplinarians, the moment they move a foot from the core of the discipline's practice, evaluate quite shoddily: we only have to look at the poor quality of test questions set by professors in most fields, or of scoring rubrics (if they exist at all), at the abuse of the interview process in choosing colleagues, at the long-time failure to use blind review of submissions to journals, at the poor quality of teacher evaluation in Carnegie 1 universities, and the poor quality of evaluations for tenure throughout post-secondary as well as K-12 education. In all these areas, a trained evaluator with zero knowledge in the subject-matter discipline can greatly improve what we might call the *fringe* evaluation performance of those in the discipline. Can they add anything at all to the *core* evaluation performance? I think so, and this year am beginning the attempt to improve the evaluation of research, a typical core evaluation activity, whose results are set out at the beginning of every article and thesis project, in the literature review. It's clear that fashion and the cult of personality have long exerted improper influence here; the question is whether there are systematic ways to reduce these biases. My vision is that in the coming century we will see considerable progress on this front, with consequent payoffs for research and teaching in substantive areas of the curriculum.

4. So, if evaluation is not the application of social science methods to solve social problems, what is it? It's a transdiscipline whose subject matter is merit/worth/significance, just as the subject of measurement is dimension and the subject of statistics is populations. The conclusions of all these and other disciplines are inferences and descriptions; in the case of evaluation, these are propositions about merit/worth/significance, or about terms that essentially involve these concepts, and we next provide a few leading features of the logic of evaluation, and a hint of the consequences of this position.

4.1 Professional evaluation is the systematic determination of merit, worth, and significance. Other terms are almost equivalent to these: quality is often used as a synonym for merit, value for worth, and importance for significance. There are a few score intrinsically evaluative terms in the language, and many technical terms, that essentially involve evaluative concepts. Here we are simply following the dictionary definitions and there are no reasons to abandon them. They provide evaluation with a reasonably well demarcated field of the greatest importance, and it's one that urgently demands a great deal of development.

4.2 Evaluation essentially involves only four logically distinct processes, not completely distinct but distinct in ways that are frequently misrepresented, even in texts on measurement and testing: grading, ranking, scoring and apportioning.

4.3 There are also just four epistemologically distinct types of evaluative claim: (1) personal preference claims, (2) market value claims, (3) contextually evaluative claims, and (4) essentially evaluative claims. Each will support certain limited evaluative conclusions using each of the four processes of 4.2. For example, personal preference claims will support conclusions about what's the best (i.e., a ranking) choice for the person whose preferences we are using. But the fourth type—for example, "the best reading programs include the following... "—is the most important kind, the kind that program evaluation centers on, and it is common in intradisciplinary and practical evaluation as well as in program/personnel/ product/etc. evaluation. It is comparable in objectivity to the best scientific claims, when the best available evaluation methodology is used, a qualification that applies equally to the kind of objectivity we seek in science itself. Such claims are not normally observation claims, although they can be; usually they are just like causal, theoretical, and other types of explanatory claims, that is, claims which are quite complex to verify, but of very great importance in science, the law, education, and practical life. When the discipline of evaluation is regarded as a pseudo-discipline, as it has been for the better part of a century, essentially evaluative claims (other than intradisciplinary ones) are classified by the intelligentsia as mere personal preference claims or market value claims, regardless of the claimant's view. In my view, this situation is changing drastically and will change completely: as the discipline gathers credibility, these come to be seen as legitimate factual claims although often still controversial until massively researched and documented. The controversiality will then merely derive from the affect load of the content, that is, the importance of the implications of evaluative claims to matters that we hold near and dear. It will no longer be possible to dismiss arguments about such matters as pointless, since they are "just a matter of taste."

4.4 I believe that one of the most important consequences of this change, albeit not one that follows deductively, is the last to which I shall call attention here. It is a consequence of accepting evaluative claims as full citizens in the empire of knowledge. In the routine practice of evaluation, the task of comparative rating is a common and highly important one. Now in this (ranking) procedure, the evaluator is typically expected to identify the key competitors for the entity being rated, whether it's a product, a program, a proposal, or a policy. To do this, the evaluator will often need to have a good command of the relevant research literature, including the results of reputable prior evaluations of a similar kind. This essential knowledge is of course field-specific, and since the field is often one in which the evaluator was not trained or has not kept current, this will require systematic review, especially of meta-analyses and of studies involving full randomized control groups. It follows that an evaluator working for an organization with a specific mission will need to develop and tend a working database that contains not only: (1) summaries of evaluations done within his or her organization, but also (2) summaries of those done by other organizations with similar missions, and (3) evaluative research results from academics working in the same fields, especially those fully-controlled studies such as those we can now find in the Cochrane and Campbell Collections. Obviously there is an opportunity here for shared work by the evaluation and research professions, since such databases will overlap substantially. The grand database comprising all such results is clearly an ideal towards which we should begin to work. I have christened it TED, for The Evaluation Database, and persuaded the Evaluation Committee of the Northern California Grantmakers to put it on their workplan, so we have a small beginning towards it.

The full plan for TED involves two further steps, controversial and experimental at this point, but in my view inevitable and desirable additions, eventually. Apart from the three relatively conventional sources of information mentioned above, there is a another one to which our attention is increasingly being called by work in organization theory related to knowledge management and knowledge engineering. The bridge to it is a fourth category, which we might call (4) impeccable but not fully controlled studies. We will need to do some work selling the larger audience about the 'impeccability' claim before these will have wide acceptance, although we are all familiar with the good case made for the quasi-experimental sub-category here. But there are a couple of other important categories as well, about which I have written elsewhere, which depend mainly on pattern recognition and the elimination of alternative explanations to demonstrate causal connection or other significance. (The best of these is perhaps the Modus Operandi Method, the mainstay of much criminalistics).

Then we will come to the fifth category, which can almost be regarded as a stretch of the fourth one. It is the tacit knowledge of experts in the field, often experienced program officers. We have too long treated it as less than respectable; but we need to reconsider this view and mine the gold that can be found there, as Michael Polanyi and the advocates of knowledge management have long been recommending. More on the details of this when some substantial examples have been developed in some detail.

5. Conclusion. There are more things in heaven and earth than were dreamed of in the positivists' philosophy, and of those things the body of evaluative knowledge may be the most important. We will eventually need to enlarge the current narrow conception of scientific knowledge built into the K-12 curriculum and the undergraduate and graduate course requirements in order to accommodate it. First we need to make sure that we who practice evaluation and teach the college courses understand it ourselves.

THE 'SOMETHING MORE' LIST

This is a draft outline of some of the insights, skills, and methodology that you won't acquire from a standard social science PhD—even one in applied social science—but that you'll need in order to do professional evaluation. The core of this package consists of the techniques that are involved in the **systematic and objective validation of evaluative claims** which is the dictionary definition of evaluation with two qualifiers in front that narrow it down to professionally competent evaluation.

To begin with, many social science PhDs have been trained to think that there is no such thing as an objective evaluative claim, that is, an unconditional claim about the merit, worth, or significance of something or someone (we here use the term 'evaluand' to refer to whatever is being evaluated). This is by contrast with a conditional claim, that is, one that begins, "If you accept the values of X, then Y is meritorious/worthy/significant." The conditional claim is not the conclusion that the client needs in such activities as program and personnel evaluation. They want to know what is really valuable, for example, what's the best reading program or the best candidate, not what would be valuable if someone valued this or that. In other words, they need to know what set of values can be justified, not just what would be valuable if such and such a set could be justified. They want an answer that is not relativized to a person or group of people such as a market. Now categorical evaluative claims, for example, "This reading program offers no significant advantages over several others currently available,"[1] are claims with the same degree of objectivity as any other non-observational, non-direct measurement claims—logical or empirical—that can be established in the social sciences, for example, claims about causation or classification or explanation. So the first item on the Something More List (SML) is:

(A) Understanding that and how objective evaluative claims are possible in principle. Now, the cognitive state of our hypothetical social science PhD is actually schizophrenic on this point. On the one hand, his/her training has not provided any support for A, as one can see by looking in any methods text used at the graduate or undergraduate level for a section on the methodology of evaluation. Indeed, it is likely that they have been taught to abjure evaluative claims and treat them as something that cannot be part of science. On the other hand, their life as a scientist, an instructor, and as a practical person, has taught them that one must be able to establish the truth of evaluative claims in order to function in any of these roles, and has even taught them how to support such claims. For example, they know how to evaluate articles in the research literature, or term papers written by their students, or the condition of lab equipment, or the validity of tests. The first requirement for an evaluator is to resolve this cognitive conflict by accepting the evidence of everyday and scientific practice that one can objectively determine the merit (etc.) of many things, including many things in science such as data quality, inferences from data to research conclusions, hence research designs and hypotheses, which immediately means abandoning the widely-held position of "value-free science." One can come to this abandonment either by look-

---

[1]Or "This candidate is outstanding" or "This paper includes many mistakes in interpreting the standard research literature on attitudes."

ing carefully at the alleged arguments establishing that position, which are fatally flawed,[2] or by realizing that one's common sense must override the philosophical underpinning of the value-free doctrine, or by looking at the procedures outlined below, which briefly cover the techniques for establishing evaluative claims. The rest of the something more list is the set of components in the "missing methodology" for verifying evaluative claims.

(B) Identifying criteria of merit. (sometimes called "dimensions of merit" or "aspects of merit"). In order to evaluate something, we almost always have to begin with a list of the criteria of merit for that thing or type/class of thing. These are the considerations that are definitionally relevant to determining the merit of the evaluand. It has to be a list that includes all of them and no more. Miss one and the evaluation may be completely invalid; add an irrelevant one, and you risk the same result. In program evaluation this list obviously starts off with items such as "reduced use of alcohol by pregnant teen-agers in the target population" but it rapidly expands into matters of maximizing the number of subjects reached, producing results with some tendency to remain in place, keeping the cost down, positive ripple effects on sibs, etc. Step B is often a considerable task: in terms of size, it is common for the list to run into dozens and sometimes more than a hundred criteria of merit. Quality of the list is equally important: in particular, it requires distinguishing *criteria* of merit from mere (empirical) *indicators* of merit (e.g., the difference between interior space and brand name in evaluating family sedans). You only use indicators if you can't get at criteria: to begin with, you must list the criteria and try for direct measures or observations of them, or of something from which you can reliably infer them. Criteria of merit are also not to be confused with logically necessary or sufficient conditions, the components of "classical definitions" like the definition of a triangle. Criteria are only jointly sufficient and only rarely are they individually necessary; however, they (logically, not empirically) 'count for' the applicability of the term for which they serve as criteria and are often used in the course of explaining the meaning of that term.[3]

---

[2] See The Logic of Evaluation; an article in Evaluation Thesaurus, 4th edition, Scriven, (Sage 1991); or the forthcoming 2nd edition of The Logic of Evaluation (Sage, 2002).

[3] For a detailed treatment, see "The Logic of Criteria" in *Journal of Philosophy* , Vol.56, October 22, 1959, pp. 857–868; reprinted in *Criteria*, ed. John V. Canfield (Garland, 1986).

Examples. (1) Hondas are good cars, most of them much better than the average car in their class. But that just shows the brand name is an *indicator* of merit. It's not a guarantee of any merit, that is, a criterion of merit. So, only buy a Honda off the showroom floor "because it's a Honda" if you don't have time to check in more detail on this particular car's performance on the criteria that collectively *define* "a good car for you." (2) If you are sure that private schools, on the average, provide a better or safer education, you still should not send your children to a private school because it's a private school unless you don't know how to check its merit by contrast with the local state school (or how to get sound advice on that). (3) The evidence is that Alcoholics Anonymous is quite successful in many cases; but that only makes its imprimatur an *indicator* of merit; you should find out *all* the problems and advantages of the local chapter, for you or the friend or relative you are recommending it to. Evaluators are the people whose job it is to check in more detail, once they have determined what they should be checking. Stereotyping or oversimplifying is the error of not doing that, of running off one indicator, with or without supporting evidence for its status as a good indicator. With respect to human beings, racism and sexism and religious prejudice are all cases of using a single label as if it's a good basis for an overall evaluative conclusion. While inferences based on a single criterion of merit are also likely to be weak, they at least prove the presence of some merit beyond any doubt, which an indicator cannot do.

The list of criteria of merit developed by a trained evaluator will, virtually always, be a longer list than any developed by either the client or an investigator untrained in evaluation, *and* it will almost always exclude some of the characteristics on the amateur's list. Standard social science texts, let alone texts from other disciplines, do not even include the requirements for a valid criteria list, let alone examples to illustrate the criteria/indicator differences.[4]

The list of criteria of merit *must* be complete: giving an objective evaluation obviously requires covering the weaknesses as well as the strengths, and that translates into reporting the performance on all dimensions that bear on merit, however poor the performance is in a particular case. Most ads and resumés are examples of alleged evaluations where the bad news is left out and we all learn to read between the lines, or at least to check other sources to see what might be there. But evaluators

---

[4] More details in the *Evaluation Thesaurus* (ibid.) and in the methodology section of a forthcoming book, *Practical Program Evaluation* (Sage, 2002).

do not force their clients to read between lines, a notoriously ambiguous and unreliable procedure. They spell out the full story.

The current fashion for "outcomes-based evaluation" usually leads to several fallacies (and one good thought, that is, look for results not just process) of which a common one is to use indicators of merit that are not criteria of merit. These are rapidly manipulated or go out of date for various reasons. The correct procedure is to list the criteria of merit and directly measure (etc.) all you can get; then cautiously use indicators for the rest, triangulating these and rechecking their validity at frequent intervals: and *then* go for all the other things that are required in order to do a decent evaluation (see for example the Key Evaluation Checklist; Scriven, 1991).

(C) Digging for the rest of the facts, that is, going far beyond the obviously relevant facts like the extent to which certain intended or desired effects have or have not been produced. In particular (but not only), this means: (1) ensuring that *performance data have been obtained on each of the criteria of merit* identified in step A; (2) *checking for side-effects*, a tricky business since there are obviously no simple rules about where to look for unanticipated effects or properties; (3) *checking for side-impacts*, that is, impacts on populations other than the target population, for example, sibs, roommates, parents, friends, coworkers; (4) *finding hidden costs*, not just the obvious ones, a very tricky business, especially since the *non-money* costs are often very important—accounting skills, even if the social scientist happens to have them, will not handle these; (5) *scrutinizing the process* by which the results were achieved. This fifth point is crucial in program evaluation for several reasons, for example, (a) to see whether the program is operating as it is said to operate (i.e., is there misrepresentation, or failure to implement an alleged test of a treatment), and for example, (b) to ensure that legal requirements on the safety and treatment of workers are respected. Hence "process acceptability" is almost always an essential criterion of merit in program evaluation, whereas in product evaluation it may not be included in the criteria of merit at all, because what counts is nearly always simply what the product can do, not how it does it. (Treating the production of clothing in sweat shops as a disbar to purchase is an example that shows this difference is not absolute).

It's rare to find a serious treatment of even one of these five points in a social science methods text, and that's important because the directed digging game, so typical of evaluation (and good investigative sciences like forensic pathology and criminalistics, and of investigative reporting, and of *some* field work in anthropology/sociology), is categorically different from the core model of hypothesis-testing that dominates much social science research. Evaluation is not "'applied social science," as the latter is currently conceived, although we may well hope, and I do expect, that in the future evaluation's existence and importance will come to affect and eventually be included in the standard social science model of investigation. The alternative is the retention of the current conception of applied social science and its inevitable marginalization.

(D) Weighting and barring the criteria of merit are methods of attaching to each of them some indication of their importance in the context of the particular evaluation. Weights may be expressed quantitatively or qualitatively: for example, we'll use the following as our standard set of qualitative weights—(1) E for Essential (i.e., the presence of this characteristic, usually at some specified level, is called a "bar"' that must be cleared), (2) * (star) for Very Important, (3) # (pound or double plus) for Important, (4) + (plus) for Minimally Important (a "tie-breaker"), and finally, (5) O (zero) for Irrelevant. In evaluating a car for your own use, you might use "seats four adults (half over 6'1" and 240 lbs) comfortably for long trips" as a criterion of merit and weight it E for Essential, whereas you weight "good fuel economy (i.e., better than 24 mpg)" as + for Minimally Important. In weighting criteria of merit for a binge drinking reduction program, one might say that impact breadth, that is, the number of people whose binge drinking is reduced), and impact depth (i.e., durability and completeness of effect on the individuals affected), are starred for Very Important, whereas cost is only a double plus (for Important), and so on.

Notice that E does not operate like the symbols. The space below E gains no points at all *and also* no scores on other dimensions can compensate for an evaluand that does not score above E on *any* scale. A line for E on any scale defines a fatal weakness; all other weights are 'compensatory', that is, poor or even 0 scores can be compensated by higher scores on other scales.

People often try to use a ten-point numerical scale to allocate weights, but making discriminations with that level of precision is difficult and likely to produce problems of inconsistency with other judges (poor inter-rater reliability) and even oneself (test-retest reliability). A five point scale is more plausible, but the qualitative scale suggested here, which has only three options within the active range, involves still fewer assumptions about the ability to weight with precision, so—this is a methodological point—one would normally begin by using it in order to avoid unnecessary risks. (Example of an assumption built into a 5 point *numerical* scale that is not built into the qualitative scale listed above: the assumption that the interval between each point on the scale is the same, that is, the assumption that the scale is an interval scale).

Notice that the two ways of assigning importance to a dimension of merit are orthogonal. No version of increasing weight will function as a bar does, except by distorting the whole representation of importance. For example, a dimension may be absolutely essential but not heavily weighted, as might be the case with the example of an E just given, since you may think it of little importance if the car can carry 5 passengers in comfort. Or it may be very important, for example, economically priced, and every reduction in price below the maximum you can afford is still very worthwhile for you.

In order to determine the relative importance of these criteria of merit, for the purpose of a particular evaluation, the evaluator takes note of the weights the client attaches to the various aspects of performance and process, but may also have to look at such matters as the needs of the impactees, legal requirements, professional standards for evaluands of this type, definitional requirements, etc. Two aspects of this step, in particular, are not covered in standard social science methodology: the problems with the use of quantitative weights (we have only mentioned one of several), and extracting weights from the many sources of value that must be scrutinized, especially needs assessment, which is commonly the most complex one. It's quite rare even to find a discussion of the difference between weights and bars, although it's a standard distinction in the field of personnel evaluation, which may explain why many procedures for evaluating proposals for funding, for example, most of those used by federal agencies, are invalid because they do not make this distinction.[5]

Grading. The dimensions of merit are the qualities of the evaluand that usually matter, to a client or to society, and the weights tell us something about how much they matter. There remains the problem of what units (of merit) to use on the vertical (performance) scale, and it has to be solved before we can produce a useful evaluation. We're not just interested in the raw scores, the performance as such, in mph or customers served. We need to bring some meaningful standards to bear within the dimensions. Steps A to D simply get us to the point of having the performance data on each criterion of merit, and the general importance of each criterion of merit.

What we have at the end of D is the basis for what we can call a "performance profile" of the evaluand. Think of this as a vertical bar chart in

---

[5] Which means, for example, that a proposal that is highly irrelevant can still win because it scores well on the other dimensions of merit, for example, personnel qualifications, infrastructure, cost controls, understanding of task, etc.

which each bar represents performance on one criterion of merit, the height of the bar being the strength of the performance. Thus, the bar representing miles per gallon will run from 5 to 125, a scale that covers all cars now on the market; for a program, the bar representing number of people served would run from 1 to some figure well above the size of the target population (because programs often turn out to serve others besides those for whom they were intended). We can use the color of the bar to represent the importance of that criterion of merit (e.g., red for essential, orange for very important, etc.) Or, in a black and white rendering, we can use shading.

While it's informative to have a profile with the raw scores of the evaluand on each dimension, plus a graphical indication of the relative importance of each of these dimensions, it leaves us a long way short of a useful evaluative portrayal. The key question still remains—what do those raw scores mean to us, or to our client, or to society? We're looking for a way to convert a performance profile into what we might call a *merit profile*.

One minor type of standardization can be done easily: we can convert all the performance scales into similar numerical scales by simply setting any point N on each of them to the point N/M x 10, where M is the maximum amount on that scale in raw score terms. But the result is just a numerical transform of the raw scores, only slightly more meaningful (because now more easily comparable across dimensions). Make sure that at least this is always done, unless one of the next two procedures are adopted.

A more important transformation, which would require considerably more research, would be to convert the vertical scales into percentile ranks, so that the mpg of the car we're looking at would not be registered as "22 mpg," but as "55th percentile mpg" amongst the cars on the market. And we could relativize the ranking even more narrowly to "midprice sedans," the group in which we're interested. For certain situations, for example, identifying the Car of the Year, or the valedictorian in a graduating high school class, or the one to buy for ourselves, this would be the relevant conversion—cases where *relative* merit on each dimension is what counts. Relative merit is indeed one kind of merit, and this process gives us "relative performance profiles."

But in most situations that is not the most important issue and it's sometimes of no importance. What's more likely to be important to us, or to our client (if we're doing the evaluation for someone else), is the absolute performance, for example, how serious the real fuel costs per year will be, not (or not just) how it compares with others on that scale; whether the performance on the exam counts as enough to be certified as a surgeon, etc. Now, the fuel costs per year, or the test scores, are still just performance figures; what's important at this point is to determine *what value should be placed on particular scores* in each category.

In a real case, for a particular buyer, that might mean that midrange economy is fine, say, 16-24mpg, but below 16 mpg would be unacceptable—in other words, "above 16 mpg" is rated as Essential on our weighting scale, that is, there's a bar at 16 mpg. It might also be the case that "25 mpg or better" would be a significant bonus—that is, it might be rated as Important or Minimally Important. Here we are just using the client's explicit preferences as the source of value from which to extract standards; but we will usually need to do some research to find out what other standards bear on this dimension and others, as in the case of certification of surgeons. Another example: there may be pollution standards set by the state affecting the merit of various mileage figures; there may be safety standards mandated by the state which may mean that we have to add a dimension of safety on which we must also rate the evaluand. Good research would turn these up when at Step B; but we'd use it at Step D.

This kind of scaling—classifying for merit, for which the usual term is *grading*—brings in some standards from the real world to give us a more general and useful presentation of the merit profile. We will simply add horizontal lines across the whole chart to separate several vertical regions by merit. For convenience, we often label these regions with the usual abbreviations for academic grades—A through F—although we'll have to be careful with this. The region under the first line is Unacceptable (corresponding to the F grade on that common scale); between the first and second is marginally acceptable but not entirely satisfactory (the D grade); and on to Satisfactory (C), Good (B), and Excellent (A). The vertical bar on a particular dimension for a particular evaluand will therefore rise up to a certain height, representing not the raw performance, not the comparative performance, but the merit of that performance, on the scale just described, in the context of this evaluation. It may show that the evaluand flunks on this dimension, or does very well, etc. Note that the absolute or relative performance may be very high, without the grade being very high: this happens when the standards only require a moderate performance (D or better) and there is no value (weight) attached to performance beyond that.

Correlatively, a flunk on one dimension is not necessarily fatal for the evaluand: in the college transcript, where each bar on the merit profile represents a course taken, a failing grade just means that that course cannot count towards the key requirements, which are an overall grade point average (GPA), and a certain number of courses passed. If a course is failed, it is usually possible to simply take another one instead.

The standard social science text does not get into any of this, especially the complex business of finding relevant standards, whereas in the methodology section of Practical Program Evaluation we identify twelve types of merit standard that should always be checked by the evaluator. Of course, we have only scratched the surface of these topics here, although hopefully enough to suggest that there are practical consequences of the logic. Our task here is just to prove that there are such details, to help toward dealing with them, and to sow that dealing with them is not part of the standard training of social scientists.

Synthesising. So now we have a merit profile *for this particular evaluand in this particular evaluation task.* (The very same performance facts would lead to a different profile if the needs of the client or impacted population were different). Sometimes that's as far as we need to push the evaluation, but more often than not, we need to go one step further and produce an overall evaluation. It's all very well to say how good something is on each of six or sixteen scales, but clients are likely to want to know if we can help them with the remaining problem: does all this mean the evaluand is very good *overall*—or just fair, or unacceptable—and does it mean that this evaluand is the best of the lot, etc. In the world of education, this is where the grade point average comes in; the usual rule is that you have to get a 2.0 overall GPA on a certain number of courses (the equivalent of 4 years of a full-time workload) in order to graduate with a baccalaureate degree. This is an example of an *overall requirement* by contrast with the ones that occur with respect to performance on each scale—the "bar." So in that context, we are using the very crude overall synthesizing device of the GPA. In most contexts, we have to do better than that. For example, there may be overall patterns that have to be matched.

To recapitulate, in these situations where any particular dimension of merit has the property that the evaluand must achieve a passing grade on it in order to avoid total disqualification, that minimum level of performance is referred to as a *stand-alone* requirement, and we often say that the whole criterion is a *stand-alone criterion.* In the academic world, the requirement that a psychology major must pass the statistics course is often a stand-alone requirement. More usually, some trade-offs are allowed between criteria, and we call such criteria *compensatory criteria*; do badly on one, you can make it up by doing well on another. Of course, the question then arises, What exactly is the rule that explains how the tradeoffs are made and the overall result judged? If there is no rule, which means it's a judgment call, then the results will typically vary depending on who happens to be doing the judging on a particular day. That is usually not an acceptable basis for the operation of evaluation as a discipline: a potential exception occurs when independent testing of the accuracy of the judge has been done. The academic rule is that the trade-offs must still result in an overall average grade of C, which is a GPA of 2.0. But it's not easy to get that kind of simplicity in most common cases of evaluating programs or personnel.

Typically, the criteria of merit are a mix of standalone and compensatory criteria. Reducing the complex features of the merit profile to a single overall measure or grade is usually a tricky business, not solved by easy rules as in the academic situation. This kind of synthesis is referred to here as *primary* or *internal* synthesis—it is the synthesis of subevaluations—and is the subject for fairly extensive discussion in the methodology section of PPE. If, for example, a funding agency wants to know whether a new policy for processing welfare claims is adequate, they need an overall synthesis against some overall standard of adequacy. Determining how to set up such an (external) standard is likely to be something which the evaluator will also have to work out if it's not already in existence *and* proven valid, a rare event. So we often have to synthesize the scores on several dimensions of merit in order to get an overall score, which we then have to appraise by developing external standards.

Now, there's another important kind of synthesis, which involves synthesizing the results of several studies or judgments of the merit of a particular evaluand, either the overall merit or the merit on one dimension. The simplest form of this occurs when we have several judges, for example, in judgments of the quality of a dive in the Olympics or the quality of the interpretation in ice skating. The more complex form arises in a special case of what's called a *meta-analysis* where all the studies are evaluative, for example the several studies that have been done on the merit of alternative models for running Head Start programs, or teen pregnancy programs. We call this *external synthesis,* also known as *secondary* synthesis. (Secondary because it builds on the internal synthesis of dimensional scores that led to each separate conclusion). It's only by doing this kind of synthesis that we can come up with recommendations to cancel a program or buy something—by showing it outperforms the alternatives. To decide that, we must have some way to compare complex merit profiles, and the usual way to do so requires the primary synthesis of reducing each to an overall score or grade; then we work out how to combine a number of these done by different investigators, or the same ones at different times, which is the secondary synthesis.

There are various ways to do these syntheses, primary or secondary, some of which are very simple, although they will only work in special cases, that is, if you get lucky. For example, in primary synthesis, if one candidate outperforms all the others on all dimensions, you do not need to do a primary synthesis for each candidate: you can already identify the best of the bunch. Even if one is better on nearly all dimensions, and loses by a little on a low-weighted dimension, you can still solve the problem without synthesis. But in more typical cases, it's useful to have a general approach, and we outline one in the Evaluation Thesaurus. It is used in quick-and-dirty form to identify the "short list" of best candidates, known as "critical competitors," then turned loose in full detail on the short list to identify the winner. The analogous case for secondary synthesis arises when all, or nearly all, the studies have the same overall winner.

The use of a single control group, especially the traditional "no-treatment" control group, in social science research is an extremely primitive example of a critical competitor but not helpful in dealing with a situation where there are several serious alternatives.

CONCLUSION

There's much more to evaluation than these bare bones, but it's just as well to be clear that there *is* a logical skeleton underpinning the process, and that it's not something we automatically acquire, in its general form, in the course of learning how to do the usual kind of social science research. It underpins our common-sense procedures of evaluation—for example, in evaluating products for purchase and jobs to take; it underpins the complex and difficult process of evaluation that underpins science itself— for example, in evaluating the design of experiments, the research of others and the quality of scientific instruments; and it underpins the whole of systematic program and policy evaluation.

REFERENCES

Rossi, P. H., Freeman, H. E., & Lipsey, M. W. (1999). *Evaluation: A systematic approach (6th Ed.).* Thousand Oaks, CA: Sage.
Scriven, M. (1959). *The logic of criteria. Journal of Philosophy, 56,* 857-868.
Scriven, M. (1991). *Evaluation thesaurus (4th Ed.).* Newbury Park, CA: Sage
Scriven, M. (2002). *Practical program evaluation.* Newbury Park, CA: Sage
Scriven, M. (2002). *The logic of evaluation (2nd Ed.).* Newbury Park, CA: Sage

3

Improving Performance and Accountability: Responding to Emerging Management Challenges

Joseph S. Wholey
University of Southern California and
U.S. General Accounting Office[1]

This conference provides a good opportunity for reflection on the past, present, and future of our evaluation profession. As Scriven has suggested, evaluation necessarily involves the selection of criteria, standards, and evaluation processes. My questions have been: Whose criteria? Whose standards? Will it be feasible to perform the evaluation in terms of those criteria and standards? How will the evaluation information be used? In particular, will evaluation information be used to improve the policies and programs evaluated? To enhance the likelihood that evaluation will be used to improve programs, I have been especially interested in evaluation efforts that provide timely feedback on program performance in terms of criteria that key stakeholders consider relevant.

For more than 20 years, I have been impressed with the potential value of regular measurement of agency and program performance; in particular, ongoing monitoring of process and outcomes in terms of performance indicators developed with the participation of managers, staff, and other key stakeholders. Early work with stakeholders could clarify evaluation criteria, monitoring systems could be tested and refined over time, performance standards could be established after baseline and

[1]The views and opinions expressed by the author are his own and should not be construed to represent the position of the U.S. General Accounting Office. The author thanks all those who have contributed to his understanding of the performance measurement, program evaluation, and the roles that evaluators may play in improving organizational performance and accountability.

trend data were available, and more timely and relevant monitoring and evaluation could strengthen accountability and lead policymakers, managers, and other stakeholders to use performance information to improve policies and programs. Fascinating questions emerge, however, when public and nonprofit organizations attempt to turn this vision into reality.

A new leadership and management approach—results-oriented management—now requires public and nonprofit organizations to measure outcomes and use outcome information. Results-oriented management involves such agencies in developing agreement among key stakeholders on outcome-oriented goals and strategies for achieving the goals, measuring performance on a regular basis, and using performance information in efforts to improve performance and strengthen accountability to key stakeholders and the public. Interesting roles for evaluators are emerging in this new management environment, where interagency networks are important to effective performance.

This paper explores results-oriented management, discusses roles that evaluators can play in overcoming challenges that arise at each stage in results-oriented management efforts, and notes that results-oriented management is likely to increase both the demand for and the supply of evaluation studies. After soliciting the readers' thoughts as to the value of such evaluator involvement, the paper suggests that our involvement is likely to be helpful in improving social programs, solving social problems, and contributing to the quality of life of those served by such programs.

RESULTS-ORIENTED MANAGEMENT

To protect societal values and meet public needs, democratic societies develop complex arrays of laws, regulations, agencies, and programs. Today, global and domestic forces demand more effective management and higher levels of organizational performance. Leaders and managers in public and nonprofit organizations face demanding constituencies, higher public expectations, and aggressive media scrutiny.

Throughout the world, both in government and in the not-for-profit sector, programs often fall short of the performance needed to meet public needs and earn public support. Some well-intentioned programs even do more harm than good. Those within and outside public and nonprofit agencies too often see poor leadership and management, inefficiency, low-quality services, and ineffective performance. Perceptions of poor management and poor performance limit the resources made available to public and nonprofit organizations. Resource constraints in turn limit the contributions of public and nonprofit organizations to the quality of life of those they serve.

A new approach, results-oriented management, has emerged as a common element in current reform efforts in the public and not-for-profit sectors. *Results-oriented management* (or *performance-based management*) is the purposeful use of resources and information in efforts to achieve and demonstrate measurable progress toward outcome-related agency and program goals. In both the public and not-for-profit sectors, where organizations lack the "bottom line" that drives private firms, results-oriented management systems seek to improve performance—and communicate the value of the organization's activities—in terms of outcomes achieved in individuals, organizations, or communities served by the organization.

Vedung (1997) likens results-oriented management to *management by objectives*, which he sees as incorporating three features thought to constitute good management practice: setting clear goals that refer to results, involving managers and staff in decisionmaking, and frequently monitoring and evaluating the results. Results-oriented management aims to shift management's focus from inputs and process to results, in order to improve program effectiveness, strengthen accountability to key stakeholders and the public, support resource allocation and other policy decisionmaking, and improve public confidence and support. Regular monitoring of program outcomes and use of the resulting information are central features of results-oriented management systems. Shifting to a focus on outcomes confronts managers with new problems, however, problems whose resolution often requires sophisticated evaluation approaches.

With the passage of the Government Performance and Results Act (GPRA) in 1993, full-scale implementation of the statute by federal agencies beginning in 1997, and related efforts at all levels of government and in foundations and other funding agencies, pressures to demonstrate outcome-related results are being felt throughout the public and not-for-profit sectors. For several years, United Way of America has been encouraging local United Ways and local human service agencies to focus on both client and community outcomes. The meaning of accountability is changing as agencies are asked to take responsibility for results that can only be achieved with the cooperation and collaboration of other organizations.

Results-oriented management is accomplished through a three-step process, each of which typically requires a series of iterations: (1) developing a reasonable level of agreement among key stakeholders on missions, outcome-oriented goals, and strategies (resources and processes) to be used to achieve the goals; (2) measuring performance (in particular, outcomes achieved) on a regular basis; (3) using performance information in efforts to improve program effectiveness and strengthen accountability to key stakeholders and the public. The first step is often accomplished through strategic planning that involves key stakeholders within and outside the organization and often results in agreements to provide managerial flexibility in return for accountability for results. All three steps provide opportunities to communicate the value of agency and program activities to stakeholders and the public. GAO's "executive guide" describes the three steps in results-oriented management, identifies practices that are important at each step, and illustrates effective implementation of those practices in public agencies (U.S. General Accounting Office, 1996).

Though annual or more frequent measurement of outputs and outcomes is emphasized in results-oriented management systems, in-depth evaluation studies can also play important roles in such management systems. A theory of results-oriented management would include assumptions that agencies and key external stakeholders will be able to reach a reasonable level of agreement on outcome-oriented goals and strategies for achieving the goals, that it will be feasible to measure and evaluate performance in implementing the strategies and achieving the goals, that managers will use performance information in efforts to improve performance and to strengthen accountability to key stakeholders and the public, and that policymakers will use performance information in resource allocation, in decisions to modify goals and strategies, and in other policy decisionmaking.

Results-oriented management is an iterative process. Results-oriented management systems are typically developed over a number of policy and management cycles as policymakers, managers, and their staffs develop and refine goals and strategies, identify factors likely to affect organizational performance and ways to leverage or mitigate the influence of such factors, implement performance measurement systems, and use performance information. Goals, strategies, and performance measurement systems may be revised to reflect changes in policies and resources, experience in implementing planned strategies, changes in stakeholders' priorities, new technologies, or changes in the availability of information on performance and on how to improve performance. When priorities change or results are unacceptable, new goals or strategies may be adopted and unproductive activities may be abandoned.

Roles for Evaluators in Results-Oriented Management

Though some might see performance measurement and evaluation issues as purely technical issues and might believe that evaluators' roles should be confined to assessment of agency and program performance, evaluators can play important roles at every stage in the results-oriented management process.

Developing agreement on goals and strategies. Performance measurement systems help define and reinforce the meaning of organizational goals and strategies. From the perspectives of different stakeholders, "performance" may focus on the products and services delivered by agencies and programs, the clients and populations served, service quality or efficiency, intermediate outcomes, unintended outcomes, or end results achieved.

Evaluators can assist policymakers and managers in identifying intended outcomes, establishing or revising agency and program goals, identifying factors that could affect achievement of the goals, and developing strategies for achieving the goals; in particular, developing partnership efforts and other strategies to leverage or mitigate the influence of external factors that are likely to affect results. Performance data and evaluation studies can be important sources of information for policymakers and managers in their efforts to develop agreement on outcome-oriented goals and the strategies to be used to achieve the goals. Such assistance may resemble evaluators' efforts to improve program design and program implementation by helping stakeholders clarify program theories (see Donaldson, this volume).

Measuring and Evaluating Performance. Given a reasonable level of agreement on goals and strategies for achieving goals, performance measurement systems play a central role in results-oriented management by providing regular feedback on the extent to which agency and program strategies have been implemented and the extent to which outcome-related performance targets have been or are being achieved. Performance information may come from measurement systems that regularly compare outputs and intermediate outcomes with performance targets, or from less-frequent evaluation studies that measure program implementation, test assumptions connecting agency and program activities to results, measure unintended outcomes, estimate the causal impact of agency and program activities, or measure other hard-to-measure outcomes.

As the General Accounting Office stated after studying experiences in leading agencies here and abroad, performance measures should "demonstrate results, [be] limited to the vital few, respond to multiple priorities, and link to responsible programs"; performance data should be sufficiently timely, complete, accurate, and consistent "to document performance and support decisionmaking at various organizational levels" (U.S. General Accounting Office, 1996, pp. 24, 27). To provide more valid measures of program performance, agencies may disaggregate performance data to reflect the degree of difficulty in achieving intended outcomes as the Occupational Safety and Health Administration has done, or statistically adjust performance standards to reflect the influence of client characteristics, economic conditions, or other degree-of-difficulty factors on client outcomes as the U.S. Department of Labor has done in job training programs (see U.S. General Accounting, 1999).

Agencies typically use numerical performance measures, but may also use peer review assessments of performance or some combination of quantitative and qualitative performance measures. The National Science Foundation (NSF), for example, uses assessments by external experts to measure the agency's success in achieving annual performance goals relating to the effectiveness of NSF-supported research and education activities (National Science Foundation, 2000). The General Accounting Office plans to use both quantitative and qualitative performance goals and measures to assess its performance (U.S. General Accounting Office, 2000a).

Rarely will a single performance measurement system or evaluation study meet the information needs of all key stakeholders. It will usually be necessary to develop hierarchies of performance measures to meet information needs at different levels. As Weiss and Morrill (1998) have noted, learning organizations use multiple feedback loops and many types of information to inform policy formulation, program improvement, and program redesign. Performance information may come from performance measurement systems, audits, case studies, benchmarking comparisons, basic and applied research, program evaluations, and experiments.

Evaluators can assist in validating performance data and improving performance measurement systems. External evaluation can be important in ensuring the accuracy and credibility of performance information intended for dissemination to policy levels and to the public. Evaluation of performance measurement systems should focus both on the technical quality of the measurement system and on the extent to which performance information is used in managing to achieve performance goals and in providing accountability to key stakeholders and the public (Wholey, 1999). Recent GAO publications explore interrelationships between performance measurement systems and evaluation studies, and show how evaluation studies can supplement and improve the data produced by performance measurement systems (U.S. General Accounting Office, 1998, 1999, 2000b).

Evaluation studies can provide a fuller and more accurate picture of program performance than either day-to-day experience or the rough sketch obtainable through typical performance measurement systems. Evaluation studies can be used to measure the extent to which a program is operating as intended, and to measure the extent to which a program achieves intended outcomes or leads to unintended outcomes. In addition, evaluation studies can be used to assess the effectiveness and cost-effectiveness of current strategies, to measure the cost savings that a program produces in other programs, to measure the net impact and net benefits caused by a program, and to measure other hard-to-measure program outcomes.

As is suggested by experiences in the Job Corps and the Special Supplemental Food Program for Women, Infants, and Children (WIC) program, impact evaluations may communicate more clearly with policy-makers if the evaluations are supplemented with benefit-cost analyses that compare program costs with cost savings and other economic benefits associated with the program's net effects. In the Reagan years, for example, an impact evaluation found that the Job Corps had a positive net effect on participants (employment service applicants who were high school dropouts) and estimated that the program's benefits to the society were greater than its costs (Mallar and others, 1980, 1982). The findings of the 1980 interim evaluation were used by Senator Hatch to help persuade his colleagues to maintain the Job Corps at a time when other employment and training programs were being eliminated or sharply reduced. Conservative Republicans, who are ordinarily skeptical of federal social programs, gave considerable weight to evaluation findings that demonstrated the effectiveness of the Job Corps and its value to society. The Job Corps, a program with little political constituency, now has an annual budget in the $1 billion range.

Similarly, WIC evaluations have been used in congressional decision-making for many years. WIC provides vouchers for food supplements, and for nutrition education and counseling, to low income pregnant women, nursing mothers, infants, and children judged to be at nutritional risk. A number of evaluation studies—some based on randomized experiments—have demonstrated that the WIC program significantly increases birthweight, significantly reduces the percentage of low-birthweight infants, and saves more money in other programs than the program costs (see, for example, U.S. General Accounting Office, 1992, which combines evaluation synthesis and benefit-cost comparisons). WIC's annual budget now exceeds $4 billion.

Using performance measurement and evaluation information. Evaluators can assist agencies in using performance measurement and evaluation information internally, to improve service quality and program effectiveness, and in using such information externally, to strengthen accountability to policymakers and the public. Within an agency or program, policymakers and managers may reallocate resources or redirect activities to improve performance, may redesign personnel management and other central management systems to focus on organizational performance, and may use performance information to create nonfinancial incentives for improved performance. The Veterans Health Administration and the U.S. Department of Transportation, for example, have used performance agreements to focus executives' attention on agency performance goals (U.S. General Accounting Office, 2000c). Agencies may also use performance information in developing partnerships with other public or private agencies to improve performance.

While performance measurement systems limit themselves to assessing the extent of progress toward agency or program goals, program evaluations typically identify opportunities to improve agency or program performance and may offer options or recommendations toward that end. For example, the U.S. Coast Guard has used performance measurement systems and evaluation studies to improve its performance as well as its accountability to key stakeholders and the public. The Coast Guard set 5-year performance goals related to deaths, injuries, and environmental damage; for example, "reduce accidental deaths and injuries from marine casualties by 20%," and "reduce the amount of oil and chemicals going into the water from marine sources by 20%." With the help of an ad hoc program evaluation group from throughout the agency, the Coast Guard then developed and refined systems for measuring and reporting on performance; for example, *worker fatalities per 100,00 workers*. The agency disaggregated performance data to help program managers understand trends and risk. By disaggregating fatality data, for example, the Coast Guard found that commercial towing was even less safe than fishing, and then entered into a partnership with the towing industry to address the problem. A collaborative study showed that, "[M]ost of the casualties were deckhands, and most of them were falling overboard—a problem which did not lend itself to an off-the-shelf regulatory program for towboats" (U.S. Coast Guard, 1996, pp. 8). As GAO noted, the Coast Guard and the towing industry developed training and guidelines to reduce the causes of fatalities. "This joint effort contributed to a significant decline in the towing industry fatality rate, from 91 per 100,000 employees in 1990 to 27 per 100,000 in 1995" (U.S. General Accounting Office, 1996, pp. 37). The U.S. Department of Transportation is now doing similar studies to determine the causes of truck crashes that now cost 5000 lives each year (Downey, 2001).

Challenges to effective use of results-oriented management. Though results-oriented management approaches may be fine in theory, a host of institutional, organizational, and technical challenges must be overcome if results-oriented management is to achieve its promise. Results-oriented management may be hampered by fragmentation of power and conflict over agency and program goals, legal and regulatory requirements, organizational cultures and capacities, interorganizational factors, overlapping information demands from key stakeholders, problems in measuring performance, lack of information on how to improve performance, and concerns over possible misuse of performance information.

Competing values, constitutional protections, and institutional and political factors. Good management is important, but other things may be equally or more important. Efforts to move to a results orientation may come into conflict with national cultures or with values like freedom, decentralization, equity, and privacy. Efforts to manage for results may run into problems if they are seen as conflicting with values that oppose unfunded mandates or favor "equitable" or "needs-based" resource allocation. Value conflicts may be magnified by institutional and political conflicts.

In this country in particular, separation of powers makes results-oriented management difficult. Power is widely fragmented: between public and private institutions (including interest groups and the media), and among the legislature, the executive branch, and the courts. Key stakeholders will often differ over goals, over strategies for achieving goals, or over the importance of unintended consequences of agency and program activities.

In a book intended to refute the notion of government bureaucracy as a monolith, Wilson (1989) identified political factors that affect the activities of government executives, managers, and staff. In an admitted oversimplification, he identified four political environments in which an agency might be situated. Wilson suggested that an agency might be the product of either (1) client politics, where agencies like the Department of Veterans Affairs face a dominant interest group that favors agency goals; (2) entrepreneurial politics, where agencies like the Environmental Protection Agency and the Food and Drug Administration face a dominant interest group like the manufacturing or pharmaceutical industry that is hostile to agency goals; (3) interest group politics, where agencies like the Occupational Safety and Health Administration face two or more interest groups like corporations and unions that are in conflict over its goals; or (4) majoritarian politics, where the agency faces no important interest group (pp. 76-83, 248-251). Wilson's categorization suggests that results-oriented management is likely to be more difficult when there is conflict over agency goals.

In addition, since most outcomes are influenced by the activities of more than a single agency, results-oriented management often requires interagency coordination, collaboration, and partnership efforts to achieve the intended results. Results-oriented management is especially challenging in decentralized systems.

Organizational cultures and capacity. Most public and nonprofit organizations focus on delivery of products and services, and focus less energy on results that lie beyond the control of agency staff. In both public and non-profit agencies, executives and managers may be so bound by internal and external rules and constraints that they have little freedom to manage for results. Agency management typically is process-oriented, and agency cultures are often dominated by standard operating procedures. Furthermore, agency executives, managers, and staff may lack the skills or the time and other resources needed to get agreement on results-oriented goals and strategies, to measure and evaluate performance, or to use performance information effectively.

Technical factors. It can be costly and difficult to get a reasonable level of agreement on outcome-oriented goals and strategies, and to get performance information that is sufficiently timely, complete, accurate, and consistent to document performance and support decision making. Resource constraints may make it difficult to obtain sufficiently accurate data on results. Further challenges will present themselves when results occur over extended periods of time.

Wilson (1989) calls particular attention to two factors affecting the cost and feasibility of managing for results: The extent to which agency goals can be precisely specified, and the extent to which progress toward agency goals can be reliably measured. Using these factors, Wilson categorizes agencies as either (1) production agencies like the Social Security Administration and the Postal Service, where staff activities and the results of those activities can be observed; (2) procedural agencies like the Occupational Safety and Health Administration and army units in peacetime, where staff activities can be observed but not the outcomes that result from those activities; (3) craft organizations like detective bureaus and army units in wartime, where staff activities cannot be observed but results are relatively easy to evaluate; or (4) coping organizations like universities and the diplomatic corps, where neither staff activities nor results are easily observed and both process-oriented and results-oriented management are likely to be difficult. Wilson's categorization suggests that results-oriented management is more likely to be difficult outside production agencies that provide direct services. Radin (1998) has suggested that, "In many ways, the [results-oriented management] process is designed for agencies that actually deliver services…; have relatively stable histories that are amenable to a planning approach; have cultures of data production (with agreement on typologies and belief in the accuracy of the information); and have manageable levels of conflict between external actors (or stakeholders)" (pp. 309).

Meeting the Challenges to Results-Oriented Management

As Drucker (1974) noted, government agencies tend to be misdirected because they are supported by budget allocations rather than being paid for results, and such agencies tend to fragment themselves by trying to please everyone. Many nonprofit organizations face similar or greater problems because of their dependence on grants and contracts from multiple sources. If public agencies and nonprofit organizations are to serve ends beyond organizational survival, however, they must find ways to focus a reasonable fraction of their resources and energies in specific directions and get external support for movement in those directions.

Public and nonprofit organizations use several approaches to overcome institutional and organizational challenges to results-oriented management: (1) using nonfinancial incentives including the time and attention of high-level officials to build senior management commitment to results-oriented goals and strategies, (2) using research and evaluation studies to assess the results of current and potential strategies, (3) negotiating with key stakeholders and if necessary revising proposed goals and strategies to get sufficient levels of support, (4) delegating authority in return for accountability for results, (5) using nonfinancial and financial incentives to build staff commitment to results-oriented goals and strategies, (6) developing partnerships to achieve results beyond the control of any one agency, (7) redesigning procurement and grants management systems to focus on performance, and (8) developing systems for using performance information to support resource allocation and decisionmaking.

Evaluators can assist in redesigning agency and program data systems to increase their value for performance measurement and results-oriented management. In more challenging assignments, evaluators may assist in redesigning program management systems, budget systems, personnel management systems, procurement systems, and grants management systems to focus on results. Evaluators may assist in developing surveys to get valid, reliable information on program results, suggesting strategies to help ensure high response rates, minimize data collection costs, and ensure that survey data are sufficiently complete, accurate, and consistent to document performance and support decisionmaking.

Public and nonprofit organizations use several more approaches to overcome institutional, organizational, and technical challenges to results-oriented management: (1) using logic models to facilitate agreement on goals, strategies, and performance measures; (2) using intermediate goals and measures (outputs and outcomes) to show progress or contributions to intended results; (3) using qualitative goals and measures when appropriate; (4) disaggregating and reporting performance information in ways useful to management; and (5) using regression models to incorporate the influence of external factors in performance measurement systems.

Performance may mean different things to different stakeholders. Logic models have been used to involve key stakeholders and to facilitate reasonable levels of agreement on goals and strategies in a broad range of programs including environmental protection programs and human service programs. Hatry's (1999) book on performance measurement presents many examples of logic models used by public and nongovernmental organizations. The Office of National Drug Control Policy has brought together interagency working groups to help develop strategic- and program-level logic models, the national drug control strategy, and action plans specifying the activities and programs to be used to achieve specific performance targets (see, e.g., Office of National Drug Control Policy, 1999, 2000). Many United Ways and United Way-funded agencies use logic models and outcome-focused performance measurement systems to clarify the purposes of funded programs, to help focus staff efforts on common goals, and to communicate the value of funded programs to potential funders and donors.

Logic models can help organizations to identify intermediate goals (outputs and intermediate outcomes) that are within the agency's span of influence and can reasonably be expected to lead to intended results. Agreement on such goals is a key ingredient in most results-oriented management efforts. A disease prevention program's goals might be stated in terms of increases in amounts of vaccines distributed and increases in immunization rates, for example, since such increases are within the program's span of influence and can be expected to help reduce communicable diseases. Highway safety programs may reward states for increasing penalties for driving under the influence and for reducing the percentage of alcohol-related fatalities, both of which can be expected to help reduce the total number of highway fatalities.

Many public and nonprofit agencies use logic models to communicate to external stakeholders, in graphic form, relevant elements of program design: key inputs, activities and processes, outputs and intermediate outcomes that reflect agency contributions, end outcomes, and causal linkages among inputs, activities, outputs, intermediate outcomes, end outcomes. Use of logic models may strengthen agency budget requests or grant applications by helping clarify agency and program contributions to intended outcomes. In Canada, logic models have been used to demonstrate linkages among program inputs or activities, outputs, and outcomes (see Auditor General of Canada, 2000). United Way of America has produced a number of guides that can be used to introduce policymakers, managers, and staff to the use of logic models and outcome data (United Way of America, 1996a, 1996b, 1996c).

In addition, as noted above, agencies may use program evaluations to explain current performance levels and learn how to improve performance, and use evaluation studies to measure hard-to-measure outcomes including net causal impact. After its weekly performance measurement system revealed a sudden outbreak of Medflies along the Mexico-Guatemala border, for example, the U.S. Department of Agriculture used program evaluation to determine why program performance had declined and how their trapping and spraying programs could be improved to control and eradicate fruit flies and thus help protect agriculture in the United States (U.S. General Accounting Office, 2000b). In the Upward Bound program, the U.S. Department of Education used program evaluation to learn about high school courses and grades, educational expectations, high school completion, and college enrollment of disadvantaged students who had been provided intensive academic experience during the summer and mentoring and tutoring over the school year in the 9th through 12th grades (U.S. General Accounting Office, 2000b). On the basis of the Upward Bound program's random assignment of students to experimental and control groups, the evaluation estimated the program's net impact in terms of college enrollment.

THE INCREASING DEMAND FOR EVALUATION SKILLS: MUTUALLY REINFORCING ROLES FOR PERFORMANCE MEASUREMENT AND EVALUATION

Given the pressures facing communities, regions, and nations across the globe and the challenges that arise as public and nongovernmental organizations work to make effective use of performance measurement and results-oriented management, there is likely to be increasing demand for those who understand qualitative and quantitative measurement and evaluation methods. Interest in performance measurement and results-oriented management is likely to grow, building on the recent progress that has been made in many public and nonprofit agencies. In this context, evaluators will be asked to help design and implement performance measurement systems, to conduct evaluation studies to explain reasons for current performance levels and measure hard-to-measure outcomes, and to assist in translating performance measurement and evaluation information into actions to improve the performance and credibility of public and non-governmental organizations.

Since few outcomes can be achieved through the efforts of a single agency, it is likely that interest will intensify in development of goals, strategies, and results-oriented management systems for "cross-cutting programs" that reflect the contributions of multiple agencies to common goals. Evaluators can make significant contributions in such complex management environments.

Effective implementation of performance measurement and results-oriented management will typically require training: in strategic planning, in involvement of stakeholders in development of goals and performance measures, in outcome measurement, in data analysis, in process and impact evaluation, and in use of performance measurement and evaluation information. Much of the needed content for such training should come from case studies, cross-case analyses, evaluation studies, and applied research on efforts to use results-oriented management systems in public and nonprofit organizations. Evaluators should be well-equipped to provide such training and to perform such studies.

Performance measurement systems and program evaluation studies can and should be mutually reinforcing. Both logic and experiences in this country and abroad suggest that the demand for and the supply of evaluation studies are likely to increase after agencies begin to measure program outcomes on a regular basis.

When policymakers and managers are regularly provided information on a program's outcomes, they are likely to want to know why the outcomes have occurred (what difference the program has made) and how performance can be improved. Such interest is likely to stimulate evaluation studies to answer the "why" and "how" questions.

Evaluation studies should be more feasible, less costly, and more useful when performance criteria have been clarified and performance data have been collected. When agencies are held accountable for improved performance, executives and managers will be more likely to use evaluation information to improve program performance and to communicate the value of agency and program activities to policy levels, other stakeholders, and the public.

PROGRESS, PROBLEMS, AND NEXT STEPS

A number of years will typically be needed to achieve effective implementation of results-oriented management systems. Improvements in program performance and accountability can take longer. Over the past several years, many state and local governments have made progress in results-oriented management, but even among leaders progress has often been followed by setbacks and disappointments in the face of political, organizational, and technical challenges.

At the federal level, 8 years after passage of the Government Performance and Results Act and approximately 4 years into government-wide implementation, federal agencies now have experience in strategic planning, annual performance planning, and performance measurement and reporting. The General Accounting Office (GAO) recently concluded that, "[N]ew and valuable information on the plans, goals, and strategies of federal agencies has been provided.... [I]ssuance of agencies' performance reports each March now represents a new and potentially more substantive stage in the implementation of GPRA...." GAO identified several continuing implementation challenges, however; for example, articulating and reinforcing a results orientation (only half of federal managers perceive strong leadership commitment to achieving results); coordinating cross-cutting programs; and building capacity to gather and use performance information (General Accounting Office, 2001, pp. 11). A focus group of current and former senior government officials and public management experts concluded that new tools such as the Government Performance and Results Act are focusing Congressional and Executive Branch attention on performance and results, but that major management problems remain. The focus group noted that some agencies and programs have improved performance. However, most programs have not developed and used outcome-oriented performance measures to track and report results and that collecting valid and reliable performance data remains a major challenge for most agencies (Reason Public Policy Institute, 2000). Similar groups convened by the National Academy of Public Administration suggested that performance-based government is important because it helps to make government more transparent, and because it provides a management framework through which leadership can implement its program agenda. They noted that the Government Performance and Results Act has increased accountability and documenting of goals and results, and has focused attention on crosscutting programs and the need to coordinate them (National Academy of Public Administration, 2001).

After several years of effort in the Canadian government, a recent report from the Auditor General concluded that, while the concept of managing for results is widely accepted and supported among senior managers and performance information is used in some programs, actual measurement and use of performance information have made only limited progress. Concluding that managing for results is still not an integral part of managing federal departments and that the evaluation function has regressed, the Auditor General called upon the Treasury Board Secretariat to assemble and communicate successful practices and suggested that it might be time for the government to consider introducing accountability legislation. The Auditor General found growing attention to "horizontal" issues that cross departmental boundaries, but found that government is still at the start of efforts to report and use performance information in managing such issues for results (Auditor General of Canada, 2000).

In the not-for-profit sector, a 3 year evaluation of the use of program outcome information in seven leading United Way communities concluded that most funded agencies believed that implementation of outcome measurement was helpful in focusing staff efforts on common goals, communicating results to stakeholders, and competing for resources. Program directors believed that implementation of program outcome measurement had a positive effect on service delivery and effectiveness. Most program directors indicated that they would recommend that directors of similar programs consider implementing outcome measurement. The limited scope and duration of the evaluation prevented the evaluators from providing findings on whether clients were in fact benefiting from the programs' outcome measurement efforts, however. Most program directors remained concerned about the cost of outcome measurement, and indicated that staff turnover resulted in a continuing need for training (see United Way of America, 2000).

My assessment of evidence to date, from different levels of government and from nonprofit organizations, suggests that results-oriented management holds great promise, but that its ultimate value is still uncertain. Progress has been made in implementing results-oriented management in many public and nonprofit organizations. Even the initial step, establishing outcome-oriented goals and strategies, has improved accountability in many agencies and programs. Performance information has been used to improve performance in specific agencies and programs. Many agency plans, and their reports, document results and strategies to achieve improved results, but many reveal difficulties in obtaining timely and valid data on program outcomes. As Greiner has suggested, research is needed on the feasibility, cost, and value of results-oriented management in various circumstances, including research on unsuccessful efforts and on best practices approaches (Greiner, 1996).

As one who has for many years worked in a public management environment, I am eager to hear readers' views as to the importance of results-oriented management, the extent to which you are interested in this management approach, and the extent to which you believe evaluation can contribute to the effective use of results-oriented management (You can reach me at wholey@usc.edu). Given the pressures facing public and nonprofit organizations and the potential value of results-oriented management in improving social programs and solving social problems, my view is that we should be involved in such efforts to move public and nonprofit organizations to a results orientation. My hope is that our efforts will eventually pay off in better lives for those served by such organizations, better communities, and increased public confidence in institutions that all of us need in our increasingly urbanized societies.

REFERENCES

Auditor General of Canada. (2000). Managing departments for results and managing horizontal issues for results. *Report of the Auditor General of Canada,* (Chapter 20). Ottawa.

Downey, M. (2001, February). *Departmental management: Experiences at DOT.* Paper Presented at the meeting of the National Academy of Public Administration, Washington, DC.

Drucker, P. F. (1974). *Management: Tasks, responsibilities, practices.* New York, NY: Harper and Row.

Greiner, J. M. (1996). Positioning performance measurement for the twenty-first century. In A. Halachmi & G. Bouckaert. (Eds.), *Organizational performance and measurement in the public sector* (pp. 11-50). Westport, CT: Quorum.

Mathematica Policy Research. *(1980). Evaluation of the economic impact of the Job Corps program: Second follow-up report.* Princeton, NJ: Author.

Mathematica Policy Research. (1982). *Evaluation of the economic impact of the Job Corps program: Third follow-up report.* Princeton, NJ: Author.

National Academy of Public Administration, Center for Improving Government Performance. (2001). *Transition briefing papers.* Washington, DC: Author.

National Science Foundation. (2000). *GPRA performance report: FY 1999.* Washington, DC: Author.

Office of National Drug Control Policy. (1999). *National drug control strategy, performance measures of effectiveness: Implementation and findings.* Washington, DC: Executive Office of the President.

Office of National Drug Control Policy. (2000). *National drug control strategy, performance measures of effectiveness: 2000 annual report.* Washington, DC: Executive Office of the President.

Radin, B. A. (1998). The Government Performance and Results Act: Hydra-headed monster or flexible management tool?. *Public Administration Review, 58,* 307-316.

Reason Public Policy Institute. (2000). *The transition dialogue series.* Washington, DC: Author.

The Urban Institute. (1999). *Performance measurement: Getting results.* Washington, DC: Hatry, H. P.

United Way of America. (1996a). *Focusing on program outcomes: Summary guide.* Alexandria, VA: Author.

United Way of America. *(1996b). Focusing on program outcomes: A guide for United Ways.* Alexandria, VA: Author.

United Way of America. (1996c). *Measuring program outcomes: A practical approach.* Alexandria, VA: Author.

United Way of America. (2000). *Agency experiences with outcome measurement: Survey findings.* Alexandria, VA: Author.

U.S. Coast Guard. (1996). *Using outcome information to redirect programs.* Washington, DC: American Society for Public Administration.

U.S. General Accounting Office. (1992) *Early intervention: Federal investments like WIC can produce savings.* Washington, DC: Author.

U.S. General Accounting Office. (1996). *Executive guide: Effectively implementing the Government Performance and Results Act.* Washington, DC: Author.

U.S. General Accounting Office. (1998). *Performance measurement and evaluation: Definitions and relationships.* Washington, DC: Author.

U.S. General Accounting Office. (1999). *Managing for results: Measuring program results that are under limited federal control.* Washington, DC: Author.

U.S. General Accounting Office. (2000a). *Performance plan: Fiscal Year 2001.* Washington, DC: Author.

U.S. General Accounting Office. (2000b). *Program evaluation: Studies helped agencies measure or explain program performance.* Washington, DC: Author.

U.S. General Accounting Office. (2000c). *Managing for results: Emerging benefits from selected agencies' use of performance agreements.* Washington, DC: Author.

U.S. General Accounting Office. (2001). *Major management challenges and program risks: A governmentwide perspective.* Washington, DC: Author.

Vedung, E. (1997). *Public policy and program evaluation.* New Brunswick, NJ: Transaction Publishers.

Weiss, H. B., & Morrill, W. A. (1998, April). Useful learning for public action. Paper presented at the American Society for Public Administration National Conference, New York, NY.

Wholey, J. S. (1999). Quality control: Assessing the accuracy and usefulness of performance measurement systems. In H. P. Hatry (Ed.), *Performance measurement: Getting results (*pp. 217-239). Washington, DC: The Urban Institute.

Wilson, J. Q. *(1989). Bureaucracy: What government agencies do and why they do it.* New York, NY: Basic Books.

Empowerment Evaluation Strikes a Responsive Cord

David Fetterman
Stanford University

Evaluation practice should strike a responsive cord in the 21st century. It should resonate with the passionate commitment to do good[1] that comes from the heart. It should be guided by values we share including love, compassion, truth, justice, loyalty, family, and community.

Evaluation has an instrumental role to play in this brave new world of our own creation. We will have to listen very closely to discern whether we can hear evaluation practice in the 21st century. I believe we will hear it—loud and clear—but will we hear the solo performance of a talented few or an orchestra of musicians ranging from percussionist to pianist playing in society harmony?

Will we hear evaluation practice playing in the foreground or the background and will we know what we hear when we hear it? Will music in the background suggest a social indifference—that evaluation is ignored, meaningless, and irrelevant or will it mean it has become such an instrumental part of our life that it is fully integrated into the hum and buzz of our culture.

We don't know the answer to many of these questions. We must listen, but we also have the obligation to compose our own music, our own harmonic vision of evaluation practice in the 21st century. Empowerment evaluation will be the leitmotif or familiar refrain you hear from me on this

---

[1]See Fetterman (1993) for examples of social scientists, particularly ethnographers, applying ethnography to evaluation and other fields in the spirit of social justice and the larger social good.

note, but I will not be singing this acapella. I am not alone. The chorus is vast and varied and growing louder all the time.

EMPOWERMENT EVALUATION

Empowerment evaluation is the use of evaluation concepts, techniques, and findings to foster improvement and self-determination (Fetterman 2000; Fetterman, Kaftarian, & Wandersman, 1996). It is guided by a commitment to truth and honesty (Fetterman, 1998). It is designed to help people help themselves and improve their programs using a form of self-evaluation and reflection. Program participants—including clients, consumers, and staff members—conduct their own evaluations; an outside evaluator often serves as a coach or additional facilitator depending on internal program capabilities. By internalizing and institutionalizing self-evaluation processes and practices, a dynamic and responsive approach to evaluation can be developed.

There are three steps involved in helping others learn to evaluate their own programs (see Figure 4.1): (1) developing a mission, vision, or unifying purpose; (2) taking stock or determining where the program stands, including strengths and weaknesses; and (3) planning for the future by establishing goals and helping participants determine their own strategies to accomplish program goals and objectives. In addition, empowerment evaluators help program staff members and participants determine the type of evidence required to document and monitor progress credibly toward their goals. These steps combined help to create a "communicative space" (Vanderplaat, 1995) to facilitate emancipatory and "communicative action" (Habermas,1984).

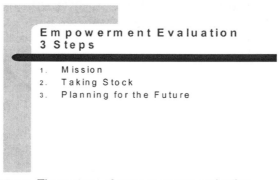

FIGURE 4.1. Three steps of empowerment evaluation.

The first step in an empowerment evaluation is to ask program staff members and participants to define their mission (see Figure 4.2). This step can be accomplished in a few hours. An empowerment evaluator facilitates an open session with as many staff members and participants as possible.

Participants are asked to generate key phrases that capture the mission of the program or project. This is done even when an existing mission statement exists, because there are typically many new participants and the initial document may or may not have been generated in a democratic open forum. Proceeding in this fashion allows fresh new ideas to become a part of the mission and it also allows participants an opportunity to voice their vision of the program. It is common for groups to learn how divergent their participants' views are about the program, even when they have been working together for years. The evaluator records these phrases, typically on a poster sheet.

Then a workshop participant is asked to volunteer to write these telescopic phrases into a paragraph or two. This document is shared with the group, revisions and corrections are made in the process, and then the group is asked to accept the document on a consensus basis: That is, they do not have to be in favor of 100% of the document; they just have to be willing to live with it. The mission statement represents the values of the group, and as such, represents the foundation for the next step, taking stock.

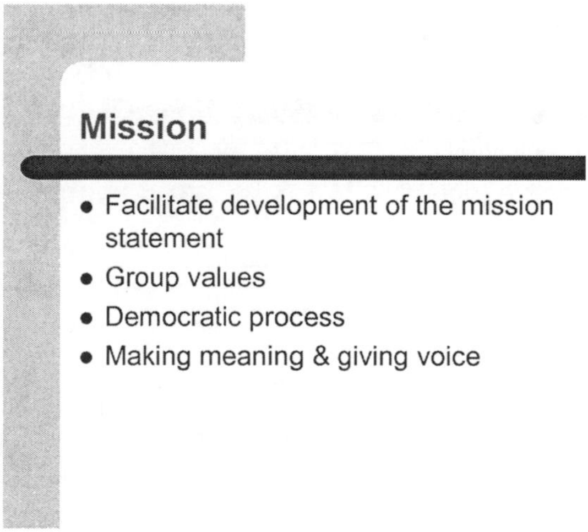

Mission

- Facilitate development of the mission statement
- Group values
- Democratic process
- Making meaning & giving voice

FIGURE 4.2. The mission statement.

TAKING STOCK

The second step in an empowerment evaluation is taking stock (see Figure 4.3). This step can also be conducted in a few hours, and has two sections. The first involves generating a list of key activities that are crucial to the functioning of the program. Once again, the empowerment evaluator serves as a facilitator, asking program staff members and participants to list the most significant features and/or activities associated with the program. A list of 10 to 20 activities is sufficient. After generating this list, it is time to prioritize and determine which are the most important activities meriting evaluation at this time.

One tool used to minimize the time associated with prioritizing activities involves voting with dots. The empowerment evaluator gives each participant five dot stickers, and asks the participants to place them by the activity on which the participant wants to focus. The participant can distribute them across five different activities or place all five on one activity. Counting the dots easily identifies the top 10 activities. The 10 activities with the most dots become the prioritized list of activities meriting evaluation at that time. (This process avoids long arguments about why one activity is valued more than another is, when both activities are included in the list of the top 10 program activities anyway.)

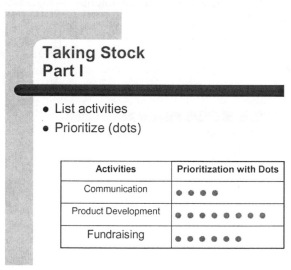

FIGURE 4.3. Taking stock (part I).

The second phase of taking stock involves rating the activities. Program staff members and participants are asked to rate how well they are doing concerning each activity on a 1 to 10 scale, with 10 as the highest level and 1 as the lowest. The staff members and participants only have minimal definitions about the components or activities at this point. Additional clarification can be pursued as needed; however, detailed definition and clarification become a significant part of the later dialogue process. (The group will never reach the rating stage if each activity is perfectly defined at this point. The rating process then sets the stage for dialogue, clarification, and communication.)

Typically, participants rate each of the activities while in their seats on their own piece of paper. Then they are asked to come up to the front of the room and record their ratings on a poster sheet of paper. This allows for some degree of independence in rating. In addition, it minimizes a long stream of second guessing and checking to see what others are rating the same activities.

At the same time, there is nothing confidential about the process. Program staff members and participants place their initials at the top of the matrix and then record their ratings for each activity. Contrary to most research designs, this system is designed to ensure that everyone knows and is influenced by each other's ratings (*after* recording them on the poster sheet). This is part of the socialization process that takes place in an empowerment evaluation, opening up the discussion and stepping toward more open disclosure—speaking one's truth.

The taking stock phase of an empowerment evaluation is conducted in an open setting for three reasons: (1) it creates a democratic flow of information and exchange of information; (2) it makes it more difficult for managers to retaliate because it is in an open forum; and (3) it increases the probability that the disclosures will be diplomatic, because program staff members and participants must remain in that environment. Open discussions in a vacuum, without regard for workplace norms, are not productive. They are often unrealistic and can be counter-productive.

Staff members and participants are more likely to give their program a higher rating if they are only asked to give an overall or gestalt rating about the program. Consequently, it is important that program staff members and participants be asked to begin by assessing individual program activities. They are more likely to give some activities low ratings if they are given an equal opportunity to speak positively about, or rate, other activities highly. The ratings can be totaled and averaged by person and by activity. This provides some insight into routinely optimistic and pessimistic participants. It allows participants to see where they stand in relation to their peers, which helps them calibrate their own assessments in the future. The more important rating, of course, is across the matrix or spreadsheet by activity. Each activity receives a total and average. Combining the individual activity averages generates a total program rating, often lower than an external assessment rating. This represents the first baseline data concerning that specific program activity. This can be used to compare change over time.

All of this work sets the tone for one of the most important parts of the empowerment evaluation process: Dialogue. The empowerment evaluator facilitates a discussion about the ratings. A survey would have accomplished the same task up to this point. However, the facilitator probes and asks why one person rated communication a 6, whereas two others rated it a 3 on the matrix.[2] Participants are asked to explain their rating and provide evidence or documentation to support the rating. This plants the seeds for the next stage of empowerment evaluation, planning for the future, where they will need to specify the evidence they plan to use to document that their activities are helping them accomplish their goals. The empowerment evaluator serves as a critical friend during this stage, facilitating discussion and making sure everyone is heard, and at the same time being critical and asking, "What do you mean by that?" or asking for additional clarification and substantiation about a particular rating or viewpoint.

Participants are asked for both the positive and negative basis for their ratings. For example, if they give communication a 3, they are asked why a 3. The typical response is because there is poor communication and they proceed to list reasons for this problem. The empowerment evaluator listens and helps record the information and then asks the question again, focusing on why it was a 3 instead of a 1. In other words, there must be something positive to report as well. An important part of empowerment evaluation involves building on strengths; even in weak areas, there is typically something positive that can be used to strengthen that activity or other activities. If the effort becomes exclusively problem focused, all participants see are difficulties instead of strengths and opportunities to build and improve on practice.

---

[2]See Fetterman (1998) for additional information about this example. Briefly, we learned that the participants were talking past each other or at least they were speaking on different levels of analysis. The individuals who rated communication a three stated that communication was poor in the school. However, the Dean rated communication a six because he was assessing communication in the school from a larger perspective. He thought we communicated much better than other departments in the Institute.

Some participants give their programs or specific activities unrealistically high ratings. The absence of appropriate documentation, peer ratings, and a reminder about the realities of their environment—such as a high drop-out rate, students bringing guns to school, and racial violence in a high school—help participants recalibrate their ratings. Participants are reminded that they can change their ratings throughout the dialogue and exchange stage of the workshop, based on what they hear and learn from their peers. The ratings are not carved in stone. However, in some cases, ratings stay higher than peers consider appropriate. The significance of this process, however, is not the actual rating so much as it is the creation of a baseline, as noted earlier, from which future progress can be measured. In addition, it sensitizes program participants to the necessity of collecting data to support assessments or appraisals.

After examining 4 or 5 examples, beginning with divergent ones and ending with similar ratings (to determine if there are totally different reasons for the same or similar ratings), this phase of the workshop is generally complete. The group or a designated subcommittee continues to discuss the ratings, and the group is asked to return to the next workshop for planning for the future with the final ratings and a brief description or explanation of what the ratings meant. (This is normally shared with the group for review, at a time in which ratings can still be changed, and then a consensus is sought concerning the document.) This process is superior to surveys because it generally has a higher response rate—close to 100% depending on how many staff members and participants are present—and it allows participants to discuss what they meant by their ratings, to recalibrate and revise their ratings based on what they learn, thus minimizing "talking past each other" about certain issues or other miscommunications such as defining terms differently and using radically different rating systems. Participants learn what a 3 and an 8 mean to individuals in the group in the process of discussing and arguing about these ratings. This is a form of norming, helping create shared meanings and interpretations within a group.

Planning for the Future

After rating their program's performance and providing documentation to support that rating, program participants are asked "Where they want to go from here?" They are asked how they would like to improve on what they do well and not so well. The empowerment evaluator asks the group

Taking Stock
Part II

- Rating 1 (low) – 10 (high)
- Dialogue

Activities	Initials of Participant	Initials of Participant	Initials of Participant	Average
Communication	3	6	3	4.00
Teaching	4	5	9	6.00
Funding	5	2	1	2.67
Product Development	1	8	4	4.33
Average	3.25	5.25	4.25	4.25

FIGURE 4.4. Taking stock (part II).

to use the taking stock list of activities (see Figure 4.4) as the basis for their plans for the future—so that their mission guides their taking stock phase, and the results of their taking stock shapes their planning for the future. This creates a thread of coherence and an audit trail for each step of their evaluation and action plans.

Goals. Program staff members and participants are asked to list their goals based on the results of their taking stock exercise. They set specific goals associated with each activity. Then the empowerment evaluator asks members of the group for strategies to accomplish each goal. They are also asked to generate forms of evidence to monitor progress toward specified goals. Program staff members and participants supply all of this information.

The empowerment evaluator is not superior or inferior in the process. They are equals. They add ideas as deemed appropriate without dominating discussion. Their primary role is to serve as a coach, facilitator, and critical evaluative friend. The empowerment evaluator must be able to serve as a facilitator, helping program members and participants process and be heard. The evaluator must also be analytical and critical, asking or prompting participants to clarify, document, and evaluate what they are doing, to ensure that specific goals are achieved. If the evaluator is only critical and analytical, the group will walk away from the endeavor. The empowerment evaluator must maintain a balance of these talents or team up with other coaches from within the group or outside the group who can help them maintain this balance.

The selected goals should be established in conjunction with supervisors and clients to ensure relevance from both perspectives. In addition, goals should be realistic, taking into consideration such factors as initial conditions, motivation, resources, and program dynamics. They should also take into consideration external standards, such as accreditation agency standards, superintendent's 5-year plan, board of trustee dictates, board standards, and so on.

In addition, it is important that goals be related to the program's activities, talents, resources, and scope of capability. One problem with traditional external evaluation is that programs have been given grandiose goals or long-term goals that participants could only contribute to in some indirect manner. There is no link between an individual's daily activities and ultimate long-term program outcomes in terms of these goals. In empowerment evaluation, program participants are encouraged to select intermediate goals that are directly linked to their daily activities. These activities can then be linked to larger, more diffuse goals, creating a clear chain of reasoning and outcomes.

Program participants are encouraged to be creative in establishing their goals. A brainstorming approach is often used to generate a new set of goals. In such a process, individuals are asked to state what they think the program should be doing. The list generated from this activity is refined, reduced, and made realistic after the brainstorming phase, through a critical review and consensual agreement process.

There are also a bewildering number of goals to strive for at any given time. As a group begins to establish goals based on this initial review of their program, they realize quickly that a consensus is required to determine the most significant issues to focus on. These are chosen according to (a) significance to the operation of the program, such as teaching in an educational setting; (b) timing or urgency, such as recruitment or budget issues; and (c) vision, including community building and learning processes.

Goal setting can be a slow process when program participants have a heavy work schedule. Sensitivity to the pacing of this effort is essential. Additional tasks of any kind and for any purpose may be perceived as simply another burden when everyone is fighting to keep their heads above water. However, individuals interested in specific goals should be asked to volunteer to be responsible for them as a team leader to ensure follow-through and internal accountability.

Developing strategies. Program participants are also responsible for selecting and developing strategies to accomplish program objectives. The same process of brainstorming, critical review, and consensual agreement is used to establish a set of strategies, which are routinely reviewed to determine their effectiveness and appropriateness. Determining appropriate strategies, in consultation with sponsors and clients, is an essential part of the empowering process. Program participants are typically the most knowledgeable about their own jobs, and this approach acknowledges and uses that expertise—and in the process, puts them back in the driver's seat.

Documenting progress. Program staff members and participants are asked what type of documentation or evidence is required to monitor progress toward their goals.[3] This is a critical step. Each form of documentation is scrutinized for relevance to avoid devoting time to collecting information that will not be useful or pertinent. Program participants are asked to explain how a given form of documentation is related to specific program goals. This review process is difficult and time-consuming, but prevents wasted time and disillusionment at the end of the process. In addition, documentation must be credible and rigorous if it is to withstand the criticism that this evaluation is self-serving (see Fetterman, 1994). The entire process of establishing a mission, taking stock, and planning for the future creates an implicit logic model[4] or program theory, demonstrating how there is nothing as practical as a good theory of action, especially one grounded in participants' own experiences (For additional discussion about program theory, see Bickman, 1987; Chen, 1990; Connell, Kubisch, Schorr, & Weiss, 1995; Cook & Shadish, 1994; Donaldson, chapter 7 of this volume; McClintock, 1990; Patton, 1989; Scriven, chapter 2 of this volume; Weiss, 1998; Wholey, 1987).

---

[3]See Linney, J.A. and Wandersman, A. (1991, 1996) for self-help documents to facilitate the process of documenting processes, outcomes, and impacts.

[4]See Dugan (1996) for an illustration of how logic models are used in empowerment evaluations.

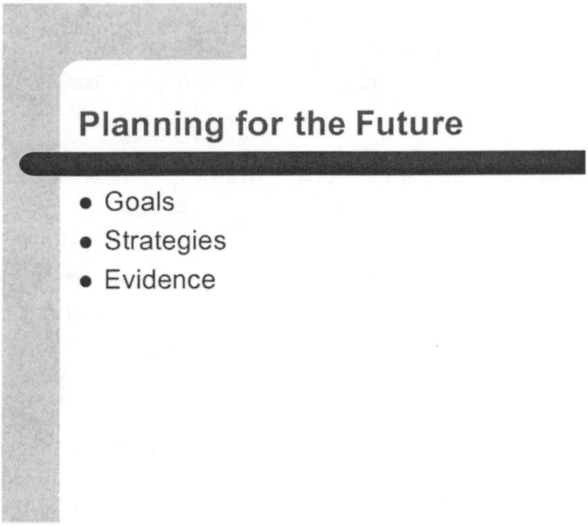

Planning for the Future

- Goals
- Strategies
- Evidence

FIGURE 4.5. Planning for the future.

COLLABORATION

Empowerment evaluation is a collaborative group activity, not an individual pursuit. An evaluator does not and can not empower anyone; people empower themselves, often with assistance and coaching. Empowerment evaluation can create an environment that is conducive to empowerment and self-determination. This process is fundamentally democratic in the sense that it invites (if not demands) participation, examining issues of concern to the entire community in an open forum. As a result, the context changes: the assessment of a program's value and worth is not the endpoint of the evaluation—as it often is in traditional evaluation—but is part of an ongoing process of program improvement. This new context acknowledges a simple but often overlooked truth: merit and worth are not static values. Populations shift, goals shift, knowledge about program practices and their value change, and external forces are highly unstable. By internalizing and institutionalizing self-evaluation processes and practices, a dynamic and responsive approach to evaluation can be developed to accommodate these shifts. As Usher (1995) explains:

> By developing the capacity to monitor and assess their own performance, program managers and staff can risk the mistakes that often occur with innovation. This is because they can detect problems and

make midcourse corrections before the results of errors due to planning or execution become widely apparent and costly. Having the capacity and responsibility to obtain such information about program operations and impact thus empowers managers and staff to explore new ways to enhance their performance. (pp. 62 - 63).

Both value assessments and corresponding plans for program improvement-developed by the group with the assistance of a trained evaluator—are subject to a cyclical process of reflection and self-evaluation. Program participants learn continually to assess their progress toward self-determined goals and to reshape their plans and strategies according to this assessment. In the process, self-determination is fostered, illumination generated, and liberation actualized. Value assessments are also highly sensitive to the life cycle of the program or organization. Goals and outcomes are geared toward the appropriate developmental level of implementation. Extraordinary improvements are not expected of a project that will not be fully implemented until the following year. Similarly, seemingly small gains or improvements in programs at an embryonic stage are recognized and appreciated in relation to their stage of development. In a fully operational and mature program, moderate improvements or declining outcomes are viewed more critically.

PROCESS USE

Empowerment evaluation ensures that each voice is heard in the chorus, but when the performance begins it is the chorus that is heard. Empowerment evaluation is about building capacity, building community, and building a future. Teaching evaluation logic and skills is a way of building capacity for ongoing self-assessment—enhancing the capacity for self-determination. According to Patton (1997), "Participation and collaboration can lead to a long-term commitment to use evaluation logic and techniques thereby building a culture of learning among those involved." (pp. 156.)

Moreover, "Learning to see the world as an evaluator sees it, often has a lasting impact on those who participate in an evaluation -- an impact that can be greater and last longer than the findings that result from that same evaluation, especially where those involved can apply that learning to future planning and evaluation situations" (Patton, 1997 pp. 156). This is process use. This is ownership.

CONCLUSION

Empowerment evaluation differs from many other forms of evaluation because the evaluator passes the baton to the orchestra. The first notes may sound dissonant. However, if you listen carefully you will hear that the chords are different, rather than dissonant. The group is playing on a different scale, a diatonic evaluative scale, but the music resonates with the group's culture, values, and aspirations.

These new sounds are not noise. If we listen we can hear how they conform to our own evaluation standards and conventions. The new sounds I hear when I work with new groups are music to my ears. The sounds I hear follow the natural rhythm of the human spirit reaching out, helping one another, and building a new world—our future.

These are the sounds of empowerment—a familiar refrain by now. They are the songs I hear in my heart and they are the songs I want to hear our children sing as we work together to compose our own world of evaluation practice in the 21st century.[5]

REFERENCES

Bickman, L. (Ed.) (1987). *Using program theory in evaluation* (New Directions for Program Evaluation, no. 33). San Francisco, CA: Jossey-Bass.

Chen, H. (1990). Issues in constructing program theory. In L. Bickman (Ed.), *Advances in program theory* (New Directions for Program Evaluation, No. 47, pp. 7-18). San Francisco, CA: Jossey-Bass.

Cook, T. & Shadish, W. (1994). Social experiments: Some developments over the past fifteen years. *Annual Review of Psychology, 45,* 545-580.

Dugan, M. (1996). Participatory and empowerment evaluation: Lessons learned in training and technical assistance. In D. M. Fetterman, S. Kaftarian, & A. Wandersman (Eds.), *Empowerment evaluation: Knowledge and tools for self-assessment and accountability*. Thousand Oaks, CA: Sage.

---

[5]This chapter is based on a plenary presentation about empowerment evaluation at the Stauffer Symposium on Applied Psychology at the Claremont Colleges. The program was titled *Evaluating Social Programs and Problems: Visions for the New Millennium*. For additional updated information refer to the empowerment evaluation website at: http://www.stanford.edu/~davidf/empowermentevaluation.html

Fetterman, D. M. (1993). *Speaking the language of power: Communication, collaboration, and advocacy* (translating ethnography into action). London, England: Falmer.

Fetterman, D. M. (1994). Steps of empowerment evaluation: From California to Cape Town. *Evaluation and Program Planning, 17* (3), 305-313.

Fetterman, D. M. (1998). Empowerment evaluation and accreditation in higher education. In E. Chelimsky & W. Shadish (Eds.), *Evaluation for the 21st century: A handbook (pp. 381-395).* Thousand Oaks, CA: Sage.

Fetterman, D. M. (2000). Foundations of empowerment evaluation. Thousand Oaks, CA: Sage.

Fetterman, D. M. (1996). Empowerment evaluation: An introduction. In D. M. Fetterman, S. Kaftarian, & A. Wandersman (Eds.), *Empowerment evaluation: Knowledge and tools for self-assessment and accountability* (pp. 13-14). Thousand Oaks, CA: Sage.

Habermas, J. (1984). *The theory of communicative action* (Vol. I). Boston, MA: Beacon Press.

Linney, J. A. & Wandersman, A. (1996). Empowering community groups with evaluation skills: The prevention plus III model. In D. M. Fetterman, S. Kaftarian, & A. Wandersman (Eds.), *Empowerment evaluation: Knowledge and tools for self-assessment and accountability.* Thousand Oaks, CA: Sage.

McClintock, C. (1990). Administrators as applied theorists. In L. Bickman (Ed.), *Advances in program theory* (New Directions for Program Evaluation, No. 47, pp. 19-33). San Francisco, CA: Jossey-Bass.

Patton, M. (1989). A context and boundaries for theory-driven approach to validity. *Evaluation and Program Planning, 12*, 375-377.

Patton, M. (1997). Toward distinguishing empowerment evaluation and placing it in a larger context. *Evaluation Practice, 18* (2), 147-163. Available online at http://www.stanford.edu/~davidf/patton.html

The Aspen Institute. (1995). *New approaches to evaluating community initiatives: Concepts, methods, and contexts.* Washington, DC: Author.

U.S. Department of Health and Human Services, Office of Substance Abuse Prevention. (1991). *Prevention Plus III: Assessing alcohol and other drug prevention programs at the school and community level: A four-step guide to useful program assessment.* Rockville, MD: Author.

Vanderplaat, M. (1995). Beyond technique: Issues in evaluating for empowerment. *Evaluation, 1*, 81-96.

Weiss, C. (1995). Nothing as practical as good theory: Exploring theory-based evaluation for comprehensive community initiatives for children and families. In J. P. Connell, A. C. Kubisch, L. B. Schorr, & C. H. Weiss (Eds.), *New approaches to evaluating community initiatives: Concepts, methods, and contexts.* Washington, DC: The Aspen Institute.

Weiss, C. (1998). *Evaluation* (2nd Ed.). Upper Saddle River, New Jersey: Prentice Hall.

Wholey, J. (Ed.). (1987). *Organizational excellence: Stimulating quality and communicating value.* Lexington, MA: Lexington Books.

5

Fourth Generation Evaluation in the New Millennium

Yvonna S. Lincoln
Texas A&M University

Speculating about the future is always both fun and difficult. On the one hand, by the time we get enough information to be accurate about the future, it is upon us. On the other hand, we seem programmed to consider what tomorrow will look like, and to search for better ways to guess about its form, even though we are more often than not surprised, astonished, delighted or dismayed.

As a consequence, it may be useful to consider fourth generation evaluation inside the structure of what I think tomorrow will look like, because even many years after the publication of *Fourth Generation Evaluation* (Guba & Lincoln, 1989), and hard on the heels of the *Handbook of Qualitative Research, 1st and 2nd Editions (Denzin & Lincoln, 1994; 2000)*, I think fourth generation evaluation was and is the way to go. There are five futures even now underway which make fourth generation evaluation strong, important, timely, and a sound base on which to build new models of evaluation. Those futures are first, postmodernism, especially the form of postmodernism which rejects nihilism in favor of a playful and more optimistic, future; second, what Best and Kellner (1997) and Bloland (1995) call "the interpretive turn" in the social sciences more broadly; third, the role of identity politics, especially its role in demanding greater inclusion for previously silenced groups; fourth, the globalism and corporatism overtaking the cultures of the world; and fifth, a growing sensitivity to postcolonial critiques throughout the Middle East, the Indian subcontinent, and the Pacific Rim, especially.

I connect these powerful social forces to fourth generation evaluation because, in telling the future, it is helpful to understand larger and sometimes subterranean forces at work in the social world, in order to see how one proposed change fits with those changes, or contradicts the changes, or resists the changes, or is completely out of touch with them. By and large, if one proposed change exhibits great consonance or resonance with other, larger, social forces, its chances of surviving, and possibly thriving, are enhanced.

I nominate these five forces because, while they began as formal academic critiques, in fact, the sentiments and political force of their arguments are being felt in a wide variety of social, economic, governmental and legislative activities around the world. Taken together, postmodernism, the interpretive turn, identity politics, globalization, and the postcolonial critique—even though each might be sensed or enacted differentially at any given time—form a powerful force field for social change. They will also, I predict, force changes in our relationships with other countries, with other cultures, and indeed, with the multiple and pluralistic subcultures inside our own country.

There are specific, albeit sometimes indistinct, linkages between these forces and fourth generation, or constructivist, or interpretivist, or inclusionary evaluation, and I would like to explore them here.

Postmodernism

First, postmodernists, unfortunately, do not wear uniforms, and so are not readily identifiable in social life. They are, nevertheless, characterized by one or more important beliefs which mark their thinking as postmodern in intent. The important thing about postmodernism is that this view represents a major disjunction—a paradigm shift—in the thinking which has guided the Western world, and especially its scientific enterprises—including research, evaluation, and policy analyses—for over a century. Modernists, primarily Enlightenment driven and Eurocentric in their orientation to social science, tend to believe that rational, orderly investigation and deduction would permit arriving at social truth, hopefully even a generalization or two. The Enlightenment narrative portion of the sociology of science drove a firm belief in the Eurocentric and Millsian idea that social engineering could proceed along the same trajectory as technological engineering. In effect, if we needed to separate the cotton seeds from the cotton, we could build a "social engine" to effect this separation.

In retrospect, it was an assumption simple, direct, highly analogous and disastrously wrong. It was wrongheaded to believe that a hyper-rationalized empiricism could undertake to accomplish in the social sciences what it accomplished in the hard sciences. "Fit" is always important, and why we believed hyper-rationalization would make sense of social life, which is clearly not necessarily rational, and sometimes even clearly nonrational, does not now seem to make good sense. As David Bakan, former president of the American Psychological Association, and premier methodologist, pointed out, the impoverished empiricism of the psychological sciences caused us to ignore, overlook, and indeed, denigrate, all that which made us human, and which gave power and meaning to human life: love, altruism, faith, heroism, forgiveness (Bakan, 1967; 1972). Because these things could not be weighed, measured, or even closely examined, they were left behind in academic scholars' investigations of human behavior.

Thus, postmodernists would argue strongly that there is no single method, design, or investigation which can produce anything more than a partial truth, one or two perspectives on a social problem, or a scientific fact which is devoid of theory. Postmodernists are characterized by doubt. Laurel Richardson (2000) observes that:

> The core of postmodernism is the *doubt* that any method or theory, discourse or genre, tradition or novelty, has a universal and general claim as the "right" or the privileged form of authoritative knowledge. Postmodernism *suspects* all truth claims of masking, and serving particular interests in local, cultural and political struggles. But it does not automatically reject conventional methods of knowing and telling as false or archaic. Rather, it opens those standard methods to inquiry and introduces new methods, which are also, then subject to critique.

> The postmodernist context of *doubt* ... distrusts all methods equally. No method has a privileged status. The superiority of "science" over "literature"—or, from another vantage point, "literature" over "science"—is challenged. But a postmodernist position does allow us to know "something" without claiming to know everything. Having a partial, local, historical knowledge is still knowing. In some ways, "knowing" is easier, however, because postmodernism recognizes the situational limitations of the knower. (p. 928)

Fourth generation evaluation—as well as most interpretivist forms of inquiry—hews to this position fairly closely. It does indeed suspect all methods and discourses, especially as those methods and discourses claim to have a lock on truth. Fourth generation evaluation is a product of

the understanding that what is called scientific truth does indeed represent ideological claims, advanced within specific political regimes of
power. In fact, in rooting itself in responsive evaluation models and interpretive anthropology, fourth generation evaluation specifically seeks to
redress some power imbalances by seeking out stakeholders remanded
to the sidelines in earlier generations of evaluation practice, and by giving
them voice.

More importantly, fourth generation evaluation has never rejected
conventional methods of knowing, whatever our critics may say. Fourth
generation's specific rejection has been the assertion that one set of
methods, and one alone, paved the way for reliable and valid knowledge
of the social world. By expanding the permissible repertoire of legitimate
data-gathering and analytic methods, fourth generation evaluation actually increases our certainty that we are getting reliable knowledge on
which we can act. Thus, a suspicious postmodernism supports the
enlargement of the methodological repertoires and tools on which evaluators can draw with confidence.

The Interpretive Turn

Second, the interpretive turn in historical, literary, and social science disciplines, can be seen as a recognition that facts are only "facts" within
some theoretical framework, and that much of what passes for science is,
in fact, some assertion within a theoretical discourse system (Bloland,
1995). This is quite close to a statement of social constructivist principles
on which naturalistic or fourth generation evaluation is predicated. Social
constructivism posits that two kinds of realities exist side by side, and
operate within the same domain: the first reality resides in tangible
objects, sites, and events, and is peopled by individuals and groups with
specific social and historical locations, and specific social interests. The
second reality resides largely in the minds of individuals and groups, and
consists of the sense people make of the tangible, physical reality. This
reality is constituted in the minds of evaluation stakeholders, and is driven
by the sense-making and meaning-imputation activities of the human
minds.

Constructivism argues that the measurable tangible realities which
normally are the focus of conventional science are only half the story; the
other half of the inquiry or evaluation effort is the sense individuals and
stakeholding groups make of those physical realities and the interactions
which go on inside the tangible and physical. Meaning-making activities
are critical because they are a deep, critical part of human cognition, and
because they are largely determinative of how people will act toward the

physical realities and events. They are also critical simply because the radical empiricism and objectivism of psychological science at the beginning of the twentieth century permitted the social-constructing mental activities of humans to languish for want of tools to measure them. Fourth generation evaluators are as interested in the *constructions* which are advanced by stakeholders as they are by the measurable dimensions and cost-benefit analyses which are normally associated with most evaluation efforts.

Clearly, the tools for collecting such social/mental constructions are those tools which enable a look into the "black box" of the human mind: qualitative methods. It is the emphasis on qualitative tools as the best means of understanding—but not "measuring"—the meaning-imputing activities of stakeholders which has no doubt given rise to the misunderstanding that fourth generation evaluators use *only* qualitative methods, but this is clearly a mistaken impression, derived from either failure to read, or misreading (see Guba & Lincoln, 1981, pp. 64 - 65; Lincoln & Guba, 1985, pp. 40; Guba & Lincoln, 1989, Guba & Lincoln, 1994, pp. 105, and Lincoln & Guba, 2000). So, for instance, while individuals refer to the shifting worldview as the "qualitative paradigm", in fact, the revolution in methods and the revolution in paradigm proposals are orthogonal to each other. The paradigm revolution—the proposal of a new metaphysics or model for research—relates most directly to the failure of conventional science to solve seemingly intractable social problems, while the revolution in qualitative methods is a result of the twin crises in anthropology and sociology, the crisis of representation (that is, representing those we study) and the crisis of authority, or legitimacy. That the two revolutions seem to parallel each other is quite likely an historical accident.

Since both meaning-making cognitive activities, and collecting data on such activities (especially collecting qualitative data), are forms of constituting, reconstituting and revising (reworking, enlarging, amplifying, reconsidering, extending, correcting) constructions, they are highly interpretive activities. Thus, social constructivism can well be included within the interpretive turn which has marked history, political science, anthropology, sociology, linguistics and various literary studies for the past 20 years.

Identity Politics

My third nomination for a global change, identity politics, is not a single entity, but rather a set of activities and concerns, circling about the central dilemma of how to live in the world as a member of a cultural or linguistic group or heritage. Identity politics probably proceeds from the various civil rights revolutions in this country as well as around the world. The civil rights movements centering on registering African-American voters in the United States, the recognition of women's rights to equal employment opportunities, the increasing sensitivity to the legal and political rights of children, the increasing visibility of gay rights protests, all have contributed to a revised and revisionist political sense of just how diverse our country—and the world—is. We now comprehend, sometimes painfully, that to speak of "our community" is both to imagine a broad public consensus which does not exist, and at the same time, to limit ourselves to speaking only for others like ourselves, who share our values, our cultural heritage, our socio-economic status, and perhaps even our gender and sexual orientation.

While fourth generation evaluation has never made any claims to being sensitive to identity politics, *per se*, by harking back to Stake's responsive evaluation as one of its intellectual roots, it does respectfully support the impulse to identity politics by attempting to take into account the social, cultural, educational and political interests of various stakeholding groups. It is in this sense that fourth generation evaluation is, of all forms of evaluation, most inclusionary. Insofar as stakeholders can be found and encouraged to participate in the overall evaluation efforts, their constructions are sought, honored, and incorporated into any and all portrayals and final evaluation reports and technical statements. Where their constructions appear to be uninformed, fourth generation evaluators provide information. Where their constructions appear to be unaware of the social constructions of other stakeholding groups and individuals, these constructions are provided to them. Where their constructions suffer from lack of data, data are freely provided.

These activities on the part of evaluators answer an urge toward greater social participation by all stakeholders, and toward more responsive, but also more democratic, forms of evaluation. They act to level the playing field in the world of social action programs. Such activities also move practitioners away from "managerially cozy" synoptic models of evaluation, in which funders and managers hold all the power cards, and toward a form of evaluation action research, in which social change, particularly around the program being evaluated, and the cogeneration of programmatic knowledge (Greenwood & Levin, 1998, Levin & Lincoln, in progress), can take place. Inclusivity (Greene, Lincoln, Mathison, Mertens, & Ryan, 1998) becomes the hallmark of such evaluation efforts, and consequently, identity politics is both incorporated, and at the same time, permitted legitimate voice in such a way as to prevent bitter power struggles in the effort to be heard.

Fourth generation evaluation, then, provides the opportunity for groups whose values may not represent those of program managers and funders to achieve voice, agency, and efficacy. This is especially critical when those who legislate and those who design implementation policies and procedures for target groups may be quite far removed from those groups (Guba, 1984, 1985). Policy personnel and implementation personnel frequently design social action and education programs without direct feedback from recipients. Rebalancing evaluation efforts to include recipient voices has the corrective effect of causing to surface the unintended side effects of which Michael Scriven made us aware, and at the same time, to create awareness of how policies are actually *experienced*. To speak in contemporary public school accountability language, policies-in-intention and policies-in-implementation are brought more into alignment with policies-as-experienced (Guba, 1984).

Globalization

The fourth major force is globalization. As we sit and watch, curious, excited, and somewhat frightened, we move into a globalized world. The world shrinks daily as economies bulge with transnational corporations, as money, currencies, whole economies move at lightning speed over the Internet. We worry, as citizens of this new world, about the effects of industrial pollution moved to other, less stringent, regulatory environments; about corporations worth more, and exerting more power, than some developing countries; about the fact that transnational corporate efforts are not under the purview or regulatory supervision of any government or governmental agency; and about what has been called the "McDonaldization" of the nonwestern world. In the midst of this new world—being created even as we sleep and work and pursue hobbies and interact with our children—we as evaluators are also working farther afield, in cross-national environments, with multinational agencies such as the WorldBank, educational and cultural organizations who represents governments or groups, and with non-governmental agencies (NGOs).

Into this globalized context, naturalistic inquiry and fourth generation travel well. They travel well because they are actively engaged in the search for stakeholders and stakeholder groups; because they are as sensitive to unintended side-effects as to program objectives; because naturalistic, phenomenological, constructivist and fourth generation evaluation is rooted in what are sometimes culturally determined meaning making activities; because they are sensitive to the ways in which Western forms of thinking impinge on conventional, Western ideas of what evaluation should be; because they are community-based and grounded, rather than simply being managerially focused; and because fourth generation evaluators see themselves less as decision-makers and more as orchestrators and facilitators of community negotiations around desired and desirable action. Fourth generation's practitioners aren't smarter than more conventional evaluators, but they do tend to be focused in ways which permit more culturally diverse perspectives to emerge. Such perspectives work well in cross-national, cross-cultural and nonwestern contexts, because they resist McDonaldization, and permit nonwestern worldviews to emerge and claim authenticity.

The Postcolonial Critique

The fifth major force is postcolonialism, the aftermath of colonialism, and the postcolonial critique. Linda Tuhiwai Smith (1999) tells a wonderful story. She comments that the term "post-colonialism" would appear to indicate that "colonialism is over, finished business (p. 24)." But she says Bobbi Sykes, an Aborigine activist, asked at some conference on postcolonialism, "What? Postcolonialism? Have they left?" Smith says that "Imperialism frames the indigenous experience. It is part of our story, our version of modernity (1999, p. 19)." She also notes that "Fragmentation is not a phenomenon of postmodernism as many might claim. For indigenous peoples fragmentation has been the consequence of imperialism (p. 28)." While not doing justice at all to either her argument, or the arguments of others who have written persuasively about postcolonialism (Nandy, 1989; Said, 1979), let me proceed to summarize one of the most important points she makes, viz., that Western forms of research are, in the main, useless for indigenous peoples. Research as practiced by European and Eurocentric colonials was, first, a method for classifying the natural and social world into categories meaningful to Europeans, even while being meaningless to indigenous peoples; second, a system of discourse which both reflected and reified imperialism as a "natural" and proper historical course; and third, a means of legitimating domination and power by imperialistic interests (Smith, 1999). She observes that, for indigenous peoples, their conversations regarding Eurocentric forms of research were quite different from the Western scientific community's conversations regarding its projects. She says:

> At a common sense level research was talked about both in terms of its absolute worthlessness to us, the indigenous world, and its absolute usefulness to those who wielded it as an instrument. It told us things already known, suggested things that would not work, and made careers for people who already had jobs. (p. 31)

If even a part of her criticism (and the critiques of others) is true, then we need some model, some paradigm, some set of methodological tools, which provides a break with more conventional Western science, and permits localized and indigenous knowledges to emerge as meaningful forms of the discourses around social action projects. Fourth generation evaluation possesses such possibilities.

Once again, fourth generation evaluation travels well because it is not tied to specific discourses, except for those of multivocal and pluralistic interests having their say. It is the most readily adaptable to action research, participatory action research (PAR), and community-centered models of generating social knowledge, and it resides within a cluster of knowledge-generating inquiry forms which seek knowledge nominated by the community, with community direction, community-devised methods, and frequently, community-dwelling, indigenous researchers.[1] This "sympathy" between fourth generation, or constructivist, evaluation and participatory approaches to inquiry[2] (Lincoln, 2000) rejects the assumption that evaluators who hold PhD's necessarily possess all the knowledge worth having regarding the merit or worth of some entity. As a different "way of knowing" itself, posited oppositionally to conventional science, it is particularly respectful of, and eager to locate, other ways of understanding, inquiring and coming to know.

As other cultures explore the long-term effects of colonization, colonialism, and imperialism (not all of it from European powers), alternative ways of knowing, and systems and discourses of inquiry "untied" (Brunswick, 1955), even partially, from Western ideas of what constitutes valid and reliable knowledge, will become more important. Grounded as it is in socially constructed realities, fourth generation evaluation is open to the possibilities of genuine cross-cultural understanding and nonwestern representational forms.

---

[1]The search for good models for fourth generation, democratic, participatory, inclusive or responsive models of evaluation should not be a difficult one. Terry Denny's "Some Still Do: River Acres, Texas" is an old, but classic example. Virtually any published work by Robert Stake, Ernest House, Jennifer Greene, or Greene and her colleagues or students, or Donna Mertens, would yield excellent examples of inclusive, or more democratic and participatory, forms of evaluation.
[2]One of the reasons fewer inclusive evaluations are available than might be hoped is that many are conducted as private contracts, with no original intention—and perhaps no permission—to publish.

Another Set of Issues

These are five ways in which fourth generation evaluation is connected to historical movements which impact the world of social policy and social action. It is a form of evaluation with built-in criteria for determining whether or not the evaluation effort has actually led to participation and to change, alteration, re-direction, and modification of existing programs, and to a more democratic level of participation by ordinary citizens. There are other ways, too, in which fourth generation evaluation represents a fresh perspective on such efforts. Two suggest themselves here, although we have little time to explore them.

First, postmodern thinking includes a dissolution in the boundaries between science and literature, and between scientific discourse and literary and artistic discourse. While others have dealt with the collapse of distinctions between science and art better and at more length, it is important to note that one consequence of this collapse has been the rise of nontechnical forms of evaluation reports (Lincoln, 1995). Nontechnical, natural-language reporting, especially in narrative forms, but also in the form of portrayals, briefings, community theater, performances, and other orally based formats, renders findings, judgments, concerns, issues, and values are both more transparent and more accessible to stakeholders beyond managers and funders. The explorations in other social sciences of experimental, literary, and "messy texts" (Marcus & Fischer, 1988) will carry over into program evaluation in ways which continue to support and prompt greater community involvement and participation in evaluation efforts. This is a good thing.

A second way in which contemporary movements in other social sciences will affect the practice of evaluation is in the psychological decentering of the subject (Gergen, 1991; Kegan, 1982; Kvale, 2000). Kvale argues that the "postmodern decentering of the subject may well lead to a decentering of the modern science of the subject" (p. 15). With the individual, the sacred self, no longer the center of a psychological, literary, cultural or psychic landscape, the practices of maintaining funders, program directors, and managers at the center of program evaluation efforts are loosed from their disciplinary support and dissolve. Two things emerge from this dissolution. First, psychology—and perhaps, as a consequence, evaluation practice—is being returned to an epistemology of practice, anti-foundational (Schwandt, 1989) and rooted in "pragmatic utility as a criterion of validity" (Kvale, 2000, p. 20). Second, it is being argued that psychology will draw increasingly on descriptive data—largely of case practice—and on interpretive modes rooted in hermeneutics and dialectics (Fishman, 1999; Kvale, 2000).

A postmodern decentering of the subject, with a concomitant focus on cases, phenomenological description and hermeneutic and interpretive modes, will link closely with fourth generation evaluation's emphasis on stakeholder groups, and with the larger political contexts of identity politics.

The larger point to be made here is that many of the explicit and implicit emphases of fourth generation evaluation—both specific critiques and alternative proposals—exhibit great fit with contemporary scientific, psychological, and literary motifs and refrains. It is not a question of whether we can ignore postmodernism, identity politics, globalizations and other pressures on our understanding of the world, in the hope that they will go away. They will not go away. Our only hope as evaluation practitioners is to choose models—or adapt those which exist—which exhibit congruence with contemporary mindsets, and practice them with integrity and cultural and political respect.

Issues Arising in the Use of Fourth Generation Evaluation

There are several other issues, far more pragmatic, which arise in discussions of new-paradigm evaluation models. Fourth generation evaluation, for instance, is a highly specific name for what is, in actual practice, a congeries of models of evaluation. The more overarching term which captures this model of evaluation might be, in fact, inclusive evaluation. Most, if not all, of the premises of inclusive evaluation are precisely the same as those of fourth generation evaluation. In the same vein, many of the evaluation methods are the same; that is, these models utilize whatever data collection and analytic techniques are required by the kind of data needed for decision-making. Some of the requisite data will be quantitative (e.g., schoolwide and districtwide test scores on statewide achievement tests), while some of the data will be qualitative (e.g., teacher constructions of what it means to "teach to the test", and whether that is even an accurate depiction of what teachers believe they are being asked to do).

Evaluating social action programs and evaluating social problems are two different activities. Clearly, evaluation practice itself frequently spends some portion of its time in defining problems, whether that is done by trying to achieve some accurate description of the program evaluators have been charged with evaluating, or providing evidence and commentary on whether or not the program is in practice addressing the problem, or trying to demonstrate that the problem as perceived by funders of the target program is that problem perceived by those who live with the problem (i.e., the difference between policy-in-intention and policy-as-experienced; see Guba, 1984). Evaluating social problems, however, is typically not the realm of the evaluator. Rather, that is the province of the social scientist, whose role it is to examine social issues and problems, and provide good definitions (grounded definitions, it is to be hoped) of social problems as the researcher uncovers them. It is then the task of policy personnel to devise social and educational programs which address those problems, and the task of evaluators to determine how well the proposed programs actually operate to ameliorate some social problem. It is the task for policy analysts (to take the analysis one step further) to "deconstruct" proposed and implemented policies to examine what the interacting effects might be when Policy A interacts with Policy B, or when Policy A is competing with Policy B as a means for addressing some social or educational problem.

There is, however, little contact between researchers who seek to define problems, policy personnel who devise policies intended to ameliorate problems, and those who evaluate the policies implemented. Furthermore, it has been well-understood for over 30 years that the connection between social scientists and policy crafters is hardly linear, nor is it direct. As Carol Weiss pointed out better than 25 years ago, evaluation data—and by extension, research data—competes in a complex arena where many kinds of data seek to be heard and acted upon. The most fruitful and insightful social science research, evaluation or policy analyses stands little chance of being heard if it does not attract "champions" who will take the data forward to legislative and policy venues with vigor. Unfortunately, many of those who are evaluation practitioners, especially those who engage in such work full-time, have little time to champion a particular piece of evaluation work, because of the press of working to attract the next evaluation contract.

Evaluation practice today is complex and fragmented at best, with an extensive array of arenas in which evaluation data are needed and desired, and many canvases on which evaluation data are painted. Those who assert that some practitioners of evaluation do not live on the same planet as others remark less about the reality of the situation than they do about the particular arenas in which they work. Many of the evaluations for which contracts are let are not major national and/or federally funded evaluation efforts. This does not mean they are less significant, but rather that evaluators are working on a smaller and more geographically-bounded canvas. One thing is clear, however. Evaluators who fail to take account of the perspectives of a growing number of pluralistic voices in social life will find those voices arrayed against a given evaluation effort. And those who choose to work in a larger and more global context must take account of indigenous voices.

Taking account of a larger throng of voices is surely a messier way to work. But as a thoughtful social scientist pointed out, if we do not, those same voices will be on CNN tomorrow, calling into question our findings, and presenting evidence to prove that we are inadequate to the tasks of our work.

REFERENCES

Bakan, D. (1972, March). Psychology can now kick the science habit. *Psychology Today, 11,* 26-28, 87-88.

Bakan, D. (1967). *On method: Toward a reconstruction of psychological investigation.* San Francisco, CA: Jossey-Bass.

Best, S. & Kellner, D. (1997). *The postmodern turn.* New York: Guildford Press.

Bloland, H. G. (1995). Postmodernism and higher education. *Journal of Higher Education, 66*:5, 522-559.

Brunswick, E. (1955). Representative design and probabilistic theory in a functional psychology. *Psychological Review, 62,* 193-217.

Denzin, N. K. & Lincoln, Y. S. (Eds.), (1994). *Handbook of qualitative research (1st Ed.).* Thousand Oaks, CA: Sage.

Denzin, N. K. & Lincoln, Y. S. (Eds.), (2000). *Handbook of qualitative research (2nd Ed.).* Thousand Oaks, CA: Sage.

Fishman, D. B. (1999). *The case for pragmatic psychology.* New York: New York University Press.

Gergen, K. J. (1991). *The saturated self: Dilemmas of identity in contemporary life.* New York: Basic Books.

Greene, J., Lincoln, Y., Mathison, S., Mertens, D., & Ryan, K. E. (1998). Advantages and challenges of using inclusive evaluation approaches in evaluation practice. *Evaluation Practice, 19,* 101-122.

Greenwood, D. J. & Levin, M. (1998). *Introduction to action research: Social research for social change.* Thousand Oaks, CA: Sage.

Guba, E. G. (1984). The effects of definitions of policy on the nature and outcome of policy analysis. *Educational Leadership, 42,* 63-70.

Guba, E. G. (1985). What can happen as a result of a policy? *Policy Studies Review, 5,* 11-16.

Guba, E. G. & Lincoln, Y. S. (1981). *Effective evaluation: Improving the usefulness of evaluation results through responsive and naturalistic approaches.* San Francisco, CA: Jossey-Bass.

Guba, E. G. & Lincoln, Y. S. (1989). *Fourth generation evaluation.* Thousand Oaks, CA: Sage.

Guba, E. G., & Lincoln, Y. S. (1994). Competing paradigms in qualitative research. In N. K. Denzin & Y.S. Lincoln, (Eds.). *Handbook of qualitative research* (1st Ed.) (pp. 105-117). Thousand Oaks, CA: Sage.

Kegan, R. (1982). *The evolving self: Problem and process in human development.* Cambridge, MA: Harvard University Press.

Kvale, S. (2000, July). *Psychology in the Postmodern Age*. Paper presented at the XXVII International Congress of Psychology, Stockholm, Sweden.

Levin, M. & Lincoln, Y. S. (in preparation). *Evaluation as social change*. Thousand Oaks, CA: Sage.

Lincoln, Y. S. (1995). The sixth moment: Emerging problems in qualitative research. *Studies in Symbolic Interaction: A Research Annual, 19*, 37-55.

Lincoln, Y. S. (2000). Engaging sympathies: Relationships between action research and social constructivism. In P. Reason & H. Bradbury (Eds.), *Handbook of action research* (pp. 124-132). London: Sage.

Lincoln, Y. S. & Denzin, N. K. (1994). The fifth moment. In N. K. Denzin & Y. S. Lincoln (Eds.), *The handbook of qualitative research (1st Ed.)* (pp. 575-586). Thousand Oaks, CA: Sage.

Lincoln, Y. S. & Guba, E. G. (1985). *Naturalistic inquiry*. Thousand Oaks, CA: Sage.

Lincoln, Y. S. & Guba, E. G. (2000). Paradigmatic controversies, contradictions and emerging confluences. In N. K.Denzin & Y. S. Lincoln (Eds.), *Handbook of qualitative research* (2nd Ed.) (pp. 163-188). Thousand Oaks, CA: Sage.

Lincoln, Y. S. & Denzin, N. K. (1994). The fifth moment. In N. K. Denzin & Y. S. Lincoln, (Eds.), *The handbook of qualitative research* (1st Ed.) (pp. 575-586). Thousand Oaks, CA: Sage.

Marcus, G. E. & Fischer, M. M. J. (1988). *Anthropology as cultural critique: An experimental moment in the human sciences*. Chicago: University of Chicago Press.

Nandy, A. (1989). *The intimate enemy: Loss and recovery of self under colonialism*. Delhi: Oxford University Press.

Reinharz, S. (1997). Who am I? The need for a variety of selves in the field. In R. Hertz (Ed.), *Reflexivity and voice* (pp. 3-20). Thousand Oaks, CA: Sage.

Richardson, L. (2000). Writing: A method of inquiry. In N. K. Denzin & Y. S. Lincoln, (Eds.), *Handbook of qualitative research (2nd Ed.)* (pp. 923-948). Thousand Oaks, CA: Sage.

Said, E. W. (1979). *Orientalism*. New York: Vintage Books.

Schratz, M. & Walker, R. (1995). *Research as social change: New opportunities for qualitative research*. London: Routledge.

Schwandt, T. A. (1996). Farewell to criteriology. *Qualitative Inquiry, 2*, 58-72.

Smith, L. T. (1999). *Decolonizing methodologies: Research and indigenous peoples*. London: Zed Books.

6

The Inclusive View of Evaluation: Visions for the New Millennium

Donna M. Mertens
Gallaudet University

Evaluators seeking direction to guide their thinking in the 21st century about the evaluation of social problems and their solutions would benefit by being cognizant of both the old things that we will carry with us into the new millenium, as well as the new things that challenge and aid us in this endeavor. A litany of social problems in the United States and around the world might seem old—crime, violence, poverty, illiteracy, un- and under-employment, disease, and drug and alcohol abuse. Yet, even in making this list within the context of the "old", it suggests that evaluators have an important role in the new millenium related to challenging the status quo in terms of the seeming intransigence of these problems, the inferred inadequacy of interventions in the face of their persistence, and the need to adopt a stance that is more conducive to uncovering the variables that contribute to these problems and to their solutions.

Evaluators are being called upon to redefine their roles by forces within and outside of the evaluation community. National trends indicate growing populations with disparate value systems and socioeconomic levels, and increasing minority populations in the United States who demand to participate more legitimately in the discussion of educational and social services that are designed to serve them (Mertens, in press; Waters, 1998). Participatory models of evaluation that evolved in Latin America, India, and Africa emphasize the need to legitimately involve all stakeholders in an evaluation, including those with the least power (Mertens, 1999a; Whitmore, 1998). Federal legislation in the United States has placed evaluation in a central position with the implementation of the Government Performance and Results Act. Such legislation, while presenting challenges, also holds the potential of increasing the power and influence of the work that evaluators do.

Advances and changes that have emerged at the end of the 20th century can contribute to the work of evaluators. Innovations in technology, such as smaller, more powerful computers; accessibility to Internet-based resources; and more sophistication in the transmission of information that is not only print, but visual and interactive, are tools that evaluators have increasingly at their disposal.

Such technological advances hold promise not only for the conduct of evaluation worldwide, but also are relevant to increasing the cooperation of evaluators on a global scale (Mertens & Russon, 2000). The emergence of many new regional and national organizations and planning for increased international cooperation amongst evaluation organizations is on going. Before 1995, only five regional and/or national evaluation organizations existed in the world. As of 2000, there are more than 30—a 500% increase in a 5 year period. However, the prospect exists for these regional and national evaluation organizations to form a networked organization, tentatively called the International Organization for Cooperation in Evaluation (IOCE). The purpose of IOCE would be to facilitate communication, promote professional development, and allow its member organizations to pursue common goals.

Building on the idea of inclusiveness in terms of participation of evaluators from all parts of the globe in the conversations about evaluation, many promising practices are emerging that emanate from new thinking by diverse groups. I will thus frame my remarks by casting a broad net around the term *inclusive* to encompass not only a specific approach to evaluation, but also the increase in opportunities for evaluators from diverse origins to participate in the process of contributing to the evolving concept of evaluation.

I will explore the territory between the need for responsiveness to the pressures of pluralism, and the role of the evaluator in relation to social change, with final implications for changes worldwide. The evaluation community has long recognized the political dimension that is inherent in its work. However, Greene (1994) articulated the nature of this relationship in such a way that supports the need for evaluators to address the political context in a more substantial way. She makes the point that what distinguishes evaluation from other forms of social inquiry is its political inherencey; that is, in evaluation, politics and science are inherently intertwined. Evaluations are conducted on the merit and worth of programs in the public domain, which are themselves responses to prioritized individual and community needs that resulted from political decisions. Greene further asserts that program evaluation "is integrally intertwined with political decision making about societal priorities, resource allocation, and power" (p. 531). Thus, as we enter the 21st millenium, evaluators are confronted with recognizing the importance of working within a political context for social change, along with the need to be responsive to increased pluralism. The growing awareness of the need to represent multiple perspectives within the political context laid the foundation for the emergence of the transformative-emancipatory paradigm which provides the basis for an inclusive approach to evaluation (Mertens, 1998; 1999).

THEORETICAL FRAMEWORK BASED ON TRANSFORMATIVE THEORY

Meaningful involvement of marginalized groups in evaluation activities has been an ongoing challenge for evaluators (Chelimsky, 1998; Mertens, 1999; Weiss, 1998). A large body of scholarly literature exists that struggles directly with the accurate and credible representation of marginalized groups in and through the research process, although it is only rarely found in research or evaluation methods or theory books. These contributions travel under a number of different names, one of these being transformative theory. Transformative scholars assume that knowledge is not neutral, but is influenced by human interests; that all knowledge reflects the power and social relationships within society; and that an important purpose of knowledge construction is to help people improve society (Banks, 1995; 1993).

Transformative theory Is used as an umbrella term that encompasses paradigmatic perspectives such as emancipatory (Lather, 1992; Mertens 1998), antidiscriminatory (Humphries & Truman, 1994; Truman, Mertens, & Humphries, 2000); participatory (De Koning & Marion, 1996; Reason, 1994; Whitmore, 1998); and Freirian approaches (McLaren & Lankshear, 1994); and is exemplified in the writings of feminists (Alcoff & Potter, 1993; Fine, 1992; Hill-Collins, 2000; Reinharz, 1992); racial/ethnic minorities (Madison, 1992; Stanfield, 1993; 1999), people with disabilities (Gill, 1999; Mertens & McLaughlin, 1995; Oliver, 1992), and people who work on behalf of marginalized groups.

The philosophical assumptions that underlie the transformative-emancipatory paradigm, and thus guide inclusive evaluators, are summarized here. For a more extensive discussion of these assumptions see Mertens (1998) and Mertens (in press). The ontological assumption describes the nature of reality as it is assumed to exist within this paradigm. The transformative-emancipatory ontological assumption holds that there are diversities of viewpoints with regard to many social realities, but those viewpoints need to be placed within political, cultural, historical, and economic value systems to understand the basis for the differences. And then, the evaluator needs to struggle with revealing those multiple constructions, as well as with decisions about privileging one perspective over another. As Greene (1994) recognized: "What importantly distinguishes one evaluation methodology from another is not methods, but rather whose questions are addressed and which values are promoted" (p. 533).

The epistemological assumption makes clear the beliefs about the relationship between the knower and what would be known. In transformative-emancipatory terms, objectivity is valued in the sense of providing a balanced and complete view of the program process and effects, such that bias is not interjected because of a lack of understanding of key viewpoints. To obtain this depth of understanding, the evaluator must be involved in the communities impacted by the service, program, or policy to a significant degree. This epistemological assumption underscores the importance of an interactive link between the evaluator and the participants with sensitivity to the impact of the social and historical factors in the relationship between the evaluator and the participants, as well as the impact of those variables for knowledge construction.

Methodologically, evaluations based in transformative theory share many commonalities with democratic deliberative evaluation, including the use of collective deliberation, stakeholder inclusiveness, and dialogical data collection methods (House & Howe, 1999; Ryan & DeStefano, 2000). However, such transformative evaluations have shades of difference in terms of the emphasis on deliberate inclusiveness of groups that have historically experienced oppression and discrimination on the basis of gender, culture, economic levels, ethnicities/races, sexual orientation, and disabilities, and in a conscious effort to build a link between the results of the evaluation and social action.

Role of the Evaluator

What is the role of the evaluator who accepts the challenge of approaching evaluation in ways that place greater emphasis on utilization for the purpose of social transformation? First, the evaluator must accept that they are part of a team whose function is to bring about social change. Underlying this acceptance is an acknowledgement that we live in a world where social injustice is part of the everyday living experience of many groups of people. House and Howe (1999) explain this perspective as, "The goal of practices like evaluation should be a more just and democratic society..." (p. 87).

The evaluator, in recognizing that social injustice exists, must also be willing to challenge the status quo. Schools are failing the poorest children of color, prisons are inordinately full of men of color, programs for youth are not universally successful in preventing drug use or teenage pregnancy, and the burden falls more on the poor, minorities, and other known segments of the population. Waters (1998) addressed this issue within the context of evaluation of educational programs when she wrote:

> On the cusp of a new millennium, we are searching for answers not in the homes, economic backgrounds, and individual disadvantages of our students in public education, it would seem that we are finally beginning to look at the quality of instructional variables that exist in schooling processes instead of 'blaming the victim.' Can we begin to ask why and how our school systems are failing our children, instead of why and how these children are failing our school systems? If schools are to be held accountable for the equitable delivery of educational opportunities and if social justice is to take place within the halls of academic opportunity, the core of the education performance indicator systems should include school and classroom information. (p. 5)

Encapsulated within the above quotation are several issues. As previously mentioned, evaluators need to acknowledge that social justice is a problem that needs to be openly discussed. Also, the evaluator's job is to challenge the status quo and seek to uncover the weaknesses within the present system that contribute to a continuation of poor education, poverty, and other social ills. To this end, the evaluator can encourage those in power to go beyond a "blaming the victim" stance to a position in which the failures within the system can be revealed.

The evaluator's role thus would include facilitating an open discourse on issues related to social justice and how these issues effect the program to be evaluated. The challenge lies in finding ways to bring the thinking of critical theorists, feminists, and others who write from the anti-discriminatory paradigm to the evaluation community and the stakeholders we serve. Within the evaluation community, there is the potential for an evaluator who adopts this stance to be criticized and marginalized for being biased, political, and value-laden (Greene, Lincoln, Mathison, Mertens, & Ryan, 1998). Society expects evaluators to be objective, and thus it is incumbent upon the inclusive evaluator working within the transformative paradigm to explain the meaning of objectivity thusly: Objectivity within this framework means a lack of bias that is achieved by inclusion of all relevant stakeholders in a way that authentic and accurate representations of their viewpoints are considered.

I made this point in my AEA presidential address that the principle of objectivity need not find itself on the opposite side of the fence from addressing the needs of marginalized and less empowered groups. "If the heart of objectivity is to avoid bias, then it seems to necessitate inclusion of perspectives of all relevant groups" (Mertens, 1999, p. 6). House and Howe (1999) described a similar concept of objectivity that means "Working toward unbiased statements through the procedures of the discipline, observing the canons of proper argument and methodology, maintaining a healthy skepticism, and being vigilant to eradicate sources of bias" (p. 9).

Such an approach to evaluation requires that the evaluator spend time reflecting upon his or her own values and how these might influence their work. Also, the logical corollary of open discourse on such issues is that the evaluator would negotiate with the client at the beginning of the evaluation to conduct a transformative, inclusive evaluation.

The Practice of Evaluation

In terms of actual practice of evaluation, the application of an inclusive approach to evaluation has implications for every step in the process: The design of the study, definition of the problem, selection of indicators of success, sampling and data collection decisions, development of intervention strategies, addressing power differentials in the study, and setting standards for a good evaluation.

The design of the study. An inclusive approach to evaluation is amenable to quantitative, qualitative, or mixed methods designs. One underlying principle that guides the choice of design is that members of the community impacted by the evaluation would be involved to some degree in the methodological and programmatic decisions. Several issues arise related to design choice, including being responsive to the community's perceptions and involvement, ethical issues concerning denial of treatment, and sharing of perks with those involved in the study.

For example, Truman (2000) addressed several ethical issues that arose in her conduct of a needs assessment regarding informational materials about safe sex and health issues amongst the gay community in Manchester, England. She selected a mixed methods design, combining qualitative and quantitative methods, based on the needs of her client (an activist group of gay men) and her own emancipatory philosophical beliefs. The client wanted her to conduct a needs assessment that they could then use to approach funding agencies to support a program of materials distribution around the topic of safe sex. She decided to use a quantitative design in deference to the client's belief that a large-scale quantitative survey for gay and bisexual men would provide factual evidence to potential funders for this need. However, she combined this quantitative approach with a qualitative review of the methods and instrument by members of the gay community as part of a pilot test. She also recruited interviewers from within the gay community to undertake face-to-face interviews. This yielded a direct benefit to the participants in terms of receiving payment for their work, training and experience in research, and increasing the credibility of the study to members of that community.

Whitmore (2000) provides another example of design choices that reflect an inclusive approach in her evaluation of a drop-in center for street-involved youth in a Canadian city. She provided the following rationale for her choice of an inclusive, participatory design: "Street involved youth were assumed experts in their own lives. Because they mistrust adults in general, especially those in authority, a peer-to-peer approach would yield better data and a deeper understanding of the key issues. The evaluation offered an opportunity to engage six street-youth in an empowering process—to build skills in evaluation, interviewing, public speaking, and writing, while developing confidence and self-esteem". This study was not without its challenges; however, the author credits its success to the choice of a design that validly and consistently involved youth from the street.

Ethical concerns arise in design choice when the design involves denial of treatment, lack of community involvement in the decision to participate, or lack of fully informed consent as to the consequences of participating, especially as it relates to the use of a control group or a placebo. Denial of treatment is one strategy used in experimental designs to establish a control group. However, this is viewed as especially problematic in terms of the ethics associated with the transformative-emancipatory paradigm. Assignment to treatments or denial of treatment on a random basis is also considered to be unethical and illegal in many schools and social service agencies. In those settings, reliance on a true experimental design with random selection and random assignment to conditions is not possible.

Recent evidence from clinical drug trials is especially troubling in that drug companies are turning to third world countries for more of their new drug tests. The third world countries do not have the same restrictions in terms of informed consent, costs are lower, and the patients that they need for testing are plentiful and more naive (Flaherty, Nelson & Stephens, 2000). *The Declaration of Helsinki*, an international medical document on ethics in research, was revised to state that "experimental therapies always should be tested against 'best current' treatments and that placebos should be used only when no treatment exists" (Okie, 2000, p. A3). If this rule is applied to social program evaluation, then evaluators might consider alternative designs, such as mixed methods, qualitative approaches, time series designs, use of known alternative treatments, comparison with an extant group, or comparison with a larger statistical base in terms of known levels of incidence (Mertens & McLaughlin, 1995).

Theoretical framework for defining the problem. Transformative-emancipatory scholars have pointed out that different theoretical frameworks have been used over the years as a basis for explaining social problems. Some of the theoretical frameworks have contributed to a negative stereotyping of women, people of color, people with disabilities, and members of other marginalized groups. For example, the medical model of disability was used to frame research geared toward fixing the person with the disability.

Theoretical frameworks that place the blame for failure inside the individual or their culture are dysfunctional, deficit models. For example, the deficit model leads to framing the problem of poverty and underachievement of children in poor urban or rural schools in terms of social deficiency or cultural deficits, rather than in terms of the marginal resources of their schools and the racialized politics of local, state, and federal governments (Mertens, 1998; Stanfield, 1999; Villegas, 1991). The transformative-emancipatory paradigm frames gender, race/ethnicity, disability, sexual orientation, and other bases of diversity from the perspective of a social, cultural, minority group such that the defining characteristic is viewed as a dimension of human difference (not a defect) (Gill, 1999; Mertens, 1998; Mertens, 2000a). Within this paradigm, the category of diversity is recognized as being socially constructed such that its meaning is derived from society's response to individuals who deviate from cultural standards.

Madison (2000) provides an example of how a theoretical framework of deficit can result in inappropriate interventions and negatively impact the self-concepts of the intended participants. She was asked to evaluate a statewide project for "at-risk" youth. She commented, "The term at-risk youth was coined to interchangeably describe both the problem and the youth. Some use the term primarily to describe a category of young people who are a problem to society. This language not only provides social group identity to this category of youth, but the contextual meanings of the language stigmatizes the youth as undesirable rather than the social situation responsible for placing them at risk" (p. 20).

Madison (2000) discovered that the problem was viewed by the agency personnel as "bad parents" She described their theoretical framework as: "The social construction of social reality is that the youth are the victims of low-income, uncaring, dysfunctional parents. None of the agencies identified systemic problems, such as educational inequities and structural unemployment, that create economic deprivation and hopelessness as factors contributing to many of the parents' inability to be available to their children" (p. 23).

Madison (2000) recommended reframing the problem as the need to provide social programs for "youth who may be at risk of not making the transition from childhood to adulthood equipped to meet the adult responsibilities required for personal growth and development, work, family life, and full participation in society" (p. 25). Thus, the agencies were able to design programs that addressed the need to provide supervision in constructive activities that would be related to successful transition from youth to adulthood.

The inclusive evaluator would seek to identify variables that help explain the failure of the status quo in terms of both external and internal factors, rather than blaming the individual or their cultural group. For example, in an evaluation of programs designed to enhance science achievement, Wang (1998) reported that the most significant predictor of science achievement was the student's opportunity to learn. An evaluator could combine this information with research that indicates that students from low socio-economic status groups, especially African American and Hispanics, are most likely to be put into classrooms with less learning opportunity even when ability is taken into account (Oakes & Guiton, 1995). Thus, the ground work is laid for examining variables that can be manipulated by the school system and for attention to groups that have not been equal beneficiaries of educational services commonly associated with greater economic prosperity in adulthood.

Evaluation questions and indicators of success. The evaluator needs to work critically to develop appropriate questions and performance indicators that reflect those factors that are related to transformation. For example, Oakes and Guiton (1995) direct evaluators and researchers in schools to query the content of school curriculum, processes that limit school achievement for poor and minority students, and the differential access to quality school facilities, programs, materials, counseling, expectations, and instruction, as well as the unequal distribution of competent teachers.

Waters (1998) addressed the issue of asking critical questions as evaluators. She wrote:

Mainstream evaluation of these reform efforts in teaching practices and educational programs misses a crucial part of the picture about how schools are functioning for all children. If we as evaluators do not ask deliberate questions about institutionalized power, democracy, quality of instruction, and inequality within the public school domain, during the process of evaluation, then we become one more vehicle that perpetuates an already neutral state of mind about the world of education and its goals for society (p. 21).

One example of how the presence of pluralism can be queried is provided by a study I am presently undertaking of a technology integration project for teacher education programs for teachers of the deaf and hard of hearing (D/HH) in the United States. One part of the project involved the development of multimedia case studies that could be used by university faculty throughout the United States with their preservice teachers to demonstrate the use of technology in K-12 classrooms. To be sure that the products were inclusive of the pluralism of the deaf community, we set as one evaluation question: "To what extent do the multi-media case studies developed in partnership with K-12 D/HH education teachers, meet these criteria: capture and explain the effective use of technology, enhance student learning, and reflect diversity in terms of gender, ethnicity, and other cultural dimensions related to communication preferences in the deaf and hard of hearing communities? The developers expected to meet the first two criteria (i.e., demonstrate effective use of technology and enhance student learning). The last set of criteria related to pluralism caused them to reflect and rethink some of their initial planning to be more inclusive.

Agar (2000) contrasts indicators of success that were defined in a study of tuberculosis screening program from the project director's and the community workers' perspectives. The traditional measures of participation in the TB screening suggested that the program was not successful. However, follow-up interviews with the community health workers revealed that they viewed the program as a success. He discovered that the workers were using a standard of caring about the people who lived in the neighborhood, rather than if they chose to have a TB screening. The workers knew that their clients often suffered from multiple life problems, including racism, violence, poverty, dysfunctional families, drug and alcohol abuse, and other health problems. From their point of view, they could not just focus on TB. They considered themselves to be successful if they could address some of the most pressing issues that the person had, if that was housing, money, food, referral to social services, or services for their children. The community health workers had expanded the notion of health care in a more holistic sense in dealing with the clients' life needs that were most salient.

Sample definitions and inclusiveness. A prerequisite to being more inclusive is the development of an appropriate sensitivity to the diversity within the populations that are served by a program, understanding the complexity of the characteristics and the cultural implications. Not all deaf people are the same. Not all Latino people are the same. Not all African Americans are the same. What are the differences within the population that are important within this context? How are the services distributed by different sub-groups? What are the values that underlie the distribution of services?

Whitmore (2000) provides an interesting list of characteristics that they considered in terms of being inclusive with the youth who were part of their participatory evaluation study of street-involved youth. They set the criteria as being a current or past participant in the Drop-In Center with an expressed interest in learning how to evaluate a program. Diversity was also sought in terms of gender, race, language (English and French), and members who were affiliated with different street subgroups that tend to compete with each other and don't mix much.

Mertens (2000) used preferred communication mode as the primary indicator of diversity in sampling in a study of court accessibility for persons who are deaf or hard of hearing. This meant including those who were highly educated and proficient users of American Sign Language; deaf adults with limited education and readings skills, some of whom communicated with sign language and gestures and pantomime; deaf/blind individuals who use an interpreter at close range; highly educated hard of hearing adults who used personal assistive listening devices; deaf adults who used Mexican Sign Language; and deaf adults who rely on oral communication (reading lips and printed English). In addition, diversity in the sample was sought on the basis of gender, race/ethnicity, and status with the court (e.g., juror, witness, victim).

Evaluators can use such question as these to help assess the inclusiveness of their samples:

• Are we including people from both genders and diverse abilities, ages, classes, culture, ethnicities, families, incomes, languages, races, disabilities, and sexualities?

• What barriers are we erecting to exclude a diversity of people?

• Have we chosen the appropriate data collection strategies for diverse groups, including providing for preferred modes of communication?

These questions were adapted from the Canadian Research Institute for Advancement of Women (1996) to guide ethics in research based on feminist principles.

Data collection strategies. Probing to discover the complexities of the populations is a first step. The evaluator must then work hard to figure out the best way to obtain authentic data from the various subgroups. This might involve using different languages or dialects, which has implications for the evaluator's own expertise linguistically or the acceptability of using an interpreter. This will definitely involve determining the appropriate method of data collection. Understanding that for some populations, a survey sent home from school or through the mail is either incomprehensible, possibly a threat, or just one more thing a person who is struggling to survive cannot deal with. Is a focus group a better way to collect data? Is a meeting in the school, church, or community center a better approach? Are meetings scheduled better during the day or at night? Is it necessary to provide food, transportation, or child care? Sensitive, careful probing can help identify appropriate data collection methods and instruments that can lead to the attainment of authentic and accurate data.

Whitmore (2000) described reasons for rejecting more traditional data collection approaches with the street-involved youth in her evaluation study. The conventional techniques such as surveys, experiments, and control groups are often considered to be inappropriate for this population. "Street involved youth have been 'surveyed to death' in recent years and are reluctant to fill out yet another form or answer yet more questions. The 'subjects' are likely to become resentful and resist in subtle ways (not answering questions truthfully or seriously) and not-so-subtle ways (refusing to respond at all). Surveys assume literacy, and many street-involved youth have low literacy skills. The questions are often framed by 'experts' who have limited understanding of street culture. Reliance on control groups ignores the transience of life on the streets; surveys and experiments may not be able to compensate for the mistrust among street youth around being 'used' for someone else's purposes. These techniques tend to further objectify and disempower an already marginalized group" (p. 9). The group decided to use modifications of Participatory Learning and Action methods that involved group mapping, direct matrix ranking, and semi-structured interviews.

Agar (2000) provides another example of a standardized research interview approach that "differs wildly from the normal ways a community health worker talks in the neighborhoods where outreach takes place" (p. 97). The community health workers were instructed to stand outside the door and speak from a standard protocol. They said the respondents considered the survey to be too long and too invasive of their privacy. The survey asked questions about income, prison, drug and alcohol use, and sexual practices, and called for time-line estimates that simply do not correspond to the way these residents think about their activities. "Needless to say, crack houses and crack users are not known for their predisposition to discuss income and hours per day spent at work with community health workers" (p. 98). Agar concludes: "We close with the hypothesis that the problem isn't acquiring and documenting information; rather, it is the scientific requirement for acquiring it in a way that contradicts the caring mode and the communicative norms of situations where interviewing was done" (p. 98).

Addressing power differentials. Intertwined with such methodological decisions are issues related to differential power for the various stakeholder groups. As House and Howe (1999) recognize, power imbalances are inherent in every human interaction. The evaluator's job is to make sure that strong power imbalances do not distort the study's findings. Power differences can be addressed by the evaluator adopting a role that facilitates the involvement of those who have had a traditionally less powerful role in discussions of social and educational programs and their impacts. For example, in the evaluation of the accessibility of court systems for deaf and hard of hearing persons that I conducted, we had an Advisory Council that represented the diversity of the deaf and hard of hearing community in terms of preferred communication modes (Mertens, 2000). However, we also had to seek input from that community that was inclusive of other types of diversity, such as gender, ethnicity/race, language, and experience with the court system.

We developed a very elaborate design for focus groups of deaf and hard of hearing people that reflected this diversity in order to determine their experiences with accessibility in the courthouse. We used their responses to develop training programs for judges and other court personnel. We invited various deaf and hard of hearing persons to appear in a video entitled "Silent Justice" that was shown at all the training sessions nation-wide. We also invited some of the focus group participants to present on panels during the training. Deaf and hard of hearing people and their advocates were invited to attend the training along with their state court representatives, and then they worked together in teams to create action plans to make their court systems more accessible for this population. These are some examples of ways to recognize and accommodate for differences in traditional positions of power amongst the various stakeholders. Evaluators who seek to be inclusive must also seek ways to redress the power imbalances by issuing invitations to those with the least power to be part of the conversation throughout the process.

CONCLUSIONS: STANDARDS, WORLD CHANGE, AND COORDINATION

The evaluator's role is to ensure that a quality evaluation is planned, conducted, and used. To this end, the evaluation community has engaged in the development of various sets of standards for good evaluations. The Program Evaluation Standards (Joint Committee on Standards for Educational Evaluation, 1994) provide one guide for evaluators to use in explaining to their clients the characteristics of a good evaluation. An addition of standards for a good evaluation based on the transformative function of evaluation would lead to a greater degree of inclusivity of previously marginalized groups. Based on the work of Kirkhart (1995), additional standards could be incorporated in order to increase the appropriateness of an evaluation in terms of multicultural and power issues. Kirkhart outlined four additional categories that evaluators could use to ensure that the quality of their evaluations is more reflective of these issues, including: methodological validity, interpersonal validity, consequential validity, and multicultural validity (see Mertens, 1998 for a complete listing).

Using this expanded set of Standards, evaluators could ask such questions of their evaluations as:

> What are the influences of personal characteristics or circumstances, such as social class, gender, race and ethnicity, language, disability, or sexual orientation in shaping interpersonal interactions, including interactions between evaluators, clients, program providers, and consumers, and other stakeholders?

> What evidence is there that the evaluation was conceptualized as a catalyst for change (e.g., shift the power relationships among cultural groups or subgroups)?

> Were the time and budget allocated to the evaluation sufficient to allow a culturally sensitive perspective to emerge?

> Did the evaluator demonstrate cultural sophistication on the cognitive, affective, and skill dimensions? Was the evaluator able to have positive

interpersonal connections, conceptualize and facilitate culturally congruent change, and make appropriate cultural assumptions in the design and implementation of the evaluation?

Adoption of the inclusive evaluator's role does not mean that the evaluator should throw away the tools that he or she has as a professional evaluator and a member of the evaluation community. The Program Evaluation Standards have value; as do the other tools that an evaluator has learned in evaluation and research methods, statistics and policy analysis classes. The role of the inclusive evaluator is enriched by adding understanding of groups that have been traditionally under-represented in methods oriented classes, through examination of scholarly literature that has emerged from feminists, people of color, people with disabilities, and their advocates, and by interacting with members of those communities in a sustained and meaningful way.

Furthermore, a global sense of involvement greets the evaluation community at the beginning of the new millenium. Collective benefits can result from international cooperation in evaluation such as building evaluation leadership and capacity in developing countries, fostering the cross-fertilization of evaluation theory and practice, and understanding the cultural limits of specific evaluation approaches. Together, inclusively, the evaluation community can make a significant contribution to the identification and solution of many of the world's social problems.

REFERENCES

Agar, M. (2000). Border lessons: Linguistic "rich points" and evaluative understanding. In R. K. Hopson (Ed.), *How and why language matters* (New Directions for Evaluation, No. 86, pp. 93-109). San Francisco, CA: Jossey-Bass.

Alcoff, L. & Potter, E. (Eds.). (1993). *Feminist epistemologies*. NY: Routledge.

Banks, J. A. (1995). The historical reconstruction of knowledge about race: Implications for transformative teaching. *Educational Researcher, 24(2)*, 15 - 25.

Banks, J. A. (1993). The canon debate, knowledge construction, and multicultural education. *Educational Researcher, 22(5)*, 4 - 14.

Canadian Research Institute for the Advancement of Women. (1996). *Feminist research ethics: A process*. Ottawa, Ontario: Author.

Chelimsky, E. (1998). The role of experience in formulating theories of evaluation practice. *American Journal of Evaluation, 19(1)*, 35 - 56.

De Koning, K., & Marion, M. (Eds.). (1996). *Participatory research in health*. London: Zed books.

Fine, M. (Ed.) (1992). *Disruptive voices*. Ann Arbor: University of Michigan Press.

Flaherty, M. P., Nelson, D., & Stephens, J. (2000). The body hunters: Overwhelming the watchdogs. *Washington Post,* Monday, Dec. 18, 2000, A1 & A16-17.

Gill, C. (1999). Invisible ubiquity: The surprising relevance of disability issues in evaluation. *American Journal of Evaluation, 20*(2), 279 - 287.

Greene, J. (1994). Qualitative program evaluation: Practice and promise. In N.K. Denzin & Y. S. Lincoln (Eds.), *The handbook of qualitative research.* (pp. 530 - 544). Thousand Oaks, CA: Sage.

Greene, J., Lincoln, Y. S., Mathison, S., Mertens, D. M. & Ryan, K. (1998). Advantages and challenges of using inclusive evaluation approaches in evaluation practice. *American Journal of Evaluation, 19(1),* 101 - 122.

Hill-Collins, P. (2000). *Black feminist thought: Knowledge, consciousness, and the politics of empowerment.* NY: Routledge.

House, E. R., & Howe, K. R. (1999*). Values in evaluation and social research.* Thousand Oaks, CA: Sage.

Humphries, B. & Truman, C. (Eds.). (1994). *Re-thinking social research.* Aldershot, UK: Avebury.

Joint Committee on Standards for Educational Evaluation (1994). *The program evaluation standards: How to assess evaluations of educational programs.* Thousand Oaks, CA: Sage.

Kirkhart, K. E. (1995). Seeking multicultural validity: A postcard from the road. *Evaluation Practice, 16* (1), 1-12.

Lather, P. (1992). Critical frames in educational research: Feminist and post-structural perspectives. *Theory into Practice, 31*(2), 1 - 13.

Madison, A. M. (2000). Language in defining social problems and in evaluating social programs. In R. K. Hopson (Ed.), *How and why language matters* (New Directions for Evaluation, No. 86, pp. 17 - 28) San Francisco, CA: Jossey-Bass.

Madison, A. M. (Ed.) (1992). *Minority issues in program evaluation* (New Directions for Program Evaluation, No. 53). San Francisco, CA: Jossey-Bass.

McLaren, P. L., & Lankshear, C. (Eds.). (1994). *Politics of liberation.* NY: Routledge.

Mertens, D. M. (in press). Mixed methods and the politics of human research: The transformative-emancipatory perspective. In C. Teddlie & A. Tashakkori, (Eds.), *Handbook of mixed methodology.* Thousand Oaks, CA: Sage.

Mertens, D. M. (2000a, January 25th). Researching disability and diversity: Merging paradigms. Paper presented at the National Institute on Disability and Rehabilitative Research Conference: *The New Paradigm on Disability: Research and Approaches,* Washington, DC.

Mertens, D. M. (2000b). Deaf and hard of hearing people in court: Using an emancipatory perspective to determine their needs. In C. Truman, D. M. Mertens, & B. Humphries (Eds.), *Research and inequality.* London: Taylor & Francis.

Mertens, D. M. (1999a). Inclusive evaluation: Implications of transformative theory for evaluation. *American Journal of Evaluation, 20(1),* 1 - 14.

Mertens, D. M. (1999b). Building an international evaluation community. In C. Russon & A. Love (Eds.), *Creating a world-wide evaluation community.* Kalamazoo, MI: University of Michigan.

Mertens, D. M. (1998). *Research methods in education and psychology: Integrating diversity with quantitative and qualitative approaches.* Thousand Oaks, CA: Sage.

Mertens, D. M. & McLaughlin, J. (1995). *Research methods in special education.* Thousand Oaks, CA: Sage.

Mertens, D. M. & Russon, C. (1999). A proposal for the International Organization for Cooperation in Evaluation. *American Journal of Evaluation, 21(2),* 275 - 283.

Oakes, J., & Guiton, G. (1995). Matchmaking: The dynamics of high school tracking decisions. *American Educational Research Journal, 32*(1), 3-33.

Oliver, M. (1992). Changing the social relations of research production? *Disability, Handicap, & Society, 7*(2), 101 - 114.

Okie, S. (2000). Health officials debate ethics of placebo use. *Washington Post,* Friday, Nov. 24, 2000, p. A3.

Reason, P. (Ed.) (1994). *Participation in human inquiry.* London: Sage.

Reinharz, S. (1992). *Feminist methods in social research.* NY: Oxford University Press.

Ryan, K. E. & DeStefano, L. (2000). (Eds.), Evaluation as a democratic process: Promoting inclusion, dialogue, and deliberation. San Francisco: Jossey-Bass.

Stanfield, J. H. II (1999). Slipping through the front door: relevant social scientific evaluation in the people-of-color century. *American Journal of Evaluation, 20(3),* 415 - 432.

Stanfield, J. H. II (1993). Methodological reflections: An introduction. In J. H. Stanfield & R. Dennis, (Eds.), *Race and ethnicity in research methods* (pp. 3 - 15). Thousand Oaks, CA: Sage.

Truman, C. (2000). New social movements and social research. In C. Truman, D. Mertens, & B. Humphries (Eds.), *Research and inequality (pp. 24-36).* London: Taylor & Frances.

Truman, C., Mertens, D., & Humphries, B. (Eds.). (2000). *Research and inequality.* London: Taylor & Frances.

Villegas, A. M. (1991*). Culturally responsive pedagogy for the 1990's and beyond.* Princeton, NJ: Educational Testing Service.

Wang, G. (1998). Critical evaluation for education reform. *Educational Policy Analysis Archives, 6(20),* 1 - 34.

Weiss, C. (1998). Have we learned anything new about the use of evaluation? *American Journal of Evaluation, 19(1),* 21 - 34.

Whitmore, E. (Ed.). (1998). *Understanding and practicing participatory evaluation* (New Directions for Program Evaluation, *No. 80)* . San Francisco: Jossey-Bass.

Whitmore, E. (2000). Six street youth who could. In P. Reason (Ed.), *Handbook of Action Research: Participative Inquiry and Practice.* London: Sage.

7

Theory-Driven Program Evaluation in the New Millennium

Stewart I. Donaldson

Claremont Graduate University

I am sometimes intrigued by those who specialize in reading palms, predicting the stock markets and outcomes of sporting events for profit, or determining personality and future behavior by studying planet alignments. While these may be fun to observe and even to engage in with friends and acquaintances on occasion, predicting the future with a reasonable degree of accuracy is well beyond my recognized expertise as an evaluator, researcher, consultant, and professor.

Fortunately, as this conference came to fruition, it became clear to me that the task of providing a vision for how we *should (not how we will)* evaluate social programs and problems in the new millennium, is actually very different from speculating or trying to predict the future. Predictions about the future can be, and often are, proven wrong by facts. Visions for a better future typically elude such harsh scrutiny. So rather than having to go out on a limb to make guesses or predictions for how evaluators will actually practice in the 21st century, I am free in this chapter to share with you my personal vision for improving the art and science of social problem solving in the new millennium.

What will you encounter if you dare to read on? First, based on my experiences as an evaluator, I will share with you my assessment of the current state of affairs. This will lead to my identification and description of major problems that are currently limiting our ability to solve social problems. Next, I will present my vision of an ideal state of affairs for program developers and evaluators to emulate in the new millennium. This vision will set the stage for discussion of one possible way to move the field closer to this ideal state. I will call the central theme of this discussion the theory-driven view of program evaluation.

SOCIAL PROBLEMS

Despite significant and continued advancements in the behavioral, social, and organizational sciences, social problems continue to thrive and wreak havoc in even the most modern, high-tech and affluent societies. Depending on one's demographic characteristics, geographic location, and socio-economic status, social problems such as drug abuse, educational underachievement or failure, inadequate training and employment opportunities, lack of access to health care and mental health services, various forms of violence and terror, prejudice and discrimination, HIV risk behaviors and the like may dramatically reduce quality of life and/or longevity. Some may speculate that many of today's social problems could be solved by reallocating national, state, and local resources. Others may opt for stricter laws and law enforcement efforts. Still others may attribute these problems to the break down of the family, social support systems, and/or moral decay. Irrespective of the differing views on the nature of social problems, most perspectives conclude that there continues to be a strong demand for societies to prevent and ameliorate a wide range of destructive social ills.

The approach to social problem solving that I will address in this chapter is called "social programming." I will define social programming for the purposes of this chapter to broadly include organized efforts (programs) to train, educate, and/or change human behavior to achieve participant and social betterment. Admittedly, my own experiences conducting program evaluations across a wide range of work settings, schools, community-based organizations, health care and health maintenance organizations (e.g., HMOs), mental health clinics, and in research and academic environments, weigh heavily on how I conceptualize the field. However, beyond my own experiences, there is a vast array of social programming efforts that fit within this discussion. Although the list presented below could easily extend into the hundreds (e.g., Lipsey & Wilson, 1993), it is intended to provide the reader with some examples of modern social programs:

1. Diversity programs implemented in corporate settings to address workplace prejudice and discrimination;
2. Career and personal development programs offered to employees in organizations or more widely through community-based organizations;
3. Drug or violence prevention programs implemented in school settings;
4. Gang violence suppression programs;

5. Community based efforts to change the risky sexual behavior of adolescents and young adults;
6. Headstart early childhood education programs;
7. Programs to prevent and solve homelessness;
8. Reemployment programs for the unemployed and underemployed.

Before I discuss my vision for improving these social problem-solving efforts in the new millennium, I will briefly describe below what I view as the "current state of affairs" in social programming, including five central problems that appear to be hindering well-intentioned efforts.

CURRENT STATE OF AFFAIRS IN SOCIAL PROGRAMMING

I see the current state of social programming to be a rather polarized black and white world. Simply put, there seem to be many skeptics and some strong believers. Let me start by briefly characterizing those who are skeptical about social programs. The clouds of skepticism seem to spread wide across the occupational and public landscape. From conservative politicians and policy makers to a broad segment of the public, social programs are often believed to be largely ineffective and a poor choice for investment. A similar spirit has been echoed by external evaluators looking back over the past three decades of evidence for the efficacy of social programs (Donaldson, 2001a). For example, many have characterized the body of evidence from systematic evaluations of social programs to be a "parade of null effects" (e.g., Rossi & Wright, 1984; Rossi, Freeman, & Lipsey, 1999). That is, one rather common impression of the history of external program evaluation has led many to believe that the establishment of policymakers, agency officials, human service professionals, and social scientists have failed to establish social programming as a legitimate endeavor (cf. Shadish, Cook, & Leviton, 1991, p. 377).

In my opinion, the other side of the argument, the pro social program position, is at least equally, if not more, convincing. First, many of the professionals working in the "social programming trenches" are skeptical about past program evaluations, and strongly believe that many social programs have been, and are currently, effective. For example, program designers, professionals delivering direct services, and the management of human service organizations often persuasively support this position. More surprisingly, a number of leading external evaluators now believe the "parade of null effects" interpretation of evaluation evidence, which has been used to dampen enthusiasm for social programs, is more likely to be due to insensitive program evaluation than to ineffective social programming (cf. Lipsey, 1988, 1990; Lipsey et al., 1985). For example, Lipsey and Wilson (1993) reported that in contrast to conventional reviews of the evaluation research, meta-analysis shows a strong, dramatic pattern of positive findings for social programs. While this reinterpretation of the entire body of evidence on the efficacy of social programs has sparked much controversy and debate, both sides of the argument seem to suggest at least five key problems that face social programming efforts in the new millennium.

FIVE PROBLEMS LIMITING SOCIAL PROGRAMMING

I will briefly list below five key problems that must be overcome in order to improve social programming in the new millennium (see Table 7.1). The first problem is *inadequate program conceptualization*. In my view, this problem is common and dooms a social program from the start. Second, the problem of *poor program implementation* is often the culprit for null effects. It is well-documented that many social programs (even those that are well conceptualized) fail because they are not implemented as planned. Third, *insensitive program evaluations* limit our ability to effectively solve social problems through social programming. A fourth problem that must be addressed in this effort to improve social problems is that of *poor stakeholder-evaluator relations,* that is, when stakeholders do not value and cooperate with the evaluation process causing social programming efforts to be severely undermined. Finally, we must overcome *barriers that prevent us from developing cumulative knowledge and wisdom.* It is highly inefficient to "reinvent the wheel" every time we are faced with a new social programming challenge.

- Inadequate Program Conceptualization
- Poor Program Implementation
- Insensitive Program Evaluations
- Poor Stakeholder-Evaluator Relations
- Scarcity of Cumulative Knowledge and Wisdom about Social Problem Solving

TABLE 7.1. Five problems limiting social programming.

SOCIAL PROGRAMMING IN THE NEW MILLENNIUM

I have shared with you my broad impressions of the current state of affairs of social programming at the turn of the century. A short list of problems limiting social programming efforts were presented to provide a baseline for discussing improvement. My vision for a more ideal situation as we move farther into the new millennium is that *most social programs* will be 1) well-designed and based on sound theory and research; 2) implemented with high fidelity; 3) evaluated in a manner that minimizes the chances of design sensitivity and validity errors; 4) evaluated in a way that empowers stakeholders to use findings to continuously improve their efforts; and 5) evaluated so that cumulative knowledge and wisdom about social programming is advanced. For the most part, it is fair to say that the gap between the current situation and the ideal state that I envision is quite wide. Therefore, the remainder of this chapter will summarize an approach for designing and evaluating social programs that promises to significantly close this gap.

THEORY-DRIVEN PROGRAM EVALUATION

Theory-driven program evaluation is a relatively recent theory of evaluation practice that attempts to build upon knowledge acquired from the practice of program evaluation over the past three decades (Chen, 1990; Chen & Rossi, 1983, 1987; Donaldson, 2001a). Shadish, Cook, & Leviton (1991) referred to theory-driven evaluation as one of the most advanced forms of evaluation theory—Stage III Evaluation Theory. They described how it has integrated and synthesized previous approaches to develop a contingency approach to evaluation practice, acknowledging that some evaluation approaches and methods work well under some circumstances but fail under others. This approach to evaluation practice has become quite popular in recent years (Donaldson & Chen, 2002), and now provides a foundation for some of the most widely used textbooks on program evaluation (e.g., Rossi, Freeman, & Lipsey, 1999; Weiss, 1998).

Program evaluation practice has a history filled with illustrations of "method-driven," "black box," "input/output," or outcome focused investigations. For example, Lipsey and Wilson (1993) meta-analyzed 111 meta-analyses of intervention studies across a wide range of program domains (representing evaluations of more than 10,000 programs) and reported that most of the literature is based on only crude outcome research with little attention to program theory or potential mediating and moderating factors. They suggested that the proper agenda for the next generation of program evaluation should focus on which program components are most effective, the mediating causal processes through which they work, and the characteristics of the participants, service providers, settings and the like that moderate the relationships between a program and its outcomes. Theory-driven evaluation provides a feasible alternative to the traditional method-driven approaches that have come up short in these respects, and is precisely focused on meeting this new agenda.

While the details of how to conduct a theory-driven program evaluation are beyond the scope of this chapter, these issues have been described in detail elsewhere (e.g., Chen, 1990; Donaldson, 2001a; Donaldson & Gooler, in press, 2001; Fitzpatrick, in press; Gooler & Donaldson, 2001; Reynolds, 1998; Rossi, Freeman, & Lipsey, 1999). Simply stated, theory-driven program evaluation is a comprehensive approach which involves three general steps:

1. Developing Program Theory
2. Formulating and Prioritizing Evaluation Questions
3. Answering Evaluation Questions

That is, evaluators typically work with stakeholders to develop a common understanding of how a program is presumed to solve the social problem(s). This common understanding of program theory helps evaluators and stakeholders identify and prioritize evaluation questions. Evaluation questions of most interest are then answered using the most rigorous methods possible given the practical constraints of the evaluation context.

Developing Program Theory

The first task of a systematic theory-driven program evaluation is to develop a conceptual framework or program theory specifying how a program intends to solve the social problem of interest (i.e., meet the needs of its target population). In some cases this may be purely the program designers' view of the program, ideally based on systematic needs assessment. However, often this view is implicit, and the task is to make it explicit and testable.

Fortunately, it is often possible and highly desirable to base the conceptual framework on multiple sources of information such as (1) prior theory and research in the program domain (Donaldson, Street, Sussman, & Tobler, 2001); (2) implicit theories held by those closest to the operation of the program (program personnel such as health educators or other human service providers); (3) observations of the program in action; and in some cases; (4) exploratory research to test critical assumptions about the nature of the program. This process seems to work well when evaluators and stakeholders approach it as a highly interactive and non-linear exercise (Donaldson & Gooler, 2001; Fitzpatrick, in press). Once a program theory or competing program theories have been developed, they are used to make informed choices about evaluation questions and methods.

It is important to note that the first step in theory-driven evaluation often reveals that a program is not ready for implementation and evaluation. Program theory development can be used to aid evaluability assessment procedures (Wholey, 1977), which are used to determine whether a program is ready to be evaluated. Therefore, developing program theory has the potential to save substantial time and resources by redirecting efforts toward further program development and/or implementation activities, as opposed to moving directly to summative evaluation that would simply expose null effects.

Formulating and Prioritizing Evaluation Questions

Formulating, prioritizing, and answering important evaluation questions are core tasks of theory-driven evaluation. First, well-developed program theories are used to identify a wide range of potential evaluation questions. Relevant stakeholders and evaluators typically generate an exhaustive list of possible questions. The group then attempts to prioritize these questions so that it is clear which questions are of most value. Differences of opinion about the value of each question across the stakeholder groups are noted and factored into final decisions about which questions to answer and which methods to use to answer those questions.

Answering Evaluation Questions

In many respects, the theory-driven view of program evaluation is method neutral, and creates a superordinate goal that helps evaluators get past old debates about which methods are superior in program evaluation (e.g., the quantitative/qualitative debate, Reichhardt & Rallis, 1994). That is, from the contingency point of view, the theory-driven approach argues that quantitative, qualitative, or mixed methods designs are neither superior nor applicable in every evaluation situation (Chen, 1997). Instead, methodological choices are informed by program theory, by specific evaluation questions ranked in order of priority, and by practical constraints (Donaldson & Gooler, 2001). Therefore, the final step in theory-driven program evaluation involves determining what type of evidence is needed to answer questions of interest with an acceptable level of confidence.

The details of this step vary considerably across program evaluations. In some cases, the group will accept nothing short of evidence based on a large-scale randomized experiment. Whereas, in other cases, rich description developed through qualitative methods are preferred over experimental designs. Further, unless data collection resources are plentiful, compromises are made to determine the most convincing design within resource and practical constraints. Unfortunately, guidelines for making these decisions are rather complex and beyond the scope of this paper. It may be said, however, that many factors typically interact to determine how to collect the evidence needed to answer the key evaluation questions (e.g., design feasibility issues, resources, stakeholder preferences, and evaluator expertise and preferences).

I have briefly introduced the theory-driven view of program evaluation as a way to overcome problems that often limit social programming and hence social problem solving. For succinctness, I have organized and condensed this view into three general steps. Recent applications of theory-driven program evaluation are presented below in an effort to be even more specific and concrete.

Recent Applications of Theory-Driven Program Evaluation

Birckmayer & Weiss (2000) and Weiss (1997) asserted that the evaluation literature is replete with arguments supporting the value of theory-driven program evaluation, but little evidence has surfaced that evaluators are adopting this approach widely. While some areas of evaluation practice have certainly been slow to adopt, theory-driven evaluation seems to have gained momentum in recent years and is now considered the "state-of-the-art" in many program areas (Crano, chapter 8 this volume; Donaldson, 2001a). Furthermore, Rossi, Freeman, and Lipsey (1999) have recently added a chapter, "Expressing and Assessing Program Theory" to their best-selling textbook, *Evaluation: A Systematic Approach.* This articulation of the role of program theory in evaluation promises to help make it a required and routine step in modern program evaluation practice. Applications of theory-driven evaluation and the use of program theory in evaluation are now widely discussed across sessions and interest groups at the annual American Evaluation Association (AEA) conferences.

Many recent applications of theory-driven evaluation are discussed and showcased by the Program Theory and Theory-driven Evaluation Topical Interest Group (TIG) of AEA. Each year the TIG sponsors a number of symposia, panels, papers, and demonstrations designed to help practicing evaluators keep abreast of the latest developments, and to improve their skills in conducting theory-driven program evaluations.

The membership of the TIG has steadily increased over the past five years, and there are now over 500 active members representing a wide range of backgrounds and evaluation expertise. A TIG Newsletter, *Mechanisms*, is published annually to document the most recent activities in the theory and practice of theory-driven program evaluation (Donaldson, 2000).

One purpose of theory-driven program evaluation is to uncover mechanisms through which a program affects desired outcomes or meets human needs. Chen (1990) describes this as intervening mechanism evaluation. Simply stated, most programs are designed to affect intervening variables which are presumed to mediate the relationship between a program and its intended outcomes. The action theory of a theory-driven evaluation specifies the nature of the program and a set of mediator variables. In contrast, conceptual theory is concerned with the relationship between the mediators and intended and/or unintended outcomes (see Chen, 1990; Donaldson, 2001). In addition, moderator variables are often examined to assess whether the nature of a program-mediator or mediator-outcome association is influenced by other factors such as participant or service provider characteristics, program dosage or strength, program delivery settings and the like. Findings from intervening mechanism evaluations inform a substantive area about why programs work or fail, for whom they work best, and what may be needed to make a program more effective.

A range of findings from theory-driven evaluations are typically discussed each year at the American Evaluation Association meeting, often under the sponsorship of the Program Theory and Theory-driven Evaluation Topical Interest Group. In recent years, informative findings from theory-driven evaluations have spanned substantive areas such as programs for "at-risk" youth, case management services, alternative programs for disruptive youth, workplace health promotion, violence prevention, teen pregnancy prevention, mental health, systemic reform in education, programs in private industry, science and literacy initiatives in the public schools, educational outreach programs, and HIV prevention programs.

Furthermore, there is a burgeoning literature of published theory-driven evaluations that illustrates the value of this evaluation approach. It is beyond the scope of this chapter to include all the published work, systematically sample the expansive literature, or describe any one study in detail. However, several studies spanning a variety of substantive domains including community youth services, breast cancer screening, pre-school scholastic development, gang crime prevention, workforce development, managed health care services, and drug abuse prevention are presented below to demonstrate that theory-driven program evaluation is making its way into mainstream evaluation practice.

Community youth services. Mercier, Piat, Peladeau, and Dagenais (2000) recently applied theory-driven evaluation to understand and evaluate the complexities of a YMCA Youth Center providing (a) sports and recreational programs, (b) educational and sensitization programs, and (c) informal counseling and referral services. They have provided a useful illustration of how to develop program theory by integrating prior theory and research, concept mapping with staff, and focus groups with youth. Findings showed a strong level of agreement among the three sources of data used to identify the critical components of a program theory of prevention in after-school-hours initiatives, such as YMCA drop-in centers. This study provides an example of how to use qualitative methods for constructing program theory to explain the expected links between program components, intervening mechanisms, and desired outcomes. The authors concluded that they now have essential information necessary to apply quantitative methods to test program theory as part of their outcome evaluation.

Breast cancer screening. Another application of theory-driven evaluation with multiple mediating mechanisms has been recently described in some detail by West and Aiken (1997). Using data from a breast cancer screening trial based on the health belief model, four factors were expected to motivate a woman to seek breast cancer screening: (1) knowing the benefits of screening mammography; (2) understanding the severity of breast cancer; (3) self-perception of susceptibility to breast cancer; and (4) knowing the barriers to screening mammography (Aiken, West, Woodward, Reno, & Reynolds, 1994). After extensive testing of this program theory, it was concluded that only perceptions of susceptibility and knowledge about benefits were key mediators of intentions to get screening. This study provides a useful example of how to test program theory using quantitative data. West & Aiken (1997) provided important instruction in how they arrived at this conclusion through systematic quantitative analyses of program theory.

Preschool scholastic development. Reynolds (1998) provided a detailed illustration of how to use confirmatory factor analysis and latent variable structural modeling to test the program theory of a preschool intervention.

In short, program theory predicted that children's early scholastic readiness for school entry and beyond would be facilitated through the provision of systematic language learning activities and opportunities for family support experiences. Reynolds (1998) demonstrated how to conduct analyses examining patterns of empirical findings against several causal criteria such as temporality of program exposure, strength of associations, dose-response functions, specificity of effects, consistency of association of program exposure and outcome, and the coherence of the empirical findings, in an effort to strengthen causal inferences about program effects. It was concluded that grade six achievement was substantially explained by two mechanisms—cognitive readiness at school entry and parent involvement in school. This article does a particularly good job of linking the evaluation practice literature with current issues related to testing program theory with quantitative analysis techniques.

Crime prevention. Kent, Donaldson, Wyrick, & Smith. (2000) demonstrated how theory-driven evaluation could overcome some of the difficulties involved in evaluating programs designed to reduce gang crime. Using data concerning incarceration and subsequent crime over a 7 year period, they were able to shed light on the mechanism that links a multiagency gang suppression effort to an overall reduction of 47% in gang crime. They found that focusing scarce resources on placing repeat gang offenders in custody, was the primary mediator of gang crime prevention program effects. Figure 7.1 summarizes these findings.

A complex work and health initiative. The nature of one's work (e.g., the presence or absence of work, or the conditions of work) is often a substantial determinant of health status, well-being, and overall quality of life (Donaldson, Gooler, & Weiss, 1998). Based on this premise, The California Wellness Foundation launched a 5 year, $20 million statewide Work and Health Initiative to promote the health and well-being of California workers and their families through work. The mission of the Work and Health Initiative was to improve the health of Californians by funding interventions that positively influence health through employment-related approaches.

Four interrelated programs comprised of over forty partner organizations working together were funded as part of this initiative. *The Future of Work and Health (FWH)* and the *Health Insurance Policy Programs (HIPP)* were expansive and comprehensive research programs designed to generate and disseminate knowledge of how the nature of work is being transformed and how that change will affect the health and well-being of Californians. Current statewide trends related to health and

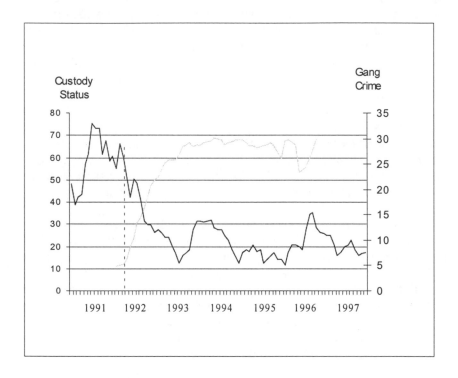

FIGURE 7.1. Trends in custody status (gray line) and gang crime (black line). Note: Broken line notes implementation of the program in January, 1992

health insurance within California were examined through extensive survey research on an annual basis. In addition, researchers throughout California systematically analyzed the changing nature of work and health, and searched for ways to improve working conditions and lower employment risks.

The Initiative also included two demonstration programs in seventeen sites throughout the state to assist both youth and adults in building job skills and finding employment. The *Winning New Jobs (WNJ)* program aimed to help workers regain employment lost due to downsizing, reengineering, and other factors driving rather dramatic changes in the California workplace, and thereby put an end to the adverse health consequences that most workers experience as a result of unemployment. The *Computers in Our Future (CIOF)* program aimed to enable youth and young adults from low-income communities to learn computer skills to improve their education and employment opportunities--thereby improving their own future health as well as the health and well-being of their families and communities (Donaldson & Gooler, in press; Donaldson, Gooler, & Weiss, 1998; Donaldson & Weiss, 1998).

The California Wellness Foundation was also deeply committed to the science of promoting health and well-being through work. As part of this commitment, systematic evaluation research by an external evaluation team was commissioned to guide the strategic development and management of each program in the Initiative, as well as inform the direction of the entire Initiative. To ensure that the perspectives and problem-solving needs of all those with a vested interest in the Initiative programs (e.g., funder, grantees, program administrators, staff, and program recipients, collectively known as stakeholders) were understood and addressed, the evaluation team adopted and facilitated a theory-driven evaluation approach. Program theories for each program were developed and used to formulate, prioritize, and answer evaluation questions. Although the evaluation designs and findings are too extensive to present here (Donaldson & Gooler, 2001; Gooler & Donaldson, 2001), the program theories used to guide these program evaluations are briefly presented below to further illustrate examples from modern evaluation practice.

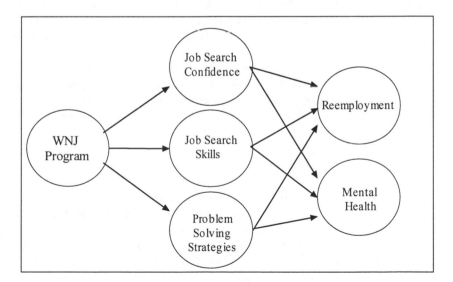

FIGURE 7.2. Winning New Jobs program theory.

Figure 7.2 illustrates that the WNJ program is presumed to improve participant job search self-confidence, job search skills, and problem solving strategies including inoculation against setbacks. These skills and psychological factors are presumed to facilitate reemployment and improve mental health.

Figure 7.3 shows that participation in the CIOF program is believed to lead to improved technology skills, career development knowledge, job search skills, and basic life skills. These acquired skills and knowledge are presumed to facilitate the pursuit of more education, intern job search skills, and basic life skills. These acquired skills and knowledge are presumed to facilitate the pursuit of more education, internship opportunities, and better employment options, which in the long term will improve participants' health status.

As shown in Figure 7.4, the HIPP program sought to increase target constituents' awareness and understanding of the status of health insurance issues in California, and to influence policy development. The program theory shows that a range of publications development, report dissemination activities, and follow-up activities were conducted in an effort to reach those desired outcomes. Support activities and potential outcomes are shown in dotted line boxes to indicate that these are expected to occur but are not required by the funding agency.

Finally, the program theory displayed in Figure 7.5 identifies the desired program outcomes for the FWH program: (1) identification of issues and trends important to the future of work and health of Californians; (2) the development of a network of people involved in building knowledge and improving practice to advance the future of work and health in California; 3) the illumination of trends important to the future of the work and health of Californians; 4) the identification of policies that can influence work and health trends to improve the health of Californians; and 5) the dissemination of research findings on California work and health trends from FWH program activities (see Donaldson & Gooler, 2001 for a detailed discussion of the development and use of these program theories).

Managed mental health care. One of the most well known examples of theory-driven evaluation in recent years is the Fort Bragg Managed Care Demonstration Project (Bickman, 1996a, 1996b). This evaluation was designed to test whether a continuum of mental health and substance abuse services for children and adolescents was more effective than standard practices in this area.

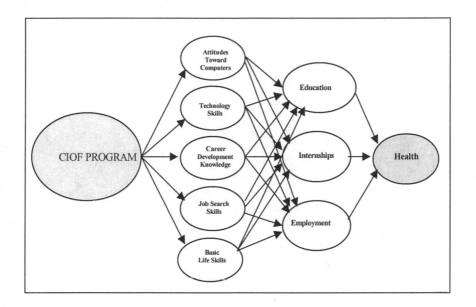

FIGURE 7.3. Computers in Our Future program theory.

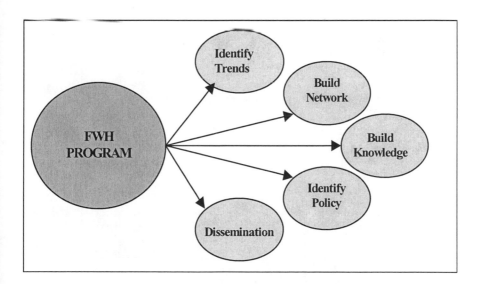

FIGURE 7.4. Future of Work and Health program theory.

FIGURE 7.5. Health Insurance Policy Program.

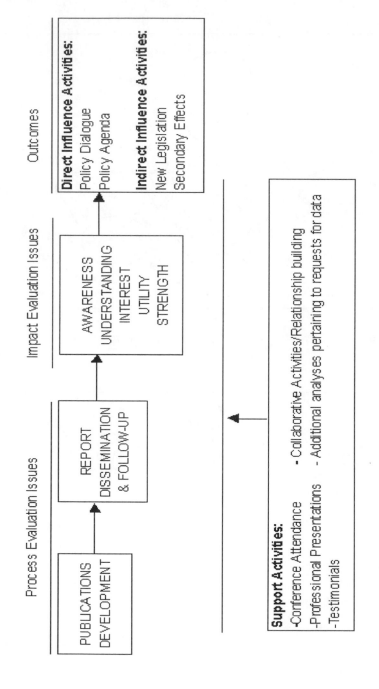

After developing and testing an elaborate program theory of this complex intervention (shown in Figure 7.6), Bickman (1996a, 1996b) concluded that the cost of this managed care delivery system was greater than traditional services, and that clinical outcomes were no better than those for the comparison site. However, Friedman & Burns (1996) point out that there were several problems with the program theory used to guide the evaluation. For example, they suggested that the theory only applied to those with serious emotional disturbances, did not specify the point at which clinical outcomes should emerge, and suggested that differences between sites (e.g., financing arrangements) may confound the findings. The debate about the program theory used to guide this evaluation illustrates the importance of considering high potential mediators (Donaldson, 2002), moderators as well as mediators (Donaldson, 2001), and dose-response and treatment-effect decay functions when formulating program theory (Lipsey, 1990).

Drug abuse prevention. Another literature that has benefited from theory-driven evaluation is the adolescent drug abuse prevention area. For example, Hansen (1993) summarized the twelve most popular drug abuse prevention strategies (and their presumed theoretical program or intervening mechanisms): (a) Normative education (decreases perceptions about prevalence and acceptability beliefs; establishes conservative norms). (b) Refusal assertion training (increases perceptions that one can effectively deal with pressure to use drugs if they are offered; increases self-efficacy). (c) Information about consequences of use (increases perceptions of personal vulnerability to common consequences of drug use). (d) Personal commitment pledges (increases personal commitment and intentions not to use drugs). (e) Values (increases perception that drug use is incongruent with lifestyle). (f) Alternatives (increases awareness of ways to engage in enjoyment without using drugs). (g) Goal setting skills (increases ability to set and achieve goals; increases achievement orientation). (h) Decision making skills (increases ability to make reasoned decisions). (i) Self-esteem (increases feeling of self-worth and valued personal identity). (j) Stress skills (increases perceptions of coping skills;reduces reported level of stress). (k) *Assistance skills* (increases availability of help). (l) Life skills (increases ability to maintain positive social relations). Hansen pointed out that most drug abuse prevention programs reflect the program developers' view of how to optimize prevention effects, rather than a combination of strategies proven to work. Furthermore, most program evaluations in this area are not able to determine which combination strategies are most effective.

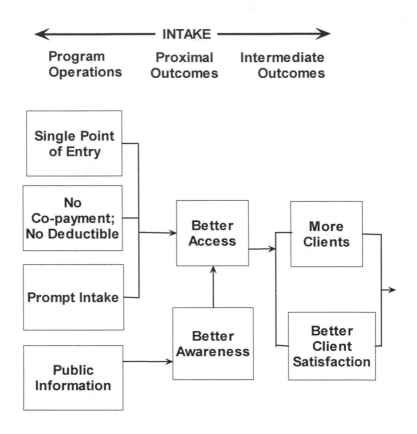

FIGURE 7.6. Fort Bragg Managed Care Demonstration Project program theory (Bickman, 1996a).

However, a series of theory-driven evaluations conducted during the last decade have shed light on the mechanisms at work in drug abuse prevention. These evaluations have shown that social influences based prevention programming is one of the most effective approaches for preventing drug abuse among young adolescents from general populations (Donaldson, 2002). For example, MacKinnon et al. (1991) found that social norms, especially among friends, and beliefs about the positive consequences of drug use appeared to be important mediators of program effects in project STAR (Students Taught Awareness and Resistance). The program did not appear to have effects through

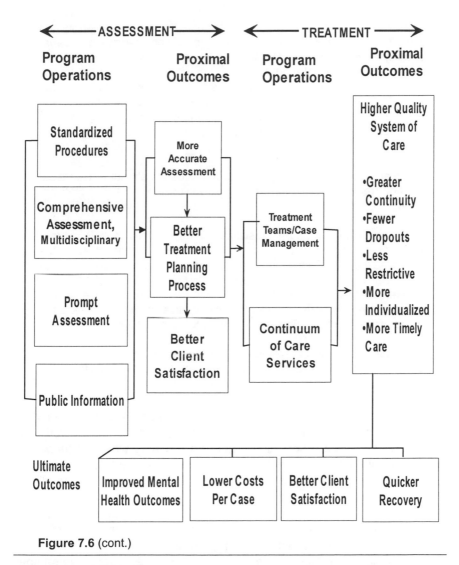

Figure 7.6 (cont.)

resistance skills (refusal training). The notion that social norms are a potent aspect of prevention programming was subsequently tested in a randomized prevention trial known as the Adolescent Alcohol Prevention Trial (AAPT; Donaldson, Graham, & Hansen, 1994; Donaldson, Graham, Piccinin, & Hansen, 1995; Hansen & Graham, 1991). Figure 7.7 represents a summary of the findings from project AAPT and shows:

(a) Normative education lowered beliefs about drug use acceptability and prevalence estimates (in 7th grade) which predicted cigarette, marijuana, and cigarette use (in 8th grade). This pattern of results was virtually the same across potential moderators of gender, ethnicity, context (public versus private school), drugs and levels of risk, and was durable across time (Donaldson, Graham, & Hansen, 1994). MacKinnon, Weber, and Pentz (1988) also failed to find strong moderator relationships across drug abuse prevention programs using gender, ethnicity, grade, socio-economic status, and urbanization

(b) Resistance skills training did improve refusal skills but refusal skills did not predict subsequent drug use (Donaldson, Graham, & Hansen, 1994)

(c) Those who received only resistance skills in public schools actually had higher prevalence estimates (a harmful effect; type of school is shown as the moderator; Donaldson, Graham, Piccinin, & Hansen, 1995)

(d) Refusal skills did predict lower alcohol use for those students who had negative intentions to drink alcohol (negative intention to drink is the moderator; Donaldson, Graham, Piccinin, & Hansen, 1995)

(e) These findings were replicated using reciprocal best friend reports of substance use (Donaldson, Thomas, Graham, Au, & Hansen, 2000)

This final example illustrates that some programs are quite complex, and that theory-driven mediator and moderator analyses conducted over a series of studies are sometimes needed to clarify why and for whom programs work. It is important to note again that the theory-driven evaluations described above are presented as relatively successful case examples to show that theory-driven program evaluation is feasible, has already made a number of important contributions across a range of program domains, appears to be gaining momentum, and is well-positioned to improve future social problem solving efforts.

Of course, these studies are just a small, non-representative sample of studies that exist throughout the vast evaluation literature. For example, Birckmayer & Weiss (2000) selected a different set of studies to examine. After critically assessing the value of six theory-driven evaluations from the health promotion literature, they concluded that there are clear benefits of using program theory to guide evaluations. Specifically,

FIGURE 7.7. Summary of findings for the Adolescent Alcohol Prevention Trial.

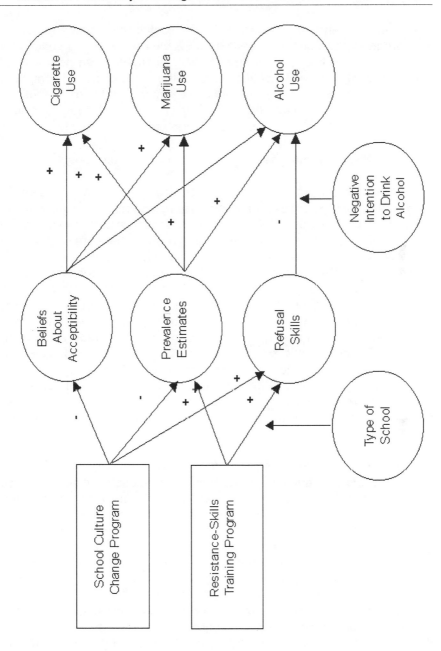

they found evidence that theory-driven evaluation can isolate unnecessary program components, highlight key issues while taking successful pilot programs to scale, locate intermediary changes, raise new evaluation questions, provide clarity and focus for the evaluation, and contribute to paradigms shifts. However, all of these examples and findings must be viewed in light of the facts that relatively unsuccessful efforts are less likely to be published, difficult to access, and are not included here.

Common Myths About Theory-Driven Program Evaluation

This volume embraces the notion of tolerance for diversity in evaluation theory and practice. Critical analysis of each perspective is valued, but is believed to be most productive when it is based on a thorough understanding of the position or approach. Unfortunately, there are examples in the history of program evaluation where critics have attacked or dismissed an approach based on a seemingly vague or incomplete understanding of the perspective. For example, Lincoln (chapter 5, this volume) pointed out "fourth generation evaluation has never rejected conventional methods of knowing, whatever our critics may say." While there have certainly been useful and sound critiques of theory-driven program evaluation (e.g., Shadish, Cook, & Levition, 1991; Crano, chapter 8 this volume; Mark, chapter 11 this volume; Thomas, chapter 9 this volume), a number of common myths seem to have been perpetuated in recent years that may prevent experienced as well as new evaluators from fully understanding theory-driven program evaluation as a theory of evaluation practice.

Program theory = social science theory. Stufflebeam (2001) asserts "there really is not much to recommend theory-based evaluation, since doing it right is usually not feasible and since failed or misrepresented attempts can be highly counterproductive." Much of his critique is grounded in the myth that well-developed social science theory (which is quite rare) is necessary for successful theory-driven program evaluation. This assertion underscores the observation that there is often confusion about the nature of program theory used in theory-driven evaluation (Donaldson & Chen, 2002; Weiss, 1997).

Although the term "program theory" often seems to conjure up images of broad social science theories about social problems, theory-driven program evaluators use the term to refer to rather small and specific theories of social programs, treatments, or interventions (Donaldson, 2001a; Lipsey, 1993). The following definitions of program theory capture the essence of how program theory is typically defined in theory-driven evaluation:

- The construction of a plausible and sensible model of how a program is suppose to work (Bickman, 1989).

- A set of propositions regarding what goes on in the black box during the transformation of input to output, that is, how a bad situation is transformed into a better one through treatment inputs (Lipsey, 1993).

- The process through which program components are presumed to affect outcomes and the conditions under which these processes are believed to operate (Donaldson, 2001a).

Of course, it is highly desirable if program theory is rooted in, or at least consistent with, behavioral or social science theory or prior research (see Donaldson et al., 2001). However, often sound theory and research are not available for the social problem of concern. If this is indeed the case, other sources of information are used to develop program theory, including implicit theories held by those closest to the operation of the program, observations of the program in action, documentation of program operations, and exploratory research to test critical assumptions about the nature of the program (For discussions on how to use these sources, see Donaldson, 2001a; Fitzpatrick, in press; Rossi, Freeman, & Lipsey, 1998). Again, the goal is to develop, in collaboration with key stakeholders, a parsimonious program theory (or competing theories to be tested) that captures the main factors that link a program with its presumed outcomes.

Theory-driven program evaluation = logic modeling. Theory-driven program evaluation is a comprehensive theory of evaluation practice. It "specifies feasible practices that evaluators can use to construct knowledge of the value of social programs that can be used to ameliorate the social problems to which programs are relevant (Shadish, Cook, & Leviton, 1991)." Whereas, logic modeling is an adaptable tool that is used across theories of evaluation practice (Funnell, 1997). That is, logic modeling can be used to develop program theory, but it is not a comprehensive theory of evaluation practice, nor required for, uniquely part of, or equivalent to theory-driven program evaluation. Furthermore, logic modeling is not only used to develop program theory. It is often used to map out other program activities such as allocation of funds, management strategies, information systems, marketing and publicity, staff recruitment and the like (Funnell, 1997).

Theory-driven program evaluation precludes simple black-box or out-come evaluation. Another myth that is sometimes used to diminish the value of theory-driven program evaluation, is that simply measuring out-comes or conducting "black-box evaluations" is sometimes an appropriate evaluation practice outside the scope of theory-driven evaluation. An example often used is that "it is not necessary to know *why* aspirin allevi-ates headaches." Putting aside the problem that most social programs are more complex in composition and are more likely to have delayed, dif-fuse, and subtle effects than aspirin in this example, there is nothing about theory-driven program evaluation that precludes black-box or out-come evaluation. Again, once program theory is developed, simple out-come evaluation may turn out to be the most appropriate design to answer the valued evaluation questions within resource and practical constraints (see Chen, 1990).

Theory-driven evaluation ignores side effects. Sometime critics seem to fear that program theory will act as blinders and prevent the discovery of harmful side effects. While the failure to detect side effects is certainly possible in most (if not all) evaluation approaches, Chen (1990) explicitly described how theory-driven evaluations should plan for potential side effects or unintended consequences. Donaldson *et al.* (1995) provided an example of how a theory-driven evaluation uncovered a serious side effect of "Just Say No" drug prevention programming, which was missed by previous evaluations. In short, once program theory is developed, evaluators and stakeholders should consider and plan for assessing potential side effects whenever possible. However, the more general problem facing evaluators across approaches is that most funders and program staff are not eager to spend resources showing that their pro-grams are harmful. It is usually the evaluator (not the approach) who must be vigilant about considering and investigating whether negative side effects result from a social program.

Competing or changing program theories are a problem. Although not as common as one might predict (Donaldson & Gooler, 2001), stakeholders can fail to reach agreement about program theory. Therefore, it is possi-ble to have two or more competing program theories to examine in an evaluation. Assuming adequate resources, testing competing program theories can lead to a very informative and useful evaluation. Having more than one program theory is often a strength, and certainly not an inherent problem. The same is true if a program theory improves or changes throughout the evaluation. This is particularly desirable when formative evaluation findings facilitate refinements in program theory, and lead to a better understanding of how to solve the social problem of interest (see Donaldson, 2001).

Theory-driven evaluation is too costly and time consuming. A common criticism of theory-driven evaluation is that it is more time consuming and costly than other evaluation approaches (Scriven, 1998). We have found many situations where this is simply not true (Donaldson & Gooler, 2001). For example, the process of developing program theory often reveals that a program is not ready for full-scale evaluation (i.e., evaluability assessment; Wholey, 1977). In this case, substantial time and resources are saved by redirecting efforts toward further program development and/or implementation activities, as opposed to summative evaluation certain to reveal null effects. Secondly, evaluation questions are prioritized in this approach, which helps stakeholders decide how to allocate evaluation resources in a cost-effective manner. The development of program theory usually enables stakeholders and evaluators to make informed decisions about evaluation design and methods, often leading to cost effective evaluation.

Notable Strengths of Theory-Driven Program Evaluation

Theory-driven program evaluation forces evaluators to "think" (and do their homework) before they "act" (employ their favorite methods). Reviewing the available literature, interviewing relevant stakeholders, observing the program in action, and possibly conducting pre-intervention research in an effort to develop sound program theory, requires evaluators to be more than general research methodologists. Theory-driven evaluators must be able to master the substantive domains related to solving the social problem of interest (or have that expertise on the evaluation team) in order to help formulate, prioritize, and answer key evaluation questions.

Fortunately, the three-step process described in this chapter is *feasible* for most evaluations of social programs. The vision for theory-driven program evaluation that I have described in this chapter aspires to *empower* stakeholders to be part of the evaluation planning process and to use evaluation findings to improve programs and solve social problems. By working collaboratively with stakeholders, theory-driven evaluation becomes much more *inclusive* (Lincoln, chapter 5 this volume; Mertens, chapter 6 this volume) than traditional method-driven evaluations (Donaldson & Chen, 2002).

However, I believe one of the greatest payoffs of this approach will come from improvements in *design sensitivity,* which is required for reaching valid conclusions in program evaluation (Lipsey, 1990). As evidenced throughout the program evaluation literature (Lipsey, 1988, 1993; Lipsey & Wilson, 1993), many evaluations are not sensitive enough to detect program effects when they truly exist. This embarrassingly prevalent form of malpractice (Lipsey, 1988), has mislead evaluators and the general social problem solving community to believe that social programs are ineffective, when in fact, they may be on their way to solving a critical social problem. The strong desire to achieve internal validity and objectivity in program evaluation (i.e., to protect against Type I error) appears to have distracted evaluators from the arguably more prevalent problem of insensitive program evaluations which commit Type II errors. In one of the most chilling analyses of this problem, Lipsey (1988) demonstrated that most published program evaluations are so insensitive that a coin toss (heads = program effect; tails = no program effect) is just as likely to conclude there is a substantial program effect when one actually exists.

One of the greatest strengths of theory-driven program evaluation is that it can dramatically improve design sensitivity in program evaluation. That is, the conceptual framework or program theory developed in the early phase of program evaluation can ultimately be used (1) to disentangle the success or failure of program implementation ("action theory") from the validity of program theory ("conceptual theory"); (2) as a basis for informed choices about evaluation methods; (3) to identify pertinent variables and how, when (e.g., dose-response and intervention-decay functions), and on whom they should be measured; (4) to carefully define and operationalize the independent (program) variables; (5) to identify and control for extraneous sources of variance; (6) to alert the program developer and evaluator to potentially important or intrusive interactions (e.g., differential participant response to the intervention); (7) to dictate the proper analytical or statistical model for data analysis and the tenability of the assumptions required in that model; and (8) to make a thoughtful and probing analysis of the validity of program evaluation in a specific context and provide feedback that can be used to improve the program under investigation, while simultaneously developing a cumulative wisdom about how and when programs work (cf. Chen 1990; Donaldson, 2001a; Lipsey 1993; Rossi, Freeman, & Lipsey, 1999).

Some Challenges Ahead

All of our visions for how to improve social programs and social problem solving in the new millennium will undoubtedly face substantial challenges. The members of our reactor panel have begun to identify and describe some of these challenges in the subsequent chapters. Although my task was to articulate a vision (for others to critique), I would be remiss not to point out at least a few of the key challenges that I see facing the practice of theory-driven program evaluation in the new millennium.

Practical advice shortage. Weiss (1997) pointed out that most of the literature on theory-driven program evaluation is written at a stratospheric level of abstraction. Practicing evaluators must search far and wide to find practical advice about the topic. The field seems in desperate need of written insights and experiences from evaluators who are actually conducting theory-driven program evaluations. Practical experiences from the trenches are needed to refine some of the initial theorizing about how best to conduct theory-driven evaluation across various settings and program areas.

It has been my experience that those who actually work with stakeholders to develop program theory and use it to guide evaluation efforts, see the world quite differently than those who offer advice about the problems or promise from the sidelines. For example, a practicing evaluator quickly learns that the nature of theory-driven evaluation is dramatically different when dealing with efficacy evaluation (evaluating a program or intervention under ideal conditions) than when conducting effectiveness evaluation (evaluating a program implemented in a "real world" organizational, community, or school setting). While many of the writings on theory-driven evaluation deal with issues relevant to efficacy evaluation, most practicing evaluators need information about effectiveness evaluation. Effectiveness evaluations must deal with a wide range of issues that stem from having less control over characteristics of the participants, service providers, and the organizational context (see Fitzpatrick, in press). I am hopeful that in the next decade there will be more work devoted to furthering the understanding of practical issues with executing theory-driven evaluations, including how to respond in a systematic manner to the numerous contingencies at work in evaluation practice.

Stakeholder relations. A second general challenge for the field is what we might call the stakeholder relations challenge (Donaldson, 2001b). Most applications of theory-driven evaluation involve considerable interaction with various stakeholders (i.e., interactive evaluation). In contrast to distanced evaluation which does not involve regular interaction with stakeholders, interactive evaluation often requires frequent interaction in an effort to develop program theory, determine evaluation questions, and to solicit appropriate input for the evaluation design (Chen, 1990, Donaldson, 2001a; Rossi, Freeman, & Lipsey, 1999). In addition, some modern theory-driven evaluations emphasize formative evaluation or continuous quality improvement as well as summative evaluation (Gooler & Donaldson, 2001). These efforts often lead to the development of learning communities or organizations, where evaluation findings are being used to improve the effectiveness of the program on an ongoing basis. While these efforts are very appealing from the armchair, they pose substantial implementation challenges in practice.

Donaldson, Gooler, & Scriven (in press) have described some of these challenges under the general rubric of managing evaluation anxiety and the psychology of evaluation. In short, the fear of negative evaluation seems deeply ingrained and inherent to the human condition. Many people avoid fully participating in activities such as program evaluation because they fear that honest participation may cause them to feel shame, embarrassment, loss of esteem and the like. When stakeholders experience dysfunctional levels of evaluation anxiety it becomes difficult to gain access to key stakeholders and program information, to collect high quality data, to use evaluation findings to improve the program, and to generally conduct a rigorous program evaluation. Therefore, for theory-driven evaluation or any other form of evaluation that requires stakeholder involvement to be effective, systematic strategies for maintaining good stakeholder relations and preventing excessive evaluation anxiety are needed. Lessons from evaluation practice about ways to deal or not to deal with these challenges, are needed to improve the implementation of interactive theory-driven evaluation.

Nomenclature. The final challenge I raise here is that the nomenclature of theory-driven program evaluation is used inconsistently and is often confusing to practicing evaluators. Weiss (1997) pointed out there is much confusion in the field over what is meant by program theory. As was described previously, the term program theory seems to conjure up images of broad social science theories, rather than small theories of treatments, programs, or interventions (Lipsey, 1993). Further compounding this problem is the fact that there are now quite a few different definitions of program theory in the literature, as well as a number of underspecified but apparently related terms such as theory-based evaluation (Weiss, 1997), program theory evaluation (Rogers, Hacsi, Petrosino, & Huebener, 2000), intervening mechanism theory (Donaldson et al., 1994), program logic (Funnell, 1997), and the like. For example, in a recent volume of *New Directions for Evaluation*, Rogers *et al.* (2000) limited their discussion to "program theory evaluation" and claimed that this is synonymous with what Chen (1990) defined as intervening mechanism evaluation, an important but relatively narrow domain of the practice of theory-driven program evaluation. Therefore, it seems essential to clarify the meanings of these various terms and concepts as we move forward, and to make them as clear and accessible as possible to practicing evaluators.

CONCLUSION

As I promised in the introduction, I have not held back in stating my vision for how to improve the art and science of social problem solving in the new millennium. In an effort to convince you this vision is more than fantasy or wild speculation about possibilities, I have provided specific evidence and examples intended to demonstrate that theory-driven program evaluation is feasible, can overcome problems currently limiting social programming, and appears to be gaining momentum as a viable approach for evaluating social programs and problems in the new millennium.

Again, I am not speculating or predicting that theory-driven program evaluation will reach its potential. I guess that time will ultimately be the judge. I am also not suggesting that theory-driven program evaluation is the only way to evaluate and solve social programs in the new millennium. I remain open to the concept of equifinality: there is more than one way to get there. The symposium and this volume have presented a range of alternatives worthy of consideration.

Rather, what I am suggesting is straightforward. If theory-driven program evaluation is practiced as described in this chapter, the social programs of the new millennium will be well-designed and based on sound theory and research, implemented with high fidelity, evaluated in a manner that minimizes the chances of design sensitivity and validity errors, evaluated in a way that is empowering and inclusive, and evaluated so that accumulation of new knowledge and wisdom about social programming will be maximized. These desirable gains promise to increase our chances of victory in the wars against the unpredictable, unimaginable, inhumane, and destructive social problems that are likely to confront us in the new millennium.

REFERENCES

Aiken, L. S., West, S.G., Woodward, C. K., Reno, R. R., & Reynolds, K. D. (1994). Increasing screening mammography in asymptomatic women:

Evaluation of a second generation, theory-based program. *Health Psychology, 13*, 526-538.

Bickman, L. B. (1996a). A continuum of care: More is not always better. *American Psychologist, 51(7)*, 689-701.

Bickman, L. B. (1996b). The evaluation of a children's mental health managed care demonstration. *The Journal of Mental Health Administration, 23*, 7-15.

Birckmayer, J. D., & Weiss, C. H. (2000). Theory-based evaluation in practice. What do we learn? *Evaluation Review, 24(4)*, 407-431.

Chen, H. T. (1990). *Theory-driven evaluations*. Newbury Park, CA: Sage.

Chen, H. T. (1997). Applying mixed methods under the framework of theory-driven evaluations. In J. C. Greene & V. J. Caracelli (Eds.), *Advances in mixed-method evaluation: The challenges and benefits of integrating diverse paradigms* (New Directions for Evaluation, No. 74). San Francisco, CA: Jossey-Bass.

Chen, H. T., & Rossi, P. H. (1983). Evaluating with sense: The theory-driven approach. *Evaluation Review, 7*, 283-302.

Chen, H. T., & Rossi, P. H. (1987). The theory-driven approach to validity. *Evaluation & Program Planning, 10*, 95-103.

Donaldson, S. I. (1995). Worksite health promotion: A theory-driven, empirically based perspective. In L. R. Murphy, J. J. Hurrel, S. L. Sauter, & G. P. Keita (Eds.), *Job stress interventions* (pp. 73-90). Washington, DC: American Psychological Association.

Donaldson, S. I. (Ed.). (2000). *Mechanisms: Newsletter for the Program Theory and Theory-driven Evaluation Topical Interest Group*. American Evaluation Association.

Donaldson, S. I. (2001a). Mediator and moderator analysis in program development. In S. Sussman (Ed.), *Handbook of program development for health behavior research* and practice (pp. 470-496). Newbury Park, CA: Sage.

Donaldson, S. I. (2001b). Overcoming our negative reputation: Evaluation becomes known as a helping profession. *American Journal of Evaluation*, 22(3), 355-361.

Donaldson, S. I. (2002). High potential mediators of drug abuse prevention program effects. In W. D. Crano & M. Burgoon (Eds.), *Mass media and drug prevention*. Mahwah, NJ: Lawrence Erlbaum Associates.

Donaldson, S. I., & Chen, H. T. (2002). *Theory-driven program evaluation: State of the art.* Manuscript under review.

Donaldson, S. I., & Gooler, L. E. (in press). Theory-driven evaluation of the Work and Health Initiative: A focus on Winning New Jobs. *American Journal of Evaluation*.

Donaldson, S. I., & Gooler, L. E. (2002). *Theory-driven evaluation in action: Lessons from a $20 million statewide work and health initiative.* Manuscript under review.

Donaldson, S. I., Gooler, L. E., & Scriven, M. (in press). Strategies for managing evaluation anxiety: Toward a psychology of program evaluation. *American Journal of Evaluation.*

Donaldson, S. I., Gooler, L. E., & Weiss, R. (1988). Promoting health and well-being through work: Science and practice. In X. B. Arriaga & S. Oskamp (Eds.), *Addressing community problems: Psychological research and intervention* (pp. 160-194). Newbury Park, CA: Sage.

Donaldson, S. I., Graham, J. W., & Hansen, W. B. (1994). Testing the generalizability of intervening mechanism theories: Understanding the effects of school-based substance use prevention interventions. *Journal of Behavioral Medicine, 17,* 195-216.

Donaldson, S. I., Graham, J. W., Piccinin, A. M., & Hansen, W. B. (1995). Resistance-skills training and onset of alcohol use: Evidence for beneficial and potentially harmful effects in public schools and in private catholic schools. *Health Psychology, 14,* 291-300.

Donaldson, S. I., Street, G., Sussman, S., & Tobler, N. (2001). Using meta-analyses to improve the design of interventions. In S. Sussman (Ed.), *Handbook of program development for health behavior research and practice* (pp. 449-466). Newbury Park, CA: Sage.

Donaldson, S. I., & Weiss, R. (1998). Health, well-being, and organizational effectiveness in the virtual workplace. In M. Igbaria & M. Tan (Eds.), *The virtual workplace* (pp. 24-44). Harrisburg, PA: Idea Group Publishing.

Donaldson, S. I., Thomas, C. W., Graham, J. W., Au, J., & Hansen, W. B. (2000). Verifying drug prevention program effects using reciprocal best friend reports. *Journal of Behavioral Medicine, 23,* 221-234.

Fitzpatrick, J. (in press). Dialogue with Stewart Donaldson about the theory-driven evaluation of the California Wellness Foundation's Work and Health Initiative. *American Journal of Evaluation.*

Friedman, R. M., & Burns, B. J. (1996). The evaluation of the Fort Bragg Demonstration Project: An alternative interpretation of the findings. *The Journal of Mental Health Administration, 23,* 7-15.

Funnell, S. (1997). Program logic: An adaptable tool for designing and evaluating programs. *Evaluation News & Comment,* 5-17.

Gooler, L. E., & Donaldson, S. I. (2002). *Evaluating for program improvement: Lessons from evaluation practice.* Manuscript under review.

Hansen, W. B. (1993). School-based alcohol prevention programs. *Alcohol Health & Research World, 17,* 54-60.

Hansen, W. B., & Graham, J. W. (1991). Preventing adolescent alcohol, marijuana, and cigarette use among adolescents: Peer pressure resistance training versus establishing conservative norms. *Preventive Medicine, 20,* 414-430.

Kent, D. R., Donaldson, S. I., Wyrick, P. A., & Smith, P. J. (2000). Evaluating criminal justice programs designed to reduce crime by targeting repeat gang offenders. *Evaluation and Program Planning, 23,* 115-124.

Lipsey, M. W. (1988). Practice and malpractice in evaluation research. *Evaluation Practice, 9*, 5-24.

Lipsey, M. W. (1990). *Design sensitivity.* Newbury Park, CA: Sage.

Lipsey, M. W. (Ed.) (1993). Theory as method: Small theories of treatments. In L. B. Sechrest & A. G. Scott (Eds.), *Understanding causes and generalizing about them* (New Directions for Program Evaluation, No. 57, pp 5-38). San Francisco, CA: Jossey-Bass.

Lipsey, M. W., Crosse, S., Dunkel, J., Pollard, J., & Stobart, G. (1985). Evaluation: The state of the art and the sorry state of the science. In D.S. Cordray (Ed.), *Utililizing prior research in evaluation planning* (New Directions for Program Evaluation, No. 27, 7-28). San Francisco, CA: Jossey-Bass.

Lipsey, M. W., & Wilson, D. B. (1993). The efficacy of psychological, educational, and behavioral treatment: Confirmation from meta-analysis. *American Psychologist, 48*, 1181-1209.

MacKinnon, D. P., Johnson, C. A., Pentz, M. A., Dwyer, J. H., Hansen, W.B. Flay, B. R., & Wang, E. Y. (1991). Mediating mechanisms in a school-based drug prevention program: First-year effects of the Midwestern prevention project. *Health Psychology, 10*, 164-172.

MacKinnon, D. P., Weber, M. D., & Pentz, M. A. (1988). How do school-based drug prevention programs work and for whom? *Drugs and Society, 3*, 125-143.

Mercier, C., Piat, M., Peladeau, N., & Dagenais, C. (2000). An application of theory-driven evaluation to a drop-in youth center. *Evaluation Review, 24*, 73-91.

Reichhardt, C., & Rallis, C. S. (Eds.) (1994). *The qualitative-quantitive debate: New perspectives* (New Directions for Program Evaluation, No. 61). San Francisco, CA: Jossey-Bass

Reynolds, A. J. (1998). Confirmatory program evaluation: A method for strengthening causal inference. *American Journal of Evaluation, 19*, 203-221.

Rogers, P. J., Hacsi, T. A., Petrosino, A., & Huebner, T. A. (Eds.) (2000). *Program theory in evaluation: Challenges and opportunities* (New Directions for Evaluation, No. 87). San Francisco, CA: Jossey-Bass.

Rossi, P. H., Freeman, H. E., & Lipsey, M. W. (1999). *Evaluation: A systematic approach (6th Ed.).* Thousand Oaks, CA: Sage.

Rossi. P. H., & Wright, J. D. (1984). Evaluation research: An assessment. *Annual Review of Sociology, 10*, 331-352.

Scriven, M. (1998). Minimalist theory: The least practice requires. *American Journal of Evaluation, 19*, 57-70.

Shadish, W. R., Cook, T. D., & Leviton, L. C. (1991). *Foundations of program evaluation: Theories of practice.* Newbury Park, CA: Sage.

Stufflebeam, D. L. (Ed.) (2001). *Evaluation models* (New Directions for Evaluation, No. 89). San Francisco, CA: Jossey-Bass.

Weiss, C. H. (1997). How can theory-based evaluation make greater headway? *Evaluation Review, 21*, 501-524.

Weiss, C. H. (1998). *Evaluation: Methods for studying programs and policies* (2nd Ed.). Upper Saddle River, NJ: Prentice Hall.

West, S. G., & Aiken, L. S. (1997). Toward understanding individual effects in multicomponent prevention programs: Design and analysis strategies. In K. J. Bryant, M. Windle, & S. G. West (Eds.), *The science of prevention: Methodological advances from alcohol and substance abuse research* (pp. 167-209). Washington, DC: American Psychological Association.

III

REACTIONS AND ALTERNATIVE VISIONS

8

Theory-Driven Evaluation and Construct Validity

William D. Crano
Claremont Graduate University

The work reported in this conference represents some of the best of evaluation today, and today's best is very good indeed. The field of evaluation research, a mere infant in the social sciences, has made impressive strides since the 1960s when it was first formalized. As we know, two of the most powerful voices at the inception of the field were Donald Campbell and Michael Scriven. Alas, Campbell cannot be here in body, but he is here in spirit, as you will see. Scriven's presence today is obvious, from the list of speakers to the organization (with Stewart Donaldson) of the conference, and for this and his past contributions I am most grateful.

Many of the papers presented in this symposium dealt directly or indirectly with an approach that has come to be called theory-driven evaluation. Although many of our speakers did not use this term in their presentations, the underlying position that is advanced by this approach was evident throughout. Accordingly, in my commentary, I will briefly consider this movement in evaluation research, with particular reference to the advances that may be facilitated by adoption of a theory-driven evaluation approach. In addition to listing some of its advantages, and noting its conceptual linkage with established psychometric theory in psychology, I also intend to show how progress on models of theory-driven evaluation might be accelerated if we attended to the linkage of this approach with established models and methods of construct validation. Given the broad reach of this conference, its gifted, productive, and influential speakers, and its ambition to reflect on the state of the art, this plan seems both feasible and appropriate, especially in light of the constraints of time and space with which we commentators must contend.

GROWING PAINS

Like most infants, the field of evaluation research experienced growing pains over the course of its early development. However, the early hit-or-miss strategies and tactics of our evaluation forbears, many of whom are still with us given the relative youth of the field, have gradually given way to more systematic approaches that promise accelerating and accumulating gains as time goes by. We now know that it is important to distinguish between the forms that a formal evaluation may take, and to understand that these forms are at once determined by knowledge of the extant context and problem under investigation, the critical variables under study, and the real and professed needs of the evaluation client. A failure to distinguish between various evaluation research forms—pre-intervention research, efficacy research, and effectiveness research—to name but one way of skinning the cat—can and has resulted in a muddle at times (e.g., see Donaldson, 1999, 2001, 2002, chapter 7 this volume; Fitzpatrick, in press; Foxhall, 1999). Failure to understand the form of evaluation we are engaged in, overstepping the boundaries of what is known, can result in evaluations that, at best, are useless, and at worst, misleading. In my view, making use of the wrong evaluation model, which often occurs when we jump the gun, rushing into effectiveness issues when pre-intervention or efficacy research is more appropriate, often results in a mismatch of research resources and research aims. Mismatching research aims and the resources necessary to support the aims is all too common in our history, but despite its regularity, a lack of fit between aim and resource remains a central problem, and still surprises us when it occurs and its negative effects are identified.

An excellent if unfortunate example of this lack of fit between research resources and evaluation goals is provided in a classic critique mounted by Campbell and Erlebacher (1970) in their review of the published evaluation of a compensatory education program conducted in Cincinnati, Ohio. Typically, such programs are provided for particularly disadvantaged populations, usually children. They often do not or cannot employ random assignment, and there's the rub, because attempts to evaluate their effectiveness often entail the use ex post facto comparisons with a control group selected from the general population and matched on theoretically relevant variables. If the two matched groups differ substantially in important respects, or, to put it another way, if they are, in fact, drawn from different populations, then the central goal of matching to produce equivalent groups will fail, bias will be introduced, and invalid conclusions fostered and probably drawn.

To lend substance to our example, consider the problems that arise when attempting to compare the effects of an intervention when the treated and comparison groups are drawn from different populations. The two samples of children studied in the research that drew Campbell and Erlebacher's ire were arguably from different populations, and this was the locus of the problem they identified in their critique. The treatment group was drawn from the poorest sections of the city, and was comprised of children doomed to fight an uphill battle for education. These children were eligible for the compensatory program precisely because they were disadvantaged educationally. The supposedly *matched* control sample was drawn from the wealthier suburbs. These children had the advantages of wealth, and all that wealth entails for educational achievement. If we compare the *populations* from which these children were drawn on any measure of academic readiness or achievement, considerable past experience suggests that they would differ substantially. But because the groups were matched on the critical achievement measure, the *samples* appeared identical. The matching procedure thus appears to have solved the problem. In this case, however, appearances are deceiving. We know without doubt that the samples are different. The apparent equality of scores on the critical matched variable is an illusion. Of course the scores on which the selection is based are the same; how could they be otherwise? Children in the comparison group were hand selected precisely because their scores matched those of children who were to receive the compensatory intervention. But we know the groups are not equivalent on anything but one highly fallible score. They vary enormously in terms of household income, race and ethnicity, family structure, and hundreds of other variables that all impinge on academic growth. Consequently, any subsequent group comparisons should disclose strong differences, and these differences are almost surely attributable to the obvious between-group nonequivalence. Unless we are willing to hypothesize that the test we use for matching purposes is not only perfectly reliable, but a perfectly valid and complete indicator of the critical construct, the matching process is doomed to failure. It cannot undo the depredations that gave rise to the initial group inequalities in the first place.

Mountains of past experience suggest that we almost certainly will obtain differences between nonequivalent groups on subsequent measures. Our most conservative (and in this instance, probably best) interpretation is that these differences are attributable to nothing more than the differences that obtained between the nonequivalent groups at the start of the study, but that were not identified by the less-than-perfect measure used to calibrate the groups. An even more difficult problem with matched data can arise when the opposite result is found, that is, when no differences are evident. In such cases, real differences often are present, but they are concealed or masked by the matching process. These statements should not be taken on faith, and so on the pages that follow, I will show why they are worthy of consideration. At the same time, this discussion will hopefully illustrate the need for theory-driven evaluation, and the requirement when making use of this form of evaluation to attend to the fit between research resources and evaluation aims.

MATCHED GROUPS PROBLEMS

Some problems with the nonequivalent matched groups that Campbell and Erlebacher (1970) discussed should be evident to anyone who has read and absorbed Campbell and Stanley's (1963) classic chapter, but to put a head on it, we will consider two ways in which the matching procedure fails to produce real (vs. apparent) equivalence between groups under comparison. First, given the nonrandom nature of selection or assignment to groups, it is highly likely that the children in the matched groups will mature at different rates, intellectually and academically. As is found almost without exception, the more advantaged group will mature faster. As such, the matching process practically guarantees differences down the line. What is worse, if the compensatory program works—if it really does help alleviate differences between treated and nontreated groups—the obtained between-group differences will be masked by this maturation process, and a null treatment effect hypothesis will be supported. If the treatment is ineffective, that is, if it fails to attenuate differences between groups, if the educational intervention merely fills time, then it will appear to have damaged the children if the hypothesized differential between-groups maturation occurs. This misdirection of research results, and the subsequent inference it supports, may do more than simply invalidate a pet theory. It may damage the very people it was designed to serve. In the present example, policymakers could use the erroneous findings mistakenly to shut down an exemplary program.

Even more subtle problems are introduced through the matching process, as will be illustrated in Figure 1, which highlights the difficulties involved in comparing samples drawn from groups having fundamentally different score distributions on the critical variable. As shown here, the *shape* of the achievement score distribution for the treated group (disadvantaged children) is identical to that of the comparison group (advantaged children). The only difference is in the mean: on average, the wealthier population, from which he comparison group is drawn, scores taged children). The only difference is in the mean: on average, the wealthier population, from which he comparison group is drawn, scores higher than the treatment group on the critical achievement test. The reasons for this difference fall outside the practical, if not the epistemological, boundaries of the research. The upshot of this lack of complete overlap between population distributions is that the so-called matched samples are drawn from *different tails* of their respective distributions. To effect a match in the present instance, that is, the researchers must draw the low-achieving sample from the upper end of its (population) achievement score distribution, whereas the comparison sample must drawn from the lower end of the more advantaged population's distribution. We know from years of research on the regression artifact that when participants are selected on the basis of an extreme score, they can be expected to regress on later testing toward the mean of their distribution. Therefore, unless the test on which the match is based is perfectly reliable, not a high likelihood, the regression pressures will be different in the two samples. Because the test scores of the children in the treatment sample fell at the higher end of their distribution, they will to regress downwards, toward the mean of their distribution, on second testing. On average, the regression artifact will tend to lower the scores of the intervention sample. Scores of the comparison group, drawn from children who fell at the lower end of their respective distribution—a necessity to allow for matching to occur—will tend to regress upwards, toward the mean of their distribution. Depending on the extent of the unreliability of the measuring instrument used to create the matches, these regression pressures will be more or less profound: ceteris paribus, the worse the test, the worse the regression artifact. Given the reliability of the standard test used to tap young children's academic achievement, it is a good bet that regression effects in this instance would be strong enough to mitigate or mask any positive changes that might have occurred as a result of the educational intervention. If this differential regression toward different means ensued, the treatment would appear much less successful in ameliorating problems than it actually is.[1] The end result of this set of nontrivial methodological errors is that a useful ameliorative program will be shelved, and the positive effects that it might have delivered to succeeding cadres of disadvantaged children will be lost.

---

[1] In this instance, given the problems that matching has introduced, a null finding might in fact be viewed as highly encouraging.

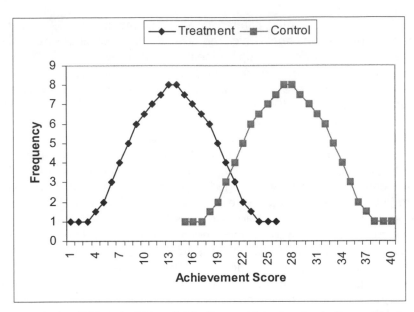

FIGURE 8.1. Different scoring distributions, which give rise to the matched group fallacy and the regression artifact.

Examples in which the treatment group is unfairly advantaged (rather than disadvantaged) by the regression artifact also could be described here, but the present illustration should suffice to warn off those who would adopt matching in a misguided attempt to offset the shortcomings of a study in which random assignment is inconvenient or impossible.

The point of this example is that the researchers who performed the original evaluation knew quite well that random assignment was the preferred approach. For practical and political reasons, however, they could not make use of this powerful research tool. They settled for what they considered the next best thing—matching. If they had not done so, they probably reasoned that they could not have performed the research. The problem with this compromise between research resources and aims is that the evaluation that ultimately was undertaken produced results that were extremely misleading, and that supported shifts in public policy that should not have been made. Research resources, in this case the necessary methodological and design factors (e.g., random assignment, control of participant assignment into conditions, etc.), were not sufficient to provide an unambiguous assessment of the compensatory program, the fundamental aim of the research. This mismatch between research resources and research goals precluded a proper evaluation.

The evaluation that consequently was produced was the "next best thing," but sometimes, second best is not worth doing. When is this observation most likely to apply? It seems to me to be most pertinent when the researcher does not know enough about the construct he or she is researching. It was the lack of construct validity that most often was at the core of the design problems identified and formalized by Campbell and Stanley (1963). We accept the fact that construct validity must be a central concern whenever we are engaged in hypothesis testing research. I argue that construct invalidity can vex the utility of even quasi-experimental or non-experimental research as well, and thus, is an equally important consideration in evaluation studies. With your indulgence, I will spend the remainder of my time—or, in this case, page—allotment attempting to persuade you of the validity of my position, and in demonstrating the relevance of this concept to theory-driven evaluation.

CONSTRUCT VALIDITY AND
THEORY–DRIVEN EVALUATION

To introduce my particular position on this issue, I want to reconstruct a conversation I had many years ago, as a young—perhaps I should say, younger—man, with my mentor. I had, probably for the 100th time, proposed a new study to him. Like all the previous ones, this study contained no less than 8 manipulated variables—I cannot remember the number of blocked variables included in these designs, but I will say with no false modesty that the order of some of my predicted interaction effects was a thing of beauty. I think the Italians would describe these studies—or at least their audacity—with the term they often used to describe Sophia Loren in her younger days.

My mentor was not amused by my youthful exuberance—some of you might call it naïveté. In fact, in this case, I think I had pushed him to the end of his tether. Flabbergasted, and more than a little baffled at how he was going to deal with his most wayward child, he responded to me with the precise and slow diction that usually signaled a storm on the near horizon. "Mr. Crano," he said, "Psychology is a science of main effects." Apparently, my predicted 7th order interactions had not impressed him.

I quite enjoyed my provocateur role as a graduate student, which one of my peers, a former friend, described as my playing the mosquito on the ass of the elephant, and decided to go on the offensive. "Not at all Professor Campbell," I replied—we couldn't call him Don until we had completed our PhD orals, and even then, most of us had trouble with this gross breach of formality. "Not at all Professor Campbell, social psychology might want to be a science of main effects, but it is assuredly a science of moderators and mediators—of interactions."

Like a shameful family secret, we never again revisited this conversation. I was not in a hurry to engage Don on this issue, though I thought I was right for once.[2] Engaging in a tough intellectual debate with Campbell always entailed at least some major bruises. But also, I do not think that he wanted to defend his position, because it was so far removed from his approach to understanding, to knowing (e.g., Campbell, 1989a, 1989b; Campbell & Overman, 1988). If we had continued our debate, I think Campbell would have argued that using an experimental design as a shotgun, as I was doing, was not a particularly good idea. To use the experiment, he would have argued, I had to have at least some idea of the construct I was attempting to investigate. This was not the inference I drew initially from his *psychology as a science of main effects* statement, but it was the one intended, I am sure. To assume he meant exactly what was said would be to deny his position on multiple operationism, the search for a heterogeneity of irrelevancies, triangulation, and so on, all of which suggest that he was far more comfortable with a complex interactionist orientation than a simplistic main effects view of the world (Crano, 1981). When designing an experiment, how could one seek a heterogeneity of irrelevancies if some grasp on the construct was not already at hand, if we did not already have some idea of the multiple forces bearing on it, giving it form and dimension? How can we know what is irrelevant if we do not have some idea of what is relevant? In fact, Campbell's ideas on construct validation, exemplified beautifully in his and Fiske's work on the multitrait-multimethod matrix, suggest that he was more intent on giving me a hard time during our interaction than in making an epistemological point (Campbell & Fiske, 1959; Crano, 2000; Fiske & Campbell, 1992). He was superb at both tasks, and although discussing the former might be more entertaining, investigating the latter will prove more informative for you, and less embarrassing for me. As such, I want to spend the remainder of my allotted space dealing with the epistemological position, especially as it has to do with the central point of our existence as social scientists, which I take to be the search for validity, or truth, to use the more vulgar term.

---

[2] As you can tell by this informal address, I did earn my PhD.

We learned in our youth that a major task, perhaps the central task, of the scientist is prediction and control; ultimately, we're in the business of understanding or establishing causation, and we cannot establish cause without understanding the constructs with which we deal. Such understanding entails a firm grasp of the network of associations in which our critical construct is enmeshed, the temporal and spatial and contextual factors that impinge on the expression of the variables with which we are concerned, which help define the psychological reality of the construct. To my mind, many of the problems of the early years of evaluation, outlined so nicely for us today by Yvonna Lincoln, had to do with a failure to understand the construct we were attempting to grasp and, ultimately, to properly assess and evaluate. If we do not have a firm grasp on our constructs, we simply are not going to produce good research, basic or applied, fundamental or evaluative, because without such understanding, we are not going to be able to see how our constructs fit with others, how they operate, and ultimately, how they define themselves.

Think about Binet's work on intelligence at the turn of the century (Binet & Simon, 1916). And now think about Richard Atkinson's SAT bombshell of last week, in which he suggested that the University of California system might do away with, or severely underweight, the Scholastic Achievement Tests in the highly competitive university admissions process. The upshot of these two thoughts should help establish my point. We still don't fully understand the construct Binet was working on, and that being the case, its evaluation, and the evaluation of traits associated or perhaps identical to it, is bound to fail, or at a minimum to produce dissatisfaction in our client base. If our client base is merely the Chancelor of the University of California system, that's one thing, but if our client base is truth, or the god of knowledge if we must personify things, that's quite another matter. Worse yet, if we can't ultimately satisfy ourselves, the ultimate arbiter of truth and goodness, good taste and value, if we can't satisfy ourselves that we understand the phenomenon with which we're dealing, then I don't know how in the world we can expect to satisfy anyone else.

When I read about theory-driven evaluation, I am, most times, both happy and distracted. I am happy because I think we're finally getting on the right track. The tie-in, or relationship, of the theory-driven approach with our best methodological work is impressive. Think about the way we establish the validity of constructs in basic experimental research. In essence, construct validation requires a theory, an understanding of the hypothetical network of causal associations and noncausal relationships among variables that we, at least as Socrates' allegory of the man in a cave, might try to come to understand (Plato, 1968). It's a tough process, but it is the fundamental job of the scientist to take it on. Campbell said it well—I can hear the tone in his voice as he spoke these words, which combined dejection with excitement: It is time, he said, that we "face up to our very unsatisfactory predicament: we have only *other invalid measures* against which to validate our tests: we have no 'criterion' to check them against" (Campbell, 1969a, p. 16). Don recognized the fact that we often do not have the horsepower to make a definitive case for a construct, that often, we are able to make our case only tentatively. That didn't stop him, and it shouldn't stop us. I am not arguing for "second best" here, in opposition to the position I took earlier. Rather, I believe it important that we recognize that perfection is never an outcome, but a goal. We use the best methods and models available, and if these inch us toward the truth, rather than toward self-deception, our work has value.[3] We are in the business of understanding cause, and in the world of evaluation the theory-driven variety provides our best shot. At its heart, theory-driven evaluation involves construct validation. The same processes apply, the same rules of evidence, the same sought-after outcomes. Understanding the link between the new (theory-driven) evaluation model and the established methods of establishing construct validity can only facilitate progress.

I am distracted by the theory-driven approach because I think there's still so much that can be done by its champions. In some ways, they're on to something new. If we consider the failures of past models, described well by Mertens and Wholey in their presentations today, for example, that is very clear. But we still have a long way to go. In my opinion, the theory-driven folks could do more, and more quickly, with fewer starts and stops, if they adopted more directly the methods we have established over the past century for developing and assessing and enhancing the validity of our constructs. If we recognize the near isomorphism between construct validation and the requirements of theory-driven evaluation, we will be more able to improve the returns on our research investments. There's help out there. It's been there for a long time. Let's take advantage of it.

Even if we do so, however, we admit our predicament is daunting. As Campbell observed, we don't know the truth, and can approach it only by pretending we do. To that I would add, if the truth be told, assuming we ever could tell it, we never will reach the truth by these approaches. And

---

[3]This observation is consistent with my position that if conditions cannot provide even small incremental movements toward understanding, if resources do not mesh with research needs, the research is best left undone.

even if we do, we won't know it. Some might have trouble with this state of affairs, but I take it as a way of life, a way of being, for the social scientist. Ours is not a fate to be decried but exulted, because the search for the grail gives meaning to our lives as scientists. It is a nonnegotiable feature of our identity. To parapharse the famous line of George Harrison, in his role of professional gigolo, Alphonso de la Pena, in the wonderful movie *Once Upon a Crime*, "It's what I do." Even better, "It's what we are."

VIRTUE

In some ways, the search for valid understanding is, or should be, a profoundly moral task. To my mind, the debate about value-free vs. value-laden evaluation was never more than public and self-righteous breast beating of social scientists who didn't know enough to hide the dirty linen, or who had too much time on their hands and too little productive work with which to occupy themselves. Unless you were willing to evaluate the quality of the ovens Krupps produced in the last great war, the reality of value-free research is nothing more than a politically correct posture. Of course our values impinge on our work. How could they not? The issue to my mind is not whether our values color our actions, but whether the values are right. Putting the issue this way gives added urgency to Scriven's observations. As with Campbell, I am reluctant to argue with Michael, and in this instance, as in most others, do not feel the need to do so. Our intellectual predecessors in ancient Greece had it right. Our job, as Aristotle saw it, was not merely to impart knowledge, but virtue. We need to produce good, not just wise, citizens. What should be my feeling if, as a professor of finance, I were to produce a Gordon Gekko, the contemptible villain of *Wall Street*? Although he was the most successful hyena in the pack, I hope and believe that I would focus on the hyena rather than the success.

I think Michael Scriven is counseling a similar road, but I will not put words in his mouth. I will say, however, that he has set a standard for evaluation, and evaluators, whose height rivals that of Campbell (1969b). Now, we must not only understand the constructs with which we are dealing, we must try to exploit them for the betterment of society, and thus must take on the added burden of guessing what a better society might be. We need more than knowledge. We must marry that almost unreachable state with wisdom, which is perhaps even more difficult to attain. There is no doubt in my mind we will fail more often than not in this quest. Indeed, I'm not sure we'll even know when we've succeeded on those rare occasions we get it right. But the trip promises to be well worth the ticket.

REFERENCES

Binet, A., & Simon, T. (1916). The development of intelligence in children (the Binet-Simon scale). (E. S. Kite, Trans.). Baltimore, MD: Williams & Wilkins.

Campbell, D. T. (1969a). Definitional versus multiple operationism. *Et al., 2*, 14-17.

Campbell, D. T. (1969b). Reforms as experiments. *American Psychologist, 24*, 409-429.

Campbell, D. T. (1989a). Being mechanistic/materialistic/realistic about the process of knowing. *Canadian Psychology, 30*, 184-185.

Campbell, D. T. (1989b). Fragments of the fragile history of psychological epistemology and theory of science. In B. Gholson & W. R. Shadish, Jr. (Eds.), *Psychology of science: Contributions to metascience* (pp. 21-46). New York: Cambridge University Press.

Campbell, D. T., & Erlebacher, A. (1970). How regression in quasi-experimental evaluation can mistakenly make compensatory education look harmful. In J. Hellmuth (Ed.), *The disadvantaged child: Vol. 3. Compensatory education: A national debate* (pp. 185-225). New York: Brunner-Mazel.

Campbell, D. T., & Fiske, D. W. (1959). Convergent and discriminant validation by the multitrait-multimethod matrix. *Psychological Bulletin, 56*, 81-105.

Campbell, D. T., & Overman, S. E. (Eds). (1988). *Methodology and epistemology for social science: Selected papers*. Chicago, IL: University of Chicago Press.

Campbell, D. T., & Stanley, J. C. (1963). Experimental and quasi-experimental designs for research on teaching. In N. L. Gage (Ed.), *Handbook of research on teaching*. Chicago: Rand-McNally (pp. 171-246). Reprinted as *Experimental and quasi-experimental designs for research*. Chicago: Rand-McNally, 1966.

Crano, W. D. (1981). Triangulation in social science: A cross-cultural example. In M. B. Brewer & B. E. Collins (Eds.), *Scientific inquiry and the social sciences: A volume in honor of Donald T. Campbell* (pp. 317-344). San Francisco: Jossey-Bass.

Crano, W. D. (2000). The multitrait-multimethod matrix as synopsis and recapitulation of Campbell's views on the proper conduct of social inquiry. In L. Bickman (Ed.), *Research design: Donald Campbell's legacy* (pp. 37-61). Thousand Oaks, CA: Sage.

Crano, W. D., & Brewer, M. B. (2002). *Principles and methods of social research* (2nd Ed.). Mahwah, NJ: Lawrence Erlbaum Associates.

Donaldson, S. I. (1999). The territory ahead for theory-driven program and organizational evaluation. *Mechanisms, 3*, 3-5.

Donaldson, S. I. (2001). Mediator and moderator analysis in program development. In S. Sussman (Ed.), *Handbook of program development for health behavior research and practice* (pp. 470-496). Newbury Park, CA: Sage.

Donaldson, S. I. (2002). High-potential mediators of drug-abuse prevention program effects. In W. D. Crano & M. Burgoon (Eds.), *Mass media and drug prevention: Classic and contemporary theories and research* (pp. 215-230). Mahwah, NJ: Lawrence Erlbaum Associates.

Fitzpatrick, J. (in press). Dialogue with Stewart Donaldson about the theory-driven evaluation of the California Wellness Foundation's Work and Health Initiative. *American Journal of Evaluation.*

Fiske, D. W., & Campbell, D. T. (1992). Citations do not solve problems. *Psychological Bulletin, 112*, 393-395.

Foxhall, K. (2000). Research for the real world: NIMH is pumping big money into effectiveness research to move promising treatments into practice. *APA Monitor, 31*, 28-36.

Plato (1968). *The Republic.* (A. D. Bloom, (trans.). New York: Basic Books.

9

EVALUATING SOCIAL PROGRAMS AND PROBLEMS: A DISCUSSANT'S VIEW

Edith P. Thomas

U.S. Department of Agriculture

VISION

Although my role here today is to be a discussant, I feel compelled to share my strong feelings about the need for evaluators with enhanced skills to assist communities and individuals to improve their quality of life. Many federally funded projects have "lived or died" because of the inappropriate or too narrow focus in their evaluations. For example, the early evaluations of the Head Start Program largely focused on raising the aptitude of children enrolled in the national program without equal concern for the other critical goals of the program. In most instances, such goals as the improvement in the nutrition and health status of the children, language development, and social skills were given less attention. To be sure, there were prominent evaluators who pointed out the shortcomings of the early evaluations of large national community-based programs in general (e.g., Campbell & Erlebacher, 1970) and Head Start in particular (e.g., Gramlich & Koshel, 1975; Rivlin & Timpane, 1975; Timpane, 1976).

It is my contention, however, that many of the underlying shortcomings were not methodological but were associated with substantive issues related to the nature of the communities that were being served; issues that may have been given more careful consideration had greater racial and ethnic diversity been reflected in the community of scholars responsible for the design and implementation of the evaluations. The current literature on program evaluation recognizes the price that is paid when community-based programs do not have influential involvement of evaluators representative of the diverse character of the communities being served. Not for face-validity, mind you, but for added-value to the quality of the evaluations being conducted.

Today, the need is even greater, as our country has grown in diversity since the 1970's. Not only in terms of ethnic and racial representation but also for evaluators with different training perspectives. The prognosis on whether the need will be met will depend on the magnitude of external forces that impact the academies.

> However, the press for evaluators of color, feminists, and those competent to serve in racially, culturally, and linguistically diverse communities will be raised beyond a recognized social need to more vocal demands by diverse communities whose voices will be in the majority during the 21st Century.

> Secondly, multiple perspectives on evaluation with a transformative and empowerment agenda will likely thrive in parallel with the redistribution of power relationships that are emerging in our rapidly changing communities.

Response to Donaldson:

As I read Stewart Donaldson's chapter, I agree that the theory-driven program evaluation (TDPE) is more prevalent than commonly assumed. I suspect, that in practice, theory-driven program evaluation has meant different things to different people. Partly, this is due to the confusion in nomenclature described in Donaldson's chapter. The problem may be that TDPE is too structurally complex for bridging the evaluator-practitioner worlds. Variations in implementation of program theory in general (the logic) also are a function of the still vast differences in the practitioner/ evaluator perspectives. The language evaluators use is symbolic of a traditional guildsmanship whereby evaluation activities have been thought to be unique to the craft. It is heavily-laden by issues that address methodology and measurement. On the other hand, practitioners' (e.g., program staff) language is action-laden, and more intuitive. The two worlds are found to be even more separate when one considers the cultural, racial, and contextual parameters that are everyday realities in the practitioner's world, while yet remaining uncharted territory for many in the world of evaluation. Much ground work has to be done to enable practitioners to internalize their rationale for conducting program functions as program theory, and to see this approach as a useful way to explicate actions and refine processes.

Reponse to Scriven:

It is heartening to hear Michael Scriven's vision about the future status and role of ethics in the practice of evaluation—one, I confess, I would have anticipated given his past discussions on the topic. Despite his optimism I see a number of challenges that must be overcome or at least considered.

Impact of technology. Technology and its impact are pervasive and ubiquitous. We have seen instances where its positive contributions to the quality of our existence have been accompanied by negative consequences. There is no reason to believe that the evaluation enterprise is immune to these effects. New ethical concerns are emerging almost daily as a function of our increased technical capabilities. These emerging issues are likely to take our program evaluation work into uncharted waters related to the ethics of social science research and evaluation.

Differences in training programs. I hope that the vision becomes a reality in so far as the training of future program evaluators. Specifically, training programs for future evaluators will necessarily need to be more experientially based at both the masters and doctoral levels. While the didactic learning of declarative and procedural knowledge is necessary, it is not sufficient. The evaluator's knowledge-base must be more comprehensive in the future to assure that he or she is prepared to conduct community-based evaluations. The watch word is: "Do No Harm." Ignorance of important community considerations and lack of sensitivity to the context and human dynamics associated with evaluation work can no longer be tolerated.

The contextually responsive skills, techniques, and awareness required to engage in community-based evaluation work in racially, culturally, and linguistically diverse settings are generally referred to as cultural competencies. It is difficult for me to believe that these skills can be developed absent social context, that is, experiential learning opportunities. Hopefully along with true experience comes a certain level of wisdom. Besides practica and internships alluded to in Scriven's chapter, I would advocate for a supervised externship to qualify for working in high priority areas (e.g., areas identified by local, state, and federal governments to be earmarked as "high stakes" areas for future funding).

The prognosis that ethical theory will have a prominent place in evaluation as a transdisciplinary field is welcomed, but one must be reminded that history tells us that the road to this vision is both long and problematic. Often the traveler must encounter egregious events such as the

Tuskegee Experiment before sufficient awareness is raised to mark the correct path to travel. We must also take periodic readings of our moral compass to assure that we include sufficient critical analyses of potentially valuable constructs (e.g., consequential and multicultural basis for validity justifications) that give us a sense of direction.

Related to Scriven's Four Processes of evaluation: the list is concise, and best of all, short. To violate the law of parsimony just a bit, I would hope that the process would include criterion-clarification (value-clarification?) this is the basis upon which merit, worth, and importance rest. The question then becomes: Whose criteria (values) will be adopted for rendering judgments? Whose will be excluded? Why? What evidence –logical and empirical-are available to provide justification?

Response to Wholey:

Joseph Wholey's chapter provided us with an excellent review of Results-oriented Management, particularly as it affects the Federal Government. The U.S. Government's services to consumers are almost always jointly financed with, and delivered through State and local governments. Some examples of these Federal Agencies are found in several Departments: Education; Health and Human Services; Housing and Urban Development; and the Department of Agriculture, to name a few.

These governmental programs generally provide:

1. Order and similarity across their projects and programs;
2. Flexibility for specific projects to respond to their respective situations, and
3. Some assessment reflecting commonalities and variations in outcomes.

Management and assessment of governmental programs at federal, state, and local levels rely on the use of common indicators by their diverse programs or projects. However, there is considerable variation that typically exists across governmental programs posing barriers generally to using quantitative indicators common to all programs/projects. I suspect that this is a major reason that evaluators seldom have examined the effectiveness of federal government programs with components at state and local levels. Another reason would be cost. Usually additional funds to evaluate such programs are limited or do not exist at all.

In government collaborative programs, tension often exist between the federal government's need for appropriate structure and similarity across programs in order to meet legislative intent and the state and local governments' need for adequate flexibility in developing and conducting individual programs, reflecting local needs. This tension is reflected in developing management and assessment indicators that are able to support both the needed structure and flexibility.

As was mentioned in the Wholey chapter, there is a great deal of variation in Intergovernmental Programming, far greater than variability of programs or projects within line agencies, because intergovernmental programs tend to allow for greater flexibility of state/local factors in shaping the design and conduct of their component programs.

It follows that line agencies would be in a better position to institute results-oriented management. However, there is light at the end of the tunnel, agencies that have a partnership rather than a line relationship are making progress with such Congressional mandates as the Government Performance and Results Act (1993), and the Agricultural Research, Extension, and Education Reform Act (1998).

Response to Lincoln and Mertens:

I have chosen to react to Lincoln's and Merten's chapters together because the issues they raise are interrelated. Both chapters address issues of human judgment and how it relates to our perception of the targets of our evaluations. Judgments have always played a prominent role in human thought, including the mental act of evaluating. Long before measurement was envisioned to be the dominant taskmaster of evaluation, judgment was the arbiter of human action. In the Bible and other sacred writings, and in other historical documents, we can view the acts of judgments and evaluation absent measurement. In one sense measurement, or more broadly speaking, methodology was viewed as a means to guide judgments, rendering them with precision, verifiability, and replicability.

It could be argued, that as greater and greater attention was placed on methodology, judgments became stepchildren consigned to the closet, only being allowed to emerge if adorned with the credentials and embellishments of scientific methods. When seen from this perspective, that of the rising to prominence of methods, then the explication of objectives can be considered as the natural consequences for meaningful measurements. The tenet that whatever can be observed, can be measured, shaped the methodology for both measurement of human actions and thought, and the development and use of objectives in evaluation.

Traditional methodologists attempted to address the inadequacies that were becoming increasingly apparent in social science research by doing what they do best—considering more complex quantitative methods such as multivariate analysis, to meet these deficiencies. The awareness of the inadequacies of traditional methodology (which are aptly pointed out in Fourth Generation Evaluation), eventually led, however to the unlocking of the closet door, but did not free the stepchildren. Judgments that were credentialed with scientific authority remained the prominent basis for reaching conclusions in disciplined inquiries. The work of Guba and Lincoln, and workers with liberation, empowerment, and capacity-building perspectives have attempted to release the multitude of judgmental perspectives from their confinement and raise their status to that of their more privileged siblings.

To be sure, paradigm wars have been fought, compromises have been made, and no clear victors have emerged. The vision, however, appears a bit clearer: Our evaluations must mirror a more representative democracy, as must our country. Guba and Lincoln, Mertens, Stake, House, among others, have given the reality to the political dimensions that must be honestly recognized in our work as evaluators and program professionals serving social needs. Most professional organizations dealing with social issues have taken a political and moral stand for the sake of democratizing and franchising all of their stakeholders. The American Evaluation Association's Guiding Principles and the Joint Committee on Standards in Testing are examples.

In all fairness, however, it should be pointed out that the danger of arrogance in the traditional orthodoxies of disciplined inquiry was recognized long before the second generation of evaluation had transpired. The Nuremberg trials and the Tuskegee experiments gave sobering awareness that racism as a social construct could conspire with scientific methods for immoral intentions. The exposure of such horrid practices to the light of the world led to the establishment of institutional review boards to provide a codification to the maxim, "Do No Harm" and respect the dignity of all human beings. To be sure, these codes fall short of the sort of empowerment called for by Fourth Generation prescriptions or Transformative Emancipatory Theory.

Has there been any evidence of changes that could be associated with the evolution of the practice and thought related to evaluation in the federal bureaucracy? If we look at one of the areas identified in Fourth Generation, that of the tendency of managerialism one can see some changes. Requirements for continuing funding, accountability and program functioning are now including structures that assure inclusive and shared power among relevant stakeholders.

An excellent example of mandating "inclusiveness" is the Congressional mandate for Agriculture. The Agricultural Research, Extension, and Education Reform Act (1998) requires that there is meaningful stakeholder input into Research, Extension, and Education programming. Albeit slow, the landscape is changing because of the changing needs of our Nation.

CLOSING

Today, the presenters have provided us with many themes in evaluation practice. They have taken us on a journey into the future by sharing their perspectives on such issues as ethical practice, multiple perspectives in judgment, improvement in accountability in government programs, diversity and inclusiveness. It also appears that apparently the creative tension between the qualitative and quantitative perspectives in evaluation will continue to be a source of intellectual exchange. The issues and challenges presented here today will remain fertile ground for evaluators in the 21st century and beyond.

REFERENCES

Campbell, D. T., & Erlebacher, A. E. (1970). How regression artifacts in quasi-experimental evaluations can mistakenly make compensatory education look harmful. In J. Hellmuth (Ed.), *The disadvantaged child* (Vol. 3., pp. 185-215). New York: Brunner/Mazel.

Gramlich, E. M. & Koshel, P. P. (1978). *Educational performance contracting.* Washington, DC: Brookings Institution.

Government Performance and Results Act. 1993. U.S. Public Law 103-62.

Agricultural Research, Extension, and Education Reform Act. 1998. U.S. Public Law 105-85.

Rivlin, A. M., & Timpane, P. M. (1975). *Planned variations in education.* Washington, DC: Brookings Institution.

Timpane, P. M. (1976). Evaluating Title I again? In C.C. Abt (Ed.), *The evaluation of social programs* (pp. 415-424). Beverly Hills, CA: Sage.

10

Examining the Role of Cultural Competency in Program Evaluation: Visions for New Millennium Evaluators

Bianca L. Guzmán

Claremont Graduate University

I had the unique opportunity to be invited to react to the presentations of several well-known evaluators during the Stauffer Symposium on Applied Psychology, Evaluating Social Programs and Problems: Visions for the New Millennium. As I listened to the presenters I began to hear many issues that are important and relevant to evaluation. As Michael Scriven discussed the transdisciplinary view of evaluation, I began to think about how appropriate and timely this issue is in relation to program evaluation. I find that as a program evaluator, I often have to cross the boundaries of several disciplines in order to create and evaluate social service programs. These boundary leaps often entail learning about the ways in which culture is ingrained in the way human beings interact and how this interaction must be examined and addressed by competent evaluators.

Donna Merten's and Yvonna Lincoln's call to action regarding how marginalized groups should be included in the evaluation process also lead me to focus my thoughts on how these groups should and could play a role in the evaluation process. In listening to Stewart Donaldson's presentation on the theory-driven view of program evaluation I continued to think about how a theory surrounding program evaluation and culture can be useful to new millennium evaluators. As I thought about these issues I realized that cultural competency should be one of the themes that new millennium evaluators should seriously address. The following reaction paper is an examination of how evaluators can begin establishing cultural competency in their own research.

As we begin this millennium, U.S. society frequently discusses and debates what it means for individuals, institutions or job settings to be politically correct. In the last decade, this discussion often focused on how to be culturally sensitive or competent as part of the politically correct agenda. Today the majority of job settings, educational institutions, and political arenas consider cultural sensitivity as an important component of their mission (McPhatter, 1997). This is certainly an indication that corporate America has taken seriously the inevitable diversity of the future labor and consumer force. Examples of this trend can be clearly seen in job solicitations. Advertisements for any type of position usually state that the organization is "an equal opportunity employer," and some solicitations state that they are also an "affirmative action employer." This is certainly the case if individuals apply for any state or federal position. Other job solicitations take a more proactive stance and state that their organization, "values diversity and is committed to providing equal career opportunities to all individuals." In educational institutions, as part of the training of certain professions, such as social work, the curriculum must include cultural diversity training in order for graduates to receive board certifications and licensures (McPhatter, 1997).

As program evaluators, many of us have also embraced the idea that cultural competence ought to be one of the central principles of our field (Mertens, this volume, chapter 6; Stanfield, 1999). Some evaluators have also stated that if evaluation work is to adequately address and create appropriate evaluations for underserved populations, a diversity perspective must be included in the process (Lincoln, this volume, chapter 5; Mertens this volume, chapter 6). To date, however, it is not clear as to how an evaluator could establish a culturally competent perspective or when this perspective would be appropriate in the evaluation process.

As U.S. society becomes increasingly multicultural and multiethnic as well as sociodemographically varied, cultural competence allows us to better understand behavior and to better interpret our findings regarding individuals and groups. This improved understanding of diverse cultural groups that are usually in oppressed and underserved positions, can also lead us to improve our evaluation plans in the direction of greater social justice (Alarcón & Foulks, 1995; Trickett, Watts, & Birman, 1994). As individuals involved in the field of program evaluation, it would seem appropriate to suggest that one of the tools evaluators of the new millennium ought to perfect is creating program evaluations that can also serve social justice functions. This concept that evaluation can also serve social justice functions is rarely explicitly articulated in the field of evaluation (Mertens, 2001). Transformative theory, however, is one of the theories that has addressed this point indirectly. This theory acknowledges that knowledge is not neutral, but that it is influenced by human interests, such as culture, and therefore power and social relationships within a culture have the ability to change. This suggests that an important purpose of knowledge construction or evaluation is to help people improve society (Banks, 1995). Scriven (2001) has also been one of the few evaluators who have suggested that in order for evaluators in the field to have merit they must not simply be involved in practicing evaluation, but they must also become a solution provider.

This is particularly important for evaluators who are working in the field of program evaluation. For example, an evaluator who is working in assessing the success of an AIDS/HIV education program should include components in the evaluation plan that suggest that the intervention being evaluated has created social justice. The change in social justice for such a program might be as basic as documenting that the intervention has impacted greater access for underrepresented ethnic groups to receive HIV testing. A more comprehensive account of whether such an intervention has achieved social justice would be to find that as a result of implementing the intervention that the health care practices of ethnic groups living with HIV had improved. These points highlight the idea that the evaluation process has the potential for being a social justice agent.

A CONTEXT FOR DEFINING CULTURE

So how do evaluators take on the task of incorporating cultural competency in their evaluation plans? One of the first things to consider is: "What does one mean when we use the term *culture*?" This question has certainly intrigued social scientist of all types for many decades. In 1952 Kroeber and Kluckhohn searched the social science literature and found that there were 164 different definitions of culture, none of which has been adopted by any particular science or field (Lonner, 1994). This is an important point because many researchers involved in the study of culture have studied many different types of cultures and have not been able to articulate a singular definition of a complex set of human behaviors.

This lack of agreement about what culture means has lead many social scientists, especially anthropologists, to either attempt to define what culture is or to declare that a definition of culture is not as relevant as discovering common behavioral patterns in human societies. Some social psychologists have expressed strong reservations for the need to understand culture especially in light of how many types of cultures are found around the world. As a matter of fact, Wheeler and Reis (1988) in an article about how mainstream social psychologists conceptualize culture write: "It takes more intellectual resources than we have to just understand our own current culture...We just don't have time to read about [other cultures]." From these examples, it follows that like any other abstract concept, theory or paradigm in the social sciences, there are individuals vested in inquiry into such topics, and there are others who would just assume that because the concept, theory or paradigm cannot be fully defined that it is not worthy of further merit or research consideration.

Another reason for this apparent lack of interest may also be that social scientists who develop theories and paradigms about human behavior, primarily by observing individuals of Euro-American descent have potentially much to lose if culture is introduced. These scientists may feel threatened by the idea that once culture is introduced into the proposed theory/paradigm that the tenets of their concepts would not generalize to other cultural groups and therefore render their theories/paradigms as not being quite as insightful as originally proposed. For example, a researcher, has spent a decade discovering how a primarily Euro-American community deals with grief due to death. This individual has proposed a theory to the general scientific community that states that when individuals experience grief they will become depressed. This might be quite relevant and insightful information to obtain, however, if another researcher conducts research on how members of X ethnic group experience grief and discovers that this group of individuals in contrast honor death with a celebration. This new researcher finds that individuals from this community do not experience depression due to the death. As can be seen from this example, it might seem appropriate to suggest that one of the tenets of the original researchers theory now comes into question. This could be the case for social scientists who have built a professional life-long career path by attempting to perfect a theory. As a proponent of the importance of cultural competency, I firmly attest that it is in the best interest of the field of evaluation to begin to create a framework by which we can begin incorporate cultural competency into our evaluation programming and research.

As has been stated previously, although there is no one definition of culture there are certain characteristics that help provide a context for how to define culture. Research suggests that existing definitions of culture have various characteristics in common (Lonner, 1994). They establish culture (1) as an abstract, human-made idea; (2) as a context or setting within which behavior occurs, is shaped, and transformed; (3) as containing values, beliefs, attitudes, and languages that have emerged as adaptations: and (4) as important enough to be passed on to other generations. Stemming from this context, it is reasonable to assert that culture affects constructions of power, gender; defines possibilities and conditions for action; and influences conceptualizations of wellness. This has implications for how evaluators carry forth program evaluation plans and assess impact.

In the following paragraphs, I will expand on how these four contextual points of culture impact the work evaluators do and critically examine what steps evaluators must take in order to begin to create evaluations that incorporate cultural competency. Figure 10.1 is a pictorial representation of how culture impacts the evaluation process and ultimately the evaluation results. Although there is debate about what cultural competency means, partly due to the debate of what culture means, I will attempt to provide a context by which we can determine if an evaluation has achieved cultural competence. Based on the four contextual points it would stand to follow that cultural competence refers to an ability to provide services that are perceived as legitimate for problems experienced by culturally diverse populations. This definition denotes the ability to transform knowledge and cultural awareness into interventions that support and sustain healthy participant-system functioning within the appropriate cultural context.

CULTURE IS AN ABSTRACT HUMAN-MADE IDEA

As point one suggests, culture is an abstract human-made idea. This conceptualization has implications for how we view reality and the field of evaluation. In fundamental scientific inquiry, we are taught to believe in established paradigms that will guide us in creating an objective reality by which we can test theories or assess impact. In other words, this form of inquiry suggests that there is one single objective reality for all humans and human society and that scientific inquiry or evaluation is a process of discovering the structure and function of that singular world (Campbell & Wasco, 2000). Many of us evaluators, who have been trained in the social sciences, have fallen into believing that this is the way to conduct evaluation research. However, there are individuals in the field who suggests that if we continue to perpetuate this form of inquiry, then we are lacking a full picture of human behavior. As Patton (1978, p. 203 as cited in Guba & Lincoln, 1989) has suggested:

> A paradigm is a worldview, a general perspective, a way of breaking down the complexity of the real world. As such, paradigms are deeply embedded in the socialization of adherents and practitioners: paradigms tell them what is important, legitimate, and reasonable. Paradigms are also normative, telling the practitioner what to do without the necessity of long existential or epistemological considerations. But it is this aspect of

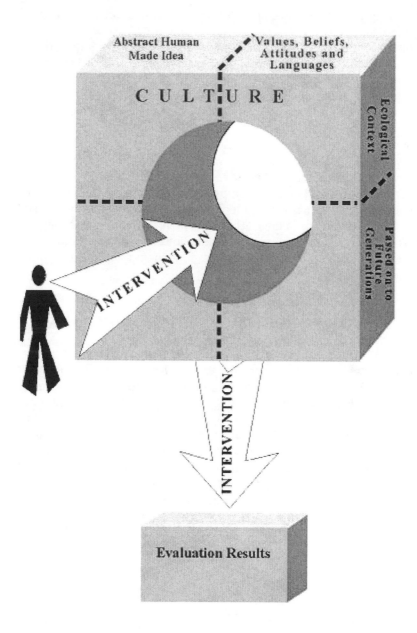

FIGURE 10.1. Depiction of how the context of culture impacts evaluation processes.

paradigms that constitutes both their strength and their weakness—their strength in that it makes action possible, their weakness in that the very reason for action is hidden in the unquestioned assumptions of the paradigm.

What Patton suggests is that it is not possible to create a paradigm without the process of human subjectivity. If we superimpose the concept that culture is a human made-idea we see that there is no such thing as objective reality when measuring culture. The argument being that when evaluators take into account culture, we must begin to admit that objective scientific methodology is not always possible. Therefore, in order to create culturally competent evaluations we must discard our scientific assumptions and create new methodologies that encompass a constructivist methodology (Guba & Lincoln, 1989). This framework suggests the following:

"Truth" is relative and a matter of consensus among informed and sophisticated constructors, not of correspondence with an objective reality.

"Facts" have no meaning except within some value framework; hence there cannot be an "objective" assessment of any proposition.

"Causes" and "effects" do not exist except by imputations; hence accountability is a relative matter and implicates all interacting parties equally.

Phenomena can be understood only within the context in which they are studied; findings from one context cannot be generalized to another; neither problems nor their solutions can be generalized from one setting to another.

At first glance all these components may appear overwhelming but once understood provide tremendous insights as to how to improve the evaluation process in general. More specifically, this framework provides evaluators with a new way of "thinking" about how culture can impact the entire evaluation process. It is important for evaluators to consider the community for whom they will create an evaluation plan. This community and the surrounding ecological framework is the key to discovering the culture of the community and the individuals who will participate in the evaluation process.

Culture as Defined by Ecological Contexts

The second point of the definition of culture is that culture is partially defined by the ecological contexts of the participants. The term ecology derives from the Greek root *iokos*, meaning, "house." The term *ecology* then in its most basic form refers to the study of houses within which organisms live, or more broadly defined, their environments/ecological contexts (Levine, & Perkins, 1987). Consideration of examining how ecological context shapes culture is important for the development of culturally competent evaluation plans.

First of all, as Lewin (1935) and other community psychologists have suggested, human behavior is a function of the person environment fit. Therefore, when we evaluate interventions, we must incorporate not only the interactions between individuals in a given intervention, but also how group dynamics emerge from repeated interactions with others as a result of and in reaction to the environment. With this point in mind, we must acknowledge that interventions by the very nature of being implemented; change the ecological environment, and this phenomena makes intervention effects variable. That is to say that a particular intervention will be as much affected or changed by the context as the participants in the evaluation. This suggests that change is not so easily assessed or engineered, but rather that it is a nonlinear process that involves the introduction of new information, and the constant reassessment of the meaning of that information in relation to the culture being examined. This interaction complicates how we create evaluation plans and how we interpret the findings of our work. As culturally competent evaluators, we must be ready to constantly reassess our evaluation plans in order to account for the neverending changes in ecological contexts. This may mean that evaluation plans will continually change as a process of the evaluation. For example, in terms of practicality, it will mean that if an evaluator has chosen to use survey methods to assess change that the survey that they have created will always change in order to capture program impact in the population who is participating in the evaluation. Furthermore, we must also be ready to discuss how these changes shape inferences that we make about our evaluation results.

To further explore this point, we must acknowledge that social contexts and interactions between and within participants are embedded within the larger social structure or meta-culture. As Bronfenbrenner's (1979) ecological model suggests, culture is embedded in a hierarchy of social forces (see Figure 10.2). These levels range from the *macrosystem* cultural attitudes and mores, through the *exosystemic* level forces such as extended family, neighbors, and social services, down to

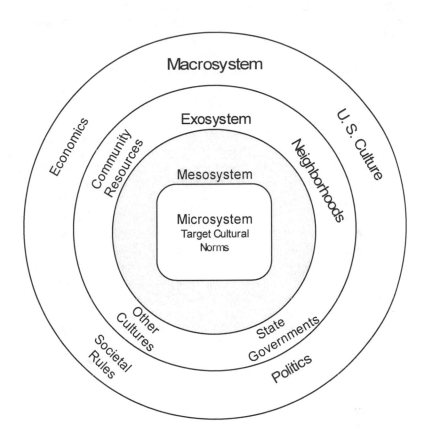

FIGURE 10.2. The ecological context of culture.

microsystemic level forces such as nuclear family, peers or any forces that directly affect the individual. Individual characteristics and dispositions exist, interact, and develop in this environment of ever-influencing forces that themselves interact across levels of the ecological hierarchy. For example, societal norms (macrosystemic) interact with participant's ability to participate in program evaluations (exosystemic) such that these two systems determine the stability of the participation of a particular underserved group. As culturally competent evaluators, we must acknowledge and seriously consider these layers of ecological context before, during, and after an evaluation assessment. As can be surmised from this analysis, if we do not take into consideration these ecological contexts, and how they interact with each other, we cannot adequately prepare an evaluation plan, and we are much less able to disseminate any evaluation results with any level of fidelity.

Culture as Values, Beliefs, Attitudes and Languages

The third part of the definition suggests that culture contains values, beliefs, attitudes and languages. The question for new millennium evaluators is: "How do these factors impact intervention programming and by default evaluation effects? In order to fully appreciate the role that values, beliefs and norms play in any given culture, I will use the example of how Latino cultural values have impacted gender roles, and how in turn these roles may impact evaluation programming.

If we examine the more traditional Latino cultural values, we find that gender roles are often dictated by two concepts, which are *marianismo* and *machismo*. *Marianismo* has been characterized as the role of the ideal woman, modeled after the Virgin Mary, based on chastity, abnegation, and sacredness, while reinforcing obedience and virginity (Ortiz-Torres, Serrano-Garcia, & Torres-Burgos, 2000). *Machismo* stresses virility, independence, physical strength, and sexual prowess. If we believe these two roles as encompassing the experiences of all individuals within Latino culture, then we have not explored how culture may change as a process of the ecological contexts in which humans live. As Latina women have joined the workforce, there have been changes in the definition of family and work relations. Many Latina women are now single heads of families, and when this is not the case, women and men are increasingly sharing financial responsibilities at home. Both of these situations promote changes in gender roles and a change in Latino societal values. Another point to consider is that as many Latinos immigrate into the United States, Euro-American culture has an impact on role transformation. Research with Latinas in the United States has demonstrated that the acculturation process is most often characterized by the adoption of less traditional beliefs and values (Soto & Shaver, 1985).

The question for evaluators is how do we account, describe or include all of these cultural nuances for example, when we are attempting to evaluate a program that promotes responsible sexual behavior in young Latina women? One of the central points that we as evaluators must acknowledge is that there are differences within a culture and that we can not logically lump individuals from a certain culture and expect that they all share the same experience or receive the same intervention impact. We must be keenly aware that because we have considered culture our evaluations will be complex and may also include findings that are not linear and may often seem contradictory to each other. As Guba and Lincoln (1989) have suggested, evaluation data has neither special status nor legitimization, but it simply represents another construction to be taken into account in the move toward understanding a social phenomena within a particular culture. Therefore, we must acknowledge that the evaluation process has just as much importance as the outcome.

With regard to how cultures develop a language, we are keenly aware and have been taught in our career paths that it is important to create programming and evaluation tools in the language that individual participants can comprehend. There are some evaluators who surmise that if an intervention can be conducted in the language of the population being impacted, and if the measurement tools can be translated, then the evaluation is culturally competent. Others may take this step as an additional burden for programming or evaluation. Some might suggest to the stakeholders who are vested in the evaluation results that having to conduct this type of evaluation will be more costly and therefore more difficult to evaluate. I have often heard evaluators suggest that *we will have to translate that measure or we will have to get someone who speaks X."* The point being that although this additional step is an unwelcome burden, once it is completed we can then conclude that we have been culturally competent. While translating a measurement tool or having someone who speaks the language of the target population is a step in the direction of culturally sensitivity these two steps do not constitute cultural competency. As sound evaluators we must realize that there is much more to how language functions in a culture, and that a mere translation of certain concepts or measures will not fully capture the experience of the participants.

It is through language that individuals convey emotion. Once again, if we examine our process of research, we can observe that our training leads us to believe that evaluation is supposed to be about thinking or discovering, not feeling. Therefore, if we just get to how the intervention has impacted the participants, we do not need to think about feelings. On the other hand, it can be argued that feelings, like beliefs and values also shape research and are a natural part of inquiry (Stanko, 1997). The emotionality of participants' lives must be acknowledged throughout the evaluation process. If an evaluator is not fully aware of a particular culture and how their linguistic patterns shape the behavioral patterns of the individuals from that culture, then the evaluator cannot make logical assessments about the impact of a certain intervention.

In Latino culture as in many other collectivist cultures, the issue of respect for elders and scholars plays a role as to how certain individuals interact with an evaluator. In many cases, the evaluator will be seen as the expert who has supreme authority over the entire evaluation process. This has implications for how Latinos will respond when interviewed about the impact of a certain intervention. It may be the case that during the interview process Latinos may feel that it is inappropriate to make direct eye contact with the evaluator or to clearly voice their concerns about what aspects of the intervention were beneficial for them and which aspects could be improved upon. The evaluator could conclude that because this individual did not seem engaged (no eye contact), which in U.S. culture is inappropriate behavior, or did not offer any thoughts about how the intervention impacted her/him that the intervention had no impact on this participant. This evaluator has assessed the situation only in relation to the objectivity of the evaluation tool and has not considered culture as part of the process of evaluation. It may be the case that this participant did benefit from the intervention or that there were pieces of the intervention that benefited her or him but because the ecological context was not conducive to allowing the participant to share emotion the participant did not do so. This situation may have been remedied if the evaluator would have enlisted someone from the target culture to interview the participants of the intervention.

Moreover, because the evaluator may be hearing emotion-laden material, the affective experiences of the evaluator must also become part of the evaluation process. This affective experience is a two-way road; the evaluator has feelings about what she or he is hearing and also has established emotional norms about certain social phenomena. Take for example the evaluator who is conducting an evaluation on a teenage pregnancy prevention program. It is probably the case that this evaluator has certain feelings about teenage pregnancy and these feelings impact the way in which this individual conducts an interview with a participant. As part of the interview process, this evaluator may also experience emotions about what the participant is disclosing. How can evaluators turn these feelings off during the evaluation process? My argument is that we cannot and that until evaluators become attuned to the feelings of their research participants as well as their own feelings an evaluation plan will not have the complexity necessary to answer the question of "did this program work?"

My suggestion to new millennium evaluators is to build into their evaluation plans a process check. This means that evaluators must constantly discourse with the members of the evaluation team and community members and check-in about their experiences with the participants. During these meetings evaluators can share their feelings while at the same time obtain feedback from community members as to how to interpret the emotions of the participants. What I am suggesting is that as new millennium evaluators we must place as much importance in the process of evaluation as in the outcome and that we cannot possibly do this if we are not aware of the role that emotions and culture play in that process.

Culture and Future Generations

In the last concept of culture, it is suggested that cultural norms are important enough to be passed on to other generations. As evaluators, we must understand how this point is important to evaluation. To return to the argument that evaluation results ought to serve to some extent social justice functions, we must be clear that if our results are culturally inappropriate, we are at risk of perpetuating or creating stereotypes of underrepresented or socially oppressed groups. An example of this would be for an evaluator to suggest that a certain successful teenage pregnancy prevention program is not decreasing the number of young Latina adolescents who become sexually active. If this finding is carried forth, there are future generations of Latina women who will carry the legacy that they are slated to become teenage mothers and dependents of the social welfare system. On the other hand, if we consider culture, we may find that Latina women on average are younger when they begin sexual activity, but there are also fewer young Latina youth who begin sexual activity at an early age when comparing them to other cultural groups as a result of that particular program (Guzmán et al., 2001). On closer inspection, we also find that young Latina women are the ones least likely to apply for social welfare programs. Within this context, I argue that we must be careful with the inferences that we make about evaluation results.

Finally, evaluators must be to some degree *Transcultural* in order to be culturally competent. Transculturalism is defined as a multidimensional construct that involves social relationships, language and media use, participation in rituals, and group identification (Ortiz-Torres et al., 2000). Although this term has been primarily used to describe the process of assimilation, I will use it here to describe how this model fits into creating a culturally competent researcher. In transculturation an individual has one culture, or identifies with one culture (dominant U.S. culture), but can incorporate or understand the behaviors of another cultural group in relation to the cultural rules of that culture rather than the dominant culture. This process suggests that an evaluator could have varied, even contradictory, manifestations of certain behaviors as they interact with different cultures. Transculturation, also suggests that evaluators can have some dissonance between what mainstream U.S. culture suggests for any given culture and what that evaluator has experienced as being so for a particular culture. This process of *being* or thinking suggests that the evaluation of culture is complex and that there are no set rules for any given culture. In other words, that evaluation of a certain cultural group is not an all or nothing process. Which leads me to suggest that becoming culturally competent cannot take on a cookbook approach. Evaluators cannot simply read a recipe or check-off a list and then attest that they are culturally competent. On the contrary, as I have suggested, becoming culturally competent involves individuals who are willing to be actively engaged with the evaluation participants and the evaluation process.

CONCLUDING REMARKS

My goal in writing this chapter has been to provide a framework that not only discusses what culture and cultural competency encompasses, but also suggests promising directions for future culturally competent evaluators. In current theories of culture, for the most part, it has been suggested that there is no universal definition of culture. It has been suggested that culture is a certain set of characteristics that help provide a context for cultural competency. The four characteristics that existing definitions of culture have in common are that culture is (1) an abstract, human-made idea; (2) a context or setting within which behavior occurs, is shaped, and transformed; (3) containing of values, beliefs, attitudes and languages that have emerged as adaptations; and (4) important enough to be passed on to other generations. I have discussed how all of these four points are relevant to cultural competency and how evaluators can begin to establish some protocols that incorporate cultural competency in their evaluation work.

REFERENCES

Alarcón, R., & Foulks, E. (1995). Personality disorders and culture: Contemporary clinical views. *Cultural Diversity and Mental Health, 1*, 3-17.

Banks, J. A. (1995). The historical reconstruction of knowledge about race: Implications for tranformative teaching. *Educational Researcher, 24*, 15-25.

Bronfenbrenner, U. (1979). *The ecology of human development: Experiments by nature and design*. Cambridge, MA: Harvard University Press.

Campbell, R. M., & Wasco, S. M. (2000). Feminist approaches to social science: Epistemological and methodological tenets. *American Journal of Community Psychology, 28*, 773-791.

Guba, E. G., & Lincoln, Y. S. (1989). *Fourth generation evaluation*. Newbury Park, CA: Sage.

Guzmán, B. L., Schlehofer-Sutton, M. M., Villanueva, C. M., Casad, B. J, Dello Stritto M. E., & Feria, A. (2002). *C.A.M.P. and Latino adolescents: A closer look at a non-traditional sex education program.* Manuscript under review.

Lewin, K. (1935). *A dynamic theory of personality.* New York: McGraw-Hill.

Levine, M., & Perkins, D. V. (1987). *Principles of community psychology: Perspectives and applications.* New York, NY: Oxford University Press.

Lonner, W. (1994). Culture and human diversity. In E. Trickett, R. Watts, & D. Birman (Eds.), *Human diversity: Perspectives on people in context* (pp. 230-243). San Francisco, CA: Jossey-Bass.

McPhatter, A. R. (1997). Cultural competence in child welfare: What is it? How do we achieve it? What happens without it? *Child Welfare, 76,* 255-278.

Ortiz-Torres, B., Serrano-García, I., & Torres-Burgos, N. (2000). Subverting culture: Promoting HIV/AIDS prevention among Puerto Rican and Dominican women. *American Journal of Community Psychology, 28,* 859-881.

Patton, M. Q. (1978). *Utilization-focused evaluation.* Beverly Hills, CA: Sage.

Stanko, E. A. (1997). "I second that emotion;" Reflections on feminism, emotionality, and research on sexual violence. In M. D. Schwartz (Ed.), *Feminism and methodology* (pp. 74-85). Bloomington: Indiana University Press.

Soto, E., & Shaver, P. (1982). Sex role traditionalism, assertiveness and symptoms of Puerto Rican women living in the United States. *Hispanic Journal of Behavioral Sciences, 4,* 1-19.

Stanfield, J. H. II (1999). Methodological reflections: An introduction. In J. H. Stanfield & R. Dennis (Eds.), *Race and ethnicity in research methods* (pp. 3-15). Thousand Oaks, CA: Sage.

Trickett, E., Watts, R., & Birman, D. (Eds.) (1994). *Human diversity: Perspectives on people in context.* San Francisco, CA: Jossey-Bass.

Wheeler, & Reis (1988). On titles, citations, and outlets: What do mainstreamers want? In M. H. Harris Bond (Eds.), *The cross-cultural challenge to social psychology* (pp. 36-47). Newbury Park, CA: Sage.

Toward an Integrative View of the Theory and Practice of Program and Policy Evaluation

Melvin M. Mark[1]

Pennsylvania State University

Visions. Contributors to this book, and to the conference on which it is based, were asked to offer a vision for evaluation for the 21st century or to respond to the visions of others. Of course, the word "vision" has come to have several meanings. A "vision" can refer to a thoughtful depiction of desired future states. Presumably contributors attempted to offer a vision in this sense. But the term "vision" can also refer to something akin to a nightmare or an hallucination. "Vision" can alternatively refer to the perceptual capacities that we have to see the things that are right in front of us. The different meanings of vision in a sense guide this chapter. The evaluators who shared their visions are too thoughtful to offer anything that should be portrayed as a nightmare or hallucination; nevertheless, reading across the different visions there are some nightmarish possibilities. And several of the visions that were offered may well be heavily influenced by what the visionaries see right in front of them, in their own areas of practice, without adequate attention to the possibilities and promises of other approaches. Metaphorically speaking, then, I will try to sort out the thoughtful portrayals of a desired future from the more nightmarish possibilities and from the possible cases of tunnel vision. In trying to sort out the different qualities of vision, I will also make suggestions toward a comprehensive view of the theory and practice of evaluation. Of course, my

[1]*Author Note*: Thanks go to Stewart Donaldson and Michael Scriven for helpful comments and for organizing this volume and the symposium on which it was based. Address correspondence to Mel Mark, Department of Psychology, 407 Moore, Penn State, University Park PA 16802, or via email at m5m@psu.edu.

view is undoubtedly influenced by my own perceptual system, and others may well see things differently than I. Such is the nature of vision!

In a relatively brief chapter, it is impossible to do justice to the observations, insights, and arguments presented by each of the contributors who offered a vision of evaluation for the new millennium. Instead, I offer a few selected observations about some of the visions, and make some general points about the current and possible future of evaluation. First, then, I offer some observations about some of the visions offered in previous chapters.

THE MEANING OF EVALUATION

Michael Scriven raises perhaps the most fundamental questions for the field of evaluation: What is evaluation? What is the nature of the field of evaluation? Drawing on his distinguished career of contributions to the field, Scriven also offers answers. Evaluation, he contends, refers to the "systematic determination of [the] merit, worth, and significance" (p. 32) of something. The field of evaluation, according to Scriven, should be accorded the status of a trans-discipline. By this he means that, like statistics, evaluation underlies a wide array of disciplines and activities. Scriven's vision seems wonderfully ambitious, perhaps suggesting (for example) that evaluation programs should be as common at universities and colleges as are statistics programs. It is also quite interesting, I believe, to think about what the issues are that the practitioners and theoreticians of an established evaluation transdiscipline would study and debate; this may be a useful "visioning" activity for all evaluators and may help lead us to a more productive research agenda for the further study of evaluation. Consistent with a point made repeatedly in this chapter, I believe that one of the central tasks in the transdiscipline of evaluation would be ongoing work on establishing the types of evaluation approaches best suited to different conditions and audiences.

Turning to Scriven's definition of evaluation, the practice of evaluation of course needs more meat on the bone than this definition provides. Scriven rightly reminds us that a common underlying logic applies to such areas of application as product evaluation, personnel evaluation, and program evaluation. But area-specific methodologies may be required to carry out this underlying logic in practice. For example, program evaluators often need to rely on different methods than do personnel or product evaluators. Thus, if there were a transdisciplinary evaluation association, it would probably have separate divisions for different types of evaluators. A second important issue arises in relation to Scriven's definition which, with its explicit focus on merit, worth, significance, and the like, is in some ways narrower than the definitions of evaluation offered by many others in the field. If evaluation is defined as Scriven prefers, we would also need to acknowledge explicitly the importance of what might described as evaluation-related services—an important form of which we now turn to.

THE AGE OF PERFORMANCE MEASUREMENT SYSTEMS

There has been a striking growth in the development of performance measurement systems, and it appears that this trend will continue in the foreseeable future (see Newcomer, 1997, on the Government Performance and Results Act, the United Way, and other forces encouraging the use of performance measurement systems). Joe Wholey offers a vision of results-oriented management (or performance-based management), with performance measurement systems serving the information needs of agency managers and staff, and with evaluators contributing in several ways to the development, operation, and perhaps even the evaluation of performance measurement systems. Wholey persuasively illustrates the potential value of using performance measurement systems to inform results-oriented management. Take in particular the example of the U.S. Coast Guard, which used a new performance measurement system to discover a surprisingly high fatality rate among commercial towing crews and then developed interventions targeted at this problem. The decline in fatalities that followed is a strong testament to the potential of results-oriented management.

Despite such successes, there are a number of concerns about performance measurement systems and, correspondingly, the results-oriented management movement (Perrin, 1998, Mark, Henry, & Julnes, 2000, chapter 7). These include the feasibility of adequately measuring outcomes for complex programs; the potential for the corruption of indicators and for goal displacement (e.g., "teaching to the test" rather than more broadly educating); the inability in most cases to draw confident causal inference that the program, rather than other forces such as a changed economy, is responsible for any observed improvement (or decline) in performance; the fear that performance measurement will drive out other forms of evaluation; and the move to a cookie cutter, one-size-fits-all approach to evaluation, with performance measurement being seen as the appropriate model for programs of all sizes and types.

In addition, an underlying problem can arise from the apparent trend of trying to use a performance measurement system simultaneously as the guiding star for multiple functions, including administration, budgeting, individual performance appraisal, and program evaluation. This problem is especially noteworthy in light of Wholey's emphasis on results-oriented management. Consider what will happen if the current trend continues and the same performance measures and reporting system are used both for program management and for reporting to Congress for its use in funding decisions. Isn't it predictable that pressures will arise in some agencies to select, measure and report indicators in a way that is expected to make the agency look good? And isn't this incompatible with having a performance measurement system that will best support effective results-based management?

Whether the use of performance measurement systems and results-oriented management has staying power, or turns out to be the latest in a long string of management fads, only time will tell. Perhaps the more appropriate question is: Under which conditions is performance measurement more and less useful, and how big a role should it have in the constellation of evaluation and evaluation related activities?

FROM LOGIC MODELS TO THEORY-DRIVEN EVALUATION: THINKING THEORETICALLY

So-called logic models are often developed as an early step in constructing a performance measurement system. In a logic model, one attempts to lay out a program's inputs, activities, outputs, and short and long term outcomes. Although sometimes the terms are used interchangeably, many evaluators differentiate between logic models and program theory. Unlike logic models, program theories generally emphasize and include the presumed mediators through which the program is expected to have its effects—the psychological, social, or (rarely) economic or structural mechanisms that the program is supposed to trigger that in turn are to lead to the desired outcomes. Stewart Donaldson, in his chapter, offers several examples. For instance, in chapter 7 (p. 129), Figure 7.7 (taken from the Adolescent Alcohol Prevention Trial) identifies psychological constructs like "refusal skills" and "beliefs about acceptability" that are expected to mediate the effect of program components on outcomes such as alcohol use. Also illustrated in that example are moderators, that is, factors that influence magnitude of a treatment effect.

In principle, theory-driven evaluation can cover a wide range of territory, including work related to implementation assessment, program improvement, effectiveness, and efficiency (Chen, 1990). It appears that in practice, however, theory-driven evaluation seems to focus primarily on testing mediators and to a lesser extent moderators (see review by Donaldson & Chen, 2002). The argument for this kind of theory-driven approach is compelling. Typically it is very useful to understand the mechanisms that underlie a program effect (Cronbach, 1982; Mark et al., 2000). If you know what processes underlie a cause-effect relationship, you can sometimes create a more effective or more efficient treatment. You can sometimes better target the intervention to the right cases. When programs are ineffective, knowing why can sometimes allow you fix the program. A case in point comes from some of Donaldson's own work on the effects of resistance skills training such as that used in DARE. Donaldson, Graham, Piccinin, & Hansen (1995) demonstrated that drug abuse resistance training is often ineffective because it makes children believe that drug use is normative, that everybody is doing it. In addition to the preceding advantages, tests of program theory can also facilitate generalization, in the sense that if you know how and why a program works, it is easier to assess whether it will operate effectively in a new setting (Cronbach, 1982; also see Mark, 1990; Shadish, Cook & Campbell, 2001). A theory-driven approach also has the potential of helping to build better connections between evaluation and the disciplines that offer theory for social programs (Yeh, 2000).

Although the theory-driven approach has important advantages, it also has limits. Despite the potential benefits of program theory, theory itself can also have some undesirable consequences (Greenwald, Pratkanis, Leippe, & Baumgardner, 1986). If theory is used to guide evaluation design and measurement selection, the consequences should be good *if* the theory is well developed and reasonably accurate. But theories are usually at best only partially correct and are often poorly developed in the intractable problem areas on which social program focus. Consequently, the theory-driven evaluation may: exclude important outcome measures that the (imperfect) theory did not specify; ignore possible mediators other than those specified in the theory; and fail to search for important moderators of the program's success. Theory-driven evaluation can forestall learning the unanticipated lessons in one's evaluation data, because the theory focuses attention and thus can operate like blinders (Mark et al., 2000, on principled discovery).

In addition, problems can arise in identifying and selecting a program theory to guide the theory-driven evaluation. In some instances, theory may be weak, with little but faith connecting program activities and key desired outcomes. Some adherents of program theory suggest that this is a sign that summative evaluation should be delayed until program theory and operations can be improved. This may sometimes be sensible but, as historical examples such as aspirin remind us, interventions are occasionally effective even if the underlying mechanism is not yet known. And program clients and funders may need and deserve to know whether an intervention is working, whether or not any program theory is tested. Alternatively, there may be an abundance of different theories, and it may be difficult to decide which of the competing theories should guide the evaluation (assuming that practical constraints will preclude a reasonable test of them all). Moreover, as Cook noted at the symposium, even the "official" program theory may change over time. In addition, evaluators are often brought in too late to help develop program theory as a guide to measurement and evaluation design.

Despite these potential problems, I believe the theory-driven approach has achieved enough successes to have earned a place in the total toolkit of evaluation approaches. Again, the question is, how big a place and under what conditions?

STAKEHOLDER INCLUSION AS A COMMONPLACE FEATURE OF EVALUATION PRACTICE

Stakeholders now represent one of the major sources of information in developing logic models and program theory. This emphasis on stakeholders as a source of guidance represents a distinct change from much of evaluation practice of decades ago, when explicit program goals were used almost exclusively to define criteria of success, and when only the funder and/or some official decision maker were thought of as evaluation users. Stakeholder-based evaluation approaches grew largely out of a concern for use, based on an assumption that if stakeholders are involved throughout in guiding an evaluation, they will be more likely to use the findings (Weiss, 1983).

More recently there has been a large and noteworthy trend in evaluation theory and practice toward a very high level of stakeholder participation. This work has occurred largely under the labels of empowerment and participatory evaluation. The visions of David Fetterman, Donna Mertens, and Yvonna Lincoln, although distinct in many important ways, all share this perspective. All of these visions give a central emphasis to stakeholder participation in evaluation. This central focus on stakeholders in a vision of evaluation can be contrasted with other, earlier approaches that tended to describe evaluation largely in terms of methods or purpose (e.g., fairly or not, Campbell, 1969, with his emphasis on experimental and quasi-experimental methods is often seen as representing an emphasis on methods, while Scriven (1967), with his classic distinction between formative and summative, is often seen as emphasizing evaluation purpose).

Whatever conception of stakeholder involvement underlies an evaluation, the very fact of stakeholder involvement raises some challenges. In general terms, these include: deciding which stakeholder groups to include; selecting and involving representatives of those groups; deciding which aspects of evaluation planning, design, implementation, analysis, and interpretation to involve stakeholders in; dealing with the practical problems of stakeholder involvement, such as when stakeholders fail to do planned evaluation work because they have other pressing demands (Schnoes et al., 2000); and somehow merging diverse stakeholder views. In addition, if some stakeholder groups rather than others are asked to participate, there may be a bias toward some kinds of evaluation activities and not others (e.g., program staff may tend to prefer formative evaluation work). Accordingly, Mertens talks about inclusiveness as a form of bias control (though of course it is not the *only* form of bias control).

Two additional, related problems appear to me to characterize the views of some empowerment and participatory evaluators. One is the seeming belief that, with adequate craft, evaluation should in fact lead to achievement of empowerment or transformation. From my perspective, although it may well be desirable to help support empowerment or transformation, it is also important not to presume that stakeholders can and will be empowered and transformed simply because of evaluation activities. As we all know, the world is complex, change often not easy, major change often slow in coming, and evaluation only part of the picture. Moreover, don't stakeholders have a right to choose to ignore us -- to remain untransformed? Can't evaluation be worthwhile, even if it contributes to modest, incremental improvements to the human condition, rather than to transformation?

A second problematic position seems to be held by *some* who march behind the participatory and empowerment banners. I am referring to the apparent belief that other evaluation approaches, those that do not equally emphasize empowerment and participation, are inappropriate and even morally wrong. I should strongly emphasize that, sadly, such thinking is hardly unique to the adherents of participatory approaches. To the contrary, it may be that parallel beliefs are equally held by those who march behind different banners[2].

---

[2]It can, however, seem more *ironic* when evaluators who espouse inclusion, empowerment, and participation would like to exclude, disempower, and see no participation by evaluators who hold different views.

Let me also emphasize that I am not saying that all (or even most) advocates of empowerment and participatory evaluation (or any other approach) take these views. Nor am I attributing these views to the contributors to this volume or to any other developers of the approaches in question. Theory developers are often quite aware of the limits of their preferred approaches. As an example, David Fetterman, seen widely as an unfailing advocate of empowerment evaluation, recently discussed why he did an important evaluation that did not follow the empowerment model (Fetterman, 2000; Fitzpatrick, 2000). But I am not sure that all empowerment and participatory evaluators would be so open to other approaches. Those who come to an approach often have less complex views and are more zealous than those who originate the approach.

My belief that this problem exists is based on what many would call anecdotal evidence. It comes from seeing journal submissions that not only advocate a position, but also (explicitly or implicitly) denigrate other positions as morally deficient. It comes too from comments at and after conference presentations, from the implicit messages of some published papers and books, and from private conversations. I hesitate to raise the issue, not simply because it can seem alarmist, but also because it can easily be misconstrued as a personal attack or unfair stereotyping. On the other hand, the personal, intellectual, and practice consequences of the paradigm war were nontrivial. So it seems to me that we should not ignore this potential problem, but should try to avoid future specious warfare in evaluation, for ourselves, the field, and those affected by the evaluations.

To reiterate, the problem I am pointing to here, what I believe is to be feared, is zealous commitment to a vision that privileges one evaluation approach while denigrating others. What I fear is that some evaluators are increasingly inclined to disparage other approaches on moral grounds, ignoring the variety of niches where different kinds of evaluation may quite appropriately fit. I have heard some participatory and empowerment evaluators, for instance, suggest that the kind of performance measurement that Joe Wholey discussed is inappropriate and perhaps intrinsically immoral (unless, perhaps, it is the result of decisions made by program clients). Although, as I noted previously, there are challenges for performance measurement systems, there are also reasonable uses. Moreover, we live in a mixed model democracy, with (what most people view as) duly elected representatives and duly appointed officials, and I find nothing immoral in trying to serve their information needs. Conversely, I have heard some quantitatively oriented evaluators disparage participatory and empowerment approaches as technically wanting and as less than evaluation. But most of us also believe in deliberative democracy, which these approaches can perhaps facilitate. And Donna Mertens reminds us that, without inclusiveness, the indicators that are chosen in any evaluation may be deficient. In short, exaggerated dismissiveness of evaluation approaches other than one's own seems to be based on a supersized version of what social psychologists would call ingroup-outgroup bias, rather than on any thoughtful analysis of the strengths and weaknesses and the appropriate range of application of each approach.

To me, then, the more nightmarish prospect suggested by the previous chapters lies, not within any vision, but looking *across* the visions.

BEYOND THE PARADIGM WARS?

There seems to be a decline in papers about the so-called paradigm war in evaluation journals and conferences. One could take this optimistically as a sign that perhaps evaluators have heeded Ernie House's (1994) suggestion that we should get beyond the perceived paradigm dichotomies and instead *do* evaluation. But at the conference on which this volume is based there were strong echoes of the paradigm wars, if not an outright resumption. Yvonna Lincoln revisited what seemed to be the same constructivist philosophy presented in *Fourth Generation Evaluation* (Guba & Lincoln, 1989), and Donna Mertens seemed to declare randomized experiments an immoral methodology. Tom Cook then responded with a description of evaluation in his world, which was in stark contrast to the depictions of Lincoln and Mertens (e.g., Cook highlighted the importance of evaluations that use random experiments or quasi-experiments to estimate the effects of social and educational programs).

Whether this exchange was an anomaly or not, whatever peace has been achieved in the paradigm wars remains an uneasy peace. Thus, there remains some need to try to identify positions that provide comfortable homes that avoid the extremities of the paradigm wars. I happen to think that a suitable home can be found in a kind of eclectic, mostly commonsense realism, integrated with an appreciation of the importance— and limits—of human sensemaking. Elsewhere I have tried to contribute to such a position (Mark et al., 2000). Not all will agree with this specific variant, but finding alternatives to the extremes of the paradigm wars remains important.

Still, even if common-sense realism, sensemaking, or another position comes to be seen as a peaceful haven amidst the extremes of the paradigm wars, it would not necessarily mean that a long peace is at hand. Looking across the chapters, one can perhaps hear the rumblings of future wars, developing perhaps from the paradigm wars but drawn along somewhat different lines. A possible dividing line for future battles may involve evaluators' views of the role of stakeholder involvement in evaluation. Some approaches—represented in varying ways in the visions of Lincoln, Mertens, and Fetterman—take stakeholder involvement both as necessary and as an intrinsic good. Others—again, represented in different ways in the visions of Scriven, Donaldson, Wholey and, I would add, Cook—seem to see stakeholder participation as beneficial, but not always necessary, and as instrumental to other evaluation activities and to evaluation use, rather than as an intrinsic good. In addition, the first set of approaches emphasize stakeholder process, while the second emphasizes evaluation findings.

Related dividing lines also exist that alternatively could come to define the sides in "Paradigm War II." One is between those who tend to see evaluation as local and interpersonal and those who tend to see it as national and policy related. Another closely related distinction can be made between those who take the goal of evaluation to be enhancing bounded practitioner wisdom versus those who take the goal to be generating generalizable knowledge about program and policy effectiveness (Schwandt, 2000 and Lipsey, 2000a, 2000b, respectively).

What is most troubling is not that there are divergent views on these and related issues. Instead, what is distressing, what suggests a nightmarish vision for the future of evaluation is that too many partisans on each side seem very ready to see the other position as inherently flawed, as intellectually defective, and as morally bankrupt. Too many advocates make it sound as though their preferred approach is suitable for all (or almost all) of evaluation practice, and that other approaches should be forever banned.[3] The resulting nightmare is that what should be a field, or profession, or transdiscipline of evaluation will become ever more fractionated, with many evaluators avoiding organizations such as the American Evaluation Association because these groups are seen as inhospitable to the person's preferred view of evaluation. The nightmare also is of opportunities lost, of programs and policies whose evaluations are shoe-horned into the evaluator's narrowly held vision of evaluation.

---

[3]Admittedly, I may here be guilty of the same kind of overstatement I am complaining about. Thoughtful advocates do often discuss the conditions under which their preferred approaches are appropriate (e.g., see Shadish et al., 2001, especially chapter 8, on the conditions supportive of randomized experiments). Nevertheless, overadvocacy seems to be the rule rather than the exception, especially when evaluators consider alternative approaches other than the one they personally espouse.

BEWARE LARGE DEFAULT OPTIONS IN EVALUATION VISIONS/THEORIES/APPROACHES

Visions of the future, like theories, can offer many benefits. They can help focus our attention on what is important, they can motivate, they can guide. But, as noted in the earlier discussion of the theory-driven approach to evaluation, theories hold potential disadvantages as well. In fact, there are entire literatures, including an extensive literature in psychology, which can be viewed as warnings about the potential dysfunctions of theories, visions, expectations, and the like. Theories can serve as blinders. They can greatly constrain what we do, how we look at the world, and therefore how we see the world. This is potentially true of theories *of* evaluation, which in a sense is what the visions offered earlier in this book are.

Of course, the better and more correct a theory is, the more the benefits outweigh the costs. This leads to the question: How correct are our evaluation theories? Let's consider the domain to which these theories are meant to apply. The world of evaluation practice is complex, diverse, with multiple arenas of application, varying types of possible users, and differing evaluation purposes. Almost certainly, many different ways of doing evaluation—or if you prefer—many different types of evaluation-related services are appropriate in different circumstances. Yet evaluation theories often seem to come with large "default options," where this term refers to explicit or implicit assumptions about how wide a range of circumstances a given evaluation approach is suitable. Evaluation theories, or visions, differ somewhat in this regard, but overall the default options within evaluation theories generally seem fairly large. In particular, most visions in this volume involve strong advocacy of one approach, with little if any attention to the likely boundary conditions under which some other approach should be practiced instead.[4] In addition, as noted above, the "disciples" who follow an evaluation approach sometimes are less sensitive to possible boundary conditions than are the people who actually develop and originally espouse those views.

---

[4]Wholey's presentation is atypical in this respect, first, because he discusses the role of evaluation activities other than those he is advocating and, second, because he explicitly acknowledges some uncertainty about the worth of his position. He indicates that his "assessment of evidence to date, from different levels of government and from nonprofit organizations, suggests that results-oriented management holds great promise, but that its ultimate value is still uncertain" (p 58).

Overadvocacy is often a natural part of the process of advocacy. Changing practice is not easy, and often requires a persistent sales effort. Psychologists at least since Festinger (1957) also would tell us that people often become highly committed to things, including presumably evaluation theories, for which they have worked hard. In addition, people often become convinced of the widespread value of an evaluation approach based on limited information. They may assess the value of their preferred approach based on what they see in front of their noses (much as program staff often become convinced of the value of their activities). Evaluators who conduct a Brand X evaluation may see benefits that arise after the evaluation. But the Brand X evaluator does not see the benefits that would have accrued if some other approach to evaluation had been followed, or even what level of improvement might have occurred without any evaluation at all. And the Brand X evaluator may have a biased view of the evidence of the evaluation's benefits, in any case. In short, then, the processes that lead to large default options within any evaluation theory or vision are fairly natural and perhaps pervasive.

Nevertheless, to think that one approach to evaluation suffices for all situations is akin to thinking that one type of social service will fit all social problems or that one type of therapy will work for all types of psychological problems. We would be aghast at program developers who held to such notions, but many evaluators appear to hold this idea when it comes to evaluation. Instead, we need to be multilingual as evaluators. We need to develop, debate, test, and refine theories (or visions) of evaluation that will help guide judgments about the conditions under which different ways of doing evaluation are appropriate.

BEYOND ADVOCACY OF DIFFERENT EVALUATION APPROACHES: SORTING AND INTEGRATING

For the most part, the previous visionaries portrayed the future with a single evaluation approach at center stage. Let me briefly offer a different kind of vision of evaluation, an alternative future. In that future we will have made progress in categorizing the vast number of choices that exist for evaluation. We will have thoughtfully discussed and studied the circumstances under which different approaches bring about various benefits. We will have developed and tried out useful and usable integrative models to help guide choices. And we will have made progress in ways to present, fairly and openly, the array of evaluation approaches to stakeholders and other evaluation users.

The history of evaluation has already seen several noteworthy attempts to develop integrative approaches. Shadish, Cook, and Leviton (1990), in their review of several major evaluation theorists' work, cite in particular Cronbach and Rossi as examples. According to Shadish et al. (1990), Cronbach and Rossi stand out among a group of evaluation scholars who attempted to focus on "the synthesis of work from preceding stages.... [and see] that the legitimacy of a method or a concept depends upon the circumstances" (p. 315). Despite the historical significance of these and other integrative theorists of evaluation, much of the more recent swell of evaluation theory has been nonintegrative. Many theorists attempt or at least claim to stake out new ground, and often seem to claim that their preferred approach will fit all potential evaluation needs.

Despite this trend, there have also been several recent attempts to try to sort at least some portion of the growing catalog of evaluation approaches and methods. For example, Cousins and Whitmore (1998) have tried to categorize different participatory approaches. Stufflebeam (2001) has offered his own assessment of some 22 approaches to evaluation. Elsewhere, my colleagues Gary Henry and George Julnes and I have tried to articulate a framework for classifying and choosing from among an array of different evaluation approaches (Mark et al., 2000).

We suggest that the selection of an evaluation purpose should follow from a thoughtful assessment, including stakeholders' perspectives, of the nature of the policy environment. In some instances, for example, the program that is to be evaluated is experiencing a stable policy environment. An extreme example is the state of Georgia's pre-kindergarten program, which by an amendment to the state constitution receives priority for state lottery revenues. With this constitutional mandate, the Pre-K program is virtually guaranteed continuation in the foreseeable future. Accordingly, an evaluation with the purpose of assessing merit and worth would effectively be moot for the Georgians funding the evaluation; in contrast, evaluation activities directed toward program and organizational improvement would likely be more helpful. Other programs and policies are in a policy environment that can be characterized as competitive. At a given historical moment, alternative courses of action may receive serious consideration. At times in the United States, for example, options have seriously been considered for the funding of primary and secondary education (e.g., vouchers). In a competitive policy environment such as this, assessment of merit and worth would generally rise to the top as the primary evaluation purpose. (see Mark et al., 2000, for additional discussion of the possible relationship between the policy environment and evaluation purpose, including two additional primary purposes, first, oversight and compliance and, second, knowledge development).

Having selected an evaluation purpose, one can then attempt to select methods that would serve that purpose. As an aid in planning, Mark et al. suggest that evaluation methods can for the most part be categorized as falling within one (or, in some cases, more) of four *inquiry modes*. Inquiry modes are clusters or functional groupings of methods that have evolved to support people's various natural sensemaking capacities. For example, the methods of causal inquiry have evolved to probe causal relations, and thereby support people's natural tendency to make causal inferences. The methods of another inquiry mode, classification, have been created to study groupings (e.g., of program clients into different types); accordingly, classification methods extend and support the natural human tendency to categorize objects. (Mark et al. describe two other inquiry modes, description and values inquiry).

Inquiry modes, Mark et al. claim, can be arrayed in terms of how well, on average, they serve a given evaluation purpose. Assume, for example, that the purpose of an evaluation is to assess the merit and worth of a social program. Given this purpose, the question of impact, of the program's effects, is often central. For instance, in evaluating a preschool program, people care about whether the program improves children's subsequent academic performance and persistence in school and, more generally, has positive effects but not negative ones. Given the centrality of such causal questions, methods of causal inquiry will typically do better when the purpose is to assess the merit and worth of a program. Notice, however, that this does not hold for all types of evaluation; in personnel evaluation, for example, the key issue may be measurement of a person's knowledge, skills, and abilities. Also notice that, even if causal methods would be the best way of evaluating a program, this does not mean that it is the only possible way. In fact, Mark et al. (2000) also encourage evaluators and stakeholders to consider the level of confidence and the quality of evidence that is required in a particular case. Less than ideal methods often suffice, but evaluators have generally lacked any guidelines (other than budget) for trying to judge how good is good enough in a particular situation (see Mark et al., 2000, pp. 92 - 93 for some tentative guidelines).

This presentation of the Mark et al. (2000) framework is necessarily cursory and incomplete. The point, however, is simply that evaluators can and should be involved in developing, using, and refining frameworks that (1) provide some taxonomy of different evaluation approaches and (2) help to guide considered judgments about what approach to use in a particular context. Ideally, such frameworks can help avoid premature and overgeneralized dismissal of those options that are not an evaluator's personal first choice. Divergent opinions are still to be expected across evaluators. Perhaps, however, disagreement can be about how wide the conditions are under which some approach is useful, rather than involving the intellectualized version of "your mother wears army boots."

SOME SUGGESTIONS TOWARD FURTHER INTEGRATION

It is relatively easy to identify the risk of further fractionation in the field and to call for us all to try to avoid it. Of course, it may not be so easy to actually avoid the problem. Let me offer some additional suggestions as to how we might move toward an integrated and integrative field of evaluation.

I have already made one suggestion, that as evaluators we should increase the esteem we give to evaluation theories that attempt to specify the conditions under which different approaches to evaluation are appropriate. Correspondingly, we should be somewhat wary of an evaluation theory that advances one approach without setting out likely boundary conditions.

Second, those in "gatekeeper" positions and those asked to evaluate work on evaluation can play a role in trying to foster integrative approaches. The people I am thinking of include our journal editors, reviewers for journals, those asked to review book prospectuses and draft manuscripts, discussants at conference sessions, and so on. People in these and similar roles can try to shape discourse away from universal claims of the moral and practical superiority of specific approaches. They can try to increase discussion of the conditions under which an evaluation approach is more versus less appropriate. They can try to reduce "straw person" and other inappropriate forms of critique of views other than one's own. I am not calling for ideas to be censored, but would simply have us encourage those advocates who are moralistically or simplistically disparaging of alternative approaches to reconsider.

Third, we can try to increase the extent to which attention is given to actual evaluation practice. Datta (2001), among others, has suggested that what can seem to be gaping divides between evaluation theories may shrink considerably when you examine actual practice. That is, Datta suggests, the actual evaluations carried out under different banners may look a lot more similar than you would think from the rhetoric of the theoretical books and articles. If we try to examine the actual practice differences associated with different approaches, rather than focusing on the rhetorical flourishes of theoretical statements, it may be easier to discuss differences collegially—and if Datta is correct, we may be surprised to learn that the differences are less than we might otherwise believe. In a sense, this recommendation echoes that of House (1994) concerning the qualitative-quantitative debate.

Fourth, integrative approaches may be more likely to flourish if we can increase the amount of research *on* evaluation. It appears that most of the effort expended on evaluation consists of people actually doing evaluation. This is fitting, of course. But it appears that the second most common type of work, and perhaps the kind that fills most of our books and many of our journals, consists of theoretical exposition and advocacy. Such work has an important role, of course, but a case can be made that we will not have achieved much more improvement in evaluation theory until we have a more sound evidence base for theory development (Shadish et al., 1990). A third kind of work also appears in the literature, and provides some evidence about the effectiveness of specific evaluation practices. This kind of work, a staple of several evaluation journals, is a sort of post-hoc case study. In these papers, the single evaluation study is offered up as the basis for one or more recommendations about how to (or how not to) do evaluation. Although this is a useful kind of scholarship, it is often limited by use of a single case, by limited data collection related to the author's recommendations (which often emerge over the course of the evaluation or at its end), and by a bias toward claiming and reporting successes rather than failures.

Most other kinds of research on evaluation are rare. Rare are evaluations that purposively and prospectively set up alternative methods to compare (though some important examples exist, e.g., Greene & McClintock, 1985). Rare too are studies that systematically compare findings, retrospectively, across different types of evaluation (though, again, noteworthy examples exist, e.g., Droitcour, Silberman, & Chelimsky, 1993). Also rare are studies that attempt to track use as a function of the evaluation approach. If we could increase the amount of research on evaluation, there would be an additional basis for supporting or refuting some of the theoretical claims that otherwise divide us. That is, research findings rather than rhetoric alone may become part of how we try to answer disputes. And evidence (e.g., on the acceptability and effectiveness of different evaluation approaches) would most likely help put the brakes on overstated claims of near-limitless applicability for any specific approach.

Of course, making research on evaluation more commonplace may not be so easy. We may need to lobby foundations and funding agencies to provide support. We may need editorial policies that encourage such work. And even if we can increase the amount of research on evaluation, this will not magically resolve all our disputes. Any empirically based area of scholarship has disputes, new and old. In evaluation, this would include disputes about what the proper criteria are for judging the success of an evaluation. And evaluators of different persuasions may even disagree, perhaps strongly, about how much can be resolved by evidence. But evidence, even if imperfect, even if based on criteria about which we do not all agree, would probably represent a major advance over the current basis for dialogue among adherents of different evaluation approaches. In addition, evaluators of any persuasion ought to be able to talk about how their preferred approach to evaluation could at least in principle be adapted for *its own* evaluation. I believe that such discussions would help clarify the limitations of single approaches and might highlight complementarities across approaches. In turn, this could encourage discussions about the possibility of more integrative views of evaluation.

Moreover, the goal is not to smother all disputes within the field. Disagreements can spur advances. But this kind of creative and stimulating debate will not happen if we split into homogeneous subsets of like-minded evaluators. At the very least, wide proliferation of research on evaluation would give us a basis for debating other than an intellectualized version of name calling.

Thus, my fifth recommendation is that we need to continue to do the things that foster what Campbell (1984) has called the "disputatious community of scholars." According to this perspective, in evaluation we probably need more criticism of each other's work, not less, but also more focused criticism. This is consistent with the calls that Scriven and others have repeatedly made for more meta-evaluation. As another example, Campbell (1984) suggests that we should encourage minority reports from members of multiple investigator evaluation teams. We also need to encourage a more cumulative approach to scholarship in evaluation. Many evaluation reports read as though there has never been another evaluation of a similar program. Published scholarship in evaluation often seems to rely more on claims that "I have something new here" rather than "I've accomplished a modest but worthwhile modification of the line of work carried out by numerous predecessors." Some change in our norms could set the stage for a more cumulative approach within the evaluation community (Lipsey, 2001).

In principle, the disputatious community of evaluation scholars can bring about the kind of integrative approaches I recommended earlier. This community would help set the procedures for argument and evidence. It is largely in this community where disputes would be played out about how valuable each evaluation approach is under various conditions. The disputatious community of scholars would also help carry out the other recommendations I have made. This community would, for example, include the people who carry out, review, read and critique research on evaluation—and this would certainly not be limited to academics![5]

To avoid a potential misinterpretation, let me emphasize that "disputatious" does not necessarily mean hostile. To the contrary, some reasonable level of civility is probably necessary to maintain a community. Perhaps it seems obvious, but we should not offer our colleagues less respect and consideration than we offer the stakeholders with whom we work. Nor should we take reasonable criticism of our work badly. After all, collegial criticism is one of the main mechanisms through which our work can improve (Campbell, 1984).

Some readers may still be doubtful about the possibility of fragmentation in the evaluation field. Some readers may be doubtful of the need for further work to develop more integrative theories of evaluation, with more nuanced views of the conditions under which different approaches are most appropriate. Some readers, pleased with the community of evaluators to which they belong, may question the need for additional efforts to try to build, maintain and enhance the disputatious community of evaluation scholars. To these readers, I ask you to keep in mind that there already are many evaluators out there who belong to different and distinct communities. It is not a new observation to point out that there are evaluators, many of them for example in economics, health care, and policy analysis, who do not belong to the same community as most AEA members, despite a shared focus on evaluation. In some cases, they have sampled the offerings of our community and found them wanting. This is, I believe, a "leading indicator" of the potential problems I have cited. In addition, take for a moment the optimistic perspective that (as I hope) my fears of further fragmentation are unfounded. Even under this rosy scenario, more efforts at integration and community building would be desirable to try to increase the number of evaluators who come into a larger evaluation community. In addition, further efforts at integration are also needed so that we can provide evaluation funders and stakeholders with a reasonable and relatively clear menu of options, rather than having their choices unduly constrained by the predilections of whatever evaluator they happen to find.

---

[5]The evaluation market, that is funders and stakeholders, can also have a voice in adjudicating these disputes, of course. At present, however, we probably do too bad a job of laying out the options to expect the market to be making informed choices overall. Also note that in this discussion of the "disputatious community of scholars" I am borrowing from some parts of the sociology of science literature, ignoring other parts, while simplifying that literature greatly.

SYSTEMATIC VALUES INQUIRY

One more change might be beneficial in moving the field toward more integrative perspectives. This change, which involves the way we think of stakeholder participation, is also, I believe, worthwhile in its own right.

As noted previously, there has been a major shift toward stakeholder involvement, at some level or another, in evaluation. At a minimum, the thoughtful inclusion of stakeholders keeps evaluation from representing only the values of a sponsor or program developer—or evaluator. But stakeholder involvement, as noted above, has limits. Two of these are particularly troubling, and lead me to the suggestion that stakeholder involvement should evolve into systematic values inquiry.

First, the conceptualization of stakeholders should be broadened to include the public in the case of most major social policies and programs. The public is typically omitted from lists when stakeholders are called to the evaluation table. This is an oversight that can be remedied, for example, with survey methods to assess public opinion concerning what things are more (or less) valued as criteria for the success of a major program. Of course, public opinion may be diverse, split along ideological or political lines, and this can make it hard to translate public opinion into action or interpretation. But this is already a problem when other stakeholders are included, and is no reason to disenfranchise the public at the evaluation table.

Second, change is called for in apparently common practice of treating stakeholder involvement as an unreported (or only minimally reported) part of evaluation process. Mark et al. (2000) contend that stakeholder input should not be viewed as a behind-the-scenes aspect of evaluation process, but as systematic values inquiry with the methods and findings fully reported. When details of methods, analysis, and results are presented, there is a kind of transparency that allows others to make judgments about the conclusions reached and about any actions based on them. Such transparency is a prerequisite for accountability. A variety of systematic methods can be used to study the value stances associated with different groups, including surveys, focus groups and, where appropriate, systematic methods to try to simulate and stimulate deliberative processes. For all of these, methods and findings can be explicitly reported, allowing a variety of interested parties to make judgments about the appropriateness of the decisions based on stakeholder input. It is probably overly optimistic, but thinking about stakeholder participation at least in part as reportable values inquiry might help bridge the gap between the two different views of stakeholder participation described previously.

CONCLUSIONS

The practice of evaluation has an important and seemingly growing role in democracies, in nonprofits, and in the private sector. Those who provided visions to this book have been among the most important contributors to the ongoing development of evaluation. Their visions deserve our careful consideration. These visions can help propel evaluation even further and enhance its contribution. But, whether or not the visionaries intended it that way, it is easy to read most of the visions as though they give a central place to one evaluation approach in the future. There are many possible explanations for this apparent overadvocacy. One possible reason is that the visionaries are overly influenced by what they see every day—which includes the successes and importance of their own preferred approach to evaluation, but not of alternative, nonpreferred approaches. The resulting overadvocacy, along with the associated large default options in most of the visions, raises the specter of a nightmarish vision. In this nightmare scenario, integration of different evaluation choices does not occur; evaluation clients are not given a full range of choices but are unduly restricted by the predilections of the evaluator; the field splinters off more rather than coalescing into a larger and more influential professional association; and, consequently, evaluators' visions become even more influenced by their limited sight, because they no longer can learn from those who take a different approach.

Desirable visions can inspire and guide. Undesirable visions can also motivate, stimulating action to avoid the unwanted future. An impressive set of evaluators have shared their visions in this book. May we all be wise in how we see fit to translate them into action.

REFERENCES

Campbell, D. T. (1969). Reforms as experiments. *American Psychologist, 24,* 409-429.

Campbell, D. T. (1984). Can we be scientific in applied social science? In R. F. Connor, D. G. Altman, & C. Jackson (Eds.), *Evaluation studies review annual* (No. 9, pp. 26-48). Thousand Oaks, CA: Sage.

Chen, H. T. (1990). *Theory-driven evaluations.* Thousand Oaks, CA: Sage.

Cousins, J. B. & Whitmore, E. (1998). Framing participatory evaluation. In E. Whitmore (Ed.), *Understanding and practicing participatory evaluation* (New Directions for Evaluation, No. 80). San Francisco: Jossey Bass.

Cronbach, L. J. (1982). *Designing evaluations of educational and social programs.* San Francisco: Jossey-Bass.

Datta, L. E. (2001). Coming attractions. *American Journal of Evaluation, 22*, 403-408.

Donaldson, S. I., & Chen, H. T. (2002). *Theory-driven program evaluation: State of the art.* Manuscript under review.

Donaldson, S. I., Graham, J. W., Piccinin, A. M., & Hansen, W. B. (1995). Resistance-skills training and onset of alcohol use: Evidence for beneficial and potentially harmful effects in public schools and in private Catholic schools. *Health Psychology, 14*, 291-300.

Droitcour, J., Silberman, G., & Chelimsky, E. (1993). Cross-design synthesis: A new form of meta-analysis for combining results from randomized clinical trials and medial-practice databases. *International Journal of Technology Assessment in Health Care, 9*, 440-449.

Festinger, L. (1957). *A theory of cognitive dissonance.* Stanford, CA: Stanford University Press.

Fetterman, D. (2000). Summary of the STEP evaluation. *American Journal of Evaluation, 21*, 239-241.

Fitzpatrick, J. (2000). Dialogue with David Fetterman. *American Journal of Evaluation, 21*, 242-259.

Greene, J. G. & McClintock, C. (1985). Triangulation in evaluation: Design and analysis issues. *Evaluation Review, 9*, 523-545.

Greenwald, A. G., Pratkanis, A. R., Leippe, M. R., & Baumgardner, M. H. (1986). Under what conditions does theory obstruct research progress? *Psychological Bulletin, 93*, 216-229.

Guba, E. G., & Lincoln, Y. S. (1989). *Fourth generation evaluation.* Thousand Oaks, CA: Sage.

House, E. R. (1994). Integrating the qualitative and the quantitative. In C. S. Reichardt & S. F. Rallis (Eds.), *The qualitative-quantitative debate: New perspectives* (New Directions for Program Evaluation, No. 61). San Francisco: Jossey-Bass.

Lipsey, M. W. (2000a). Meta-evaluation and the learning curve in evaluation practice. *American Journal of Evaluation, 20*, 207-212.

Lipsey, M. W. (2000b). Method and rationality are not social diseases. *American Journal of Evaluation, 20*, 221-224.

Lipsey, M. W. (2001). Re: Unsolved problems and unfinished business. *American Journal of Evaluation, 21*, 325 -328.

Mark, M. M. (1990). From program theory to tests of program theory. In L. Bickman (Ed.), *Advances in program theory* (New Directions for Program Evaluation, No. 47, pp. 37-51). San Francisco: Jossey-Bass.

Mark, M. M., Henry, G.T., & Julnes, G. (2000). *Evaluation: An integrated framework for understanding, guiding, and improving policies and programs.* San Francisco: Jossey-Bass.

Newcomer, K. E. (Ed.) (1997). *Using performance measurement to improve public and nonprofit programs* (New Directions for Evaluation, No. 75). San Francisco: Jossey-Bass.

Perrin, B. (1998). Effective use and misuse of performance measurement. *American Journal of Evaluation, 19*, 367-379.

Schnoes, C. J., Murphey-Berman, V., & Chambers, J. M. (2000). Empowerment evaluation applied: Experiences, analysis, and recommendations from a case study. *American Journal of Evaluation, 21,* 53-64.

Scriven, M. S. (1967). The methodology of evaluation. In R. W. Tyler, R. M. Gagne, & M. S. Scriven (Eds.), *Perspectives of curriculum evaluation* (AERA Monograph Series on Curriculum Evaluation, No. 1, pp. 39-83). Skokie, IL: Rand McNally.

Shadish, W. R., Cook, T. D., & Leviton, L. C. (1990). *Foundations of program evaluation: Theories of practice.* Newbury Park, CA: Sage.

Shadish, W.R., Cook, T.D., & Campbell, D.T. (2001). *Experimental and quasi-experimental designs for generalized causal inference.* Boston: Houghton-Mifflin.

Schwandt, T. A. (2000). Meta-analysis and everyday life: The good, the bad, and the ugly. *American Journal of Evaluation, 20,* 213-219.

Stufflebeam, D. L. (2001). *Evaluation models* (New Directions for Evaluation, No. 89). San Francisco: Jossey-Bass.

Weiss, C. H. (1983). The stakeholder approach to evaluation: Origins and promise. In A. S. Bryk (Ed.), *Stakeholder-based evaluation* (New Directions for Program Evaluation, No. 17, pp. 3-14). San Francisco: Jossey-Bass.

Yeh, S. S. (2000). Improving educational and social programs: A planned variation cross-validation model. *American Journal of Evaluation, 21,* 171-184.

ABOUT THE CONTRIBUTORS

Dr. Thomas D. Cook is Professor of Sociology, Psychology, Education and Social Policy Faculty Fellow, Institute for Policy Research, North-western University. One of Dr. Cook's major research interests is examining routes out of poverty, especially for racial minorities in the inner city, with special emphasis on how material and social resources activate self-help activities. A second line of research is methodological, dealing with the design and execution of social experiments, methods for promoting causal generalization and theories of evaluation practice. Dr. Cook has written or edited seven books and published numerous articles and book chapters. He received the Myrdal Prize for Science from the Evaluation Research Society in 1982 and the Donald Campbell Prize for Innovative Methodology from the Policy Sciences Organization in 1988. He is a trustee of the Russell Sage Foundation and a member of its Committee on the Future of Work. Dr. Cook was elected to the American Academy of Arts and Sciences in 2000.

Dr. William D. Crano is Professor of Psychology at Claremont Graduate University. He has served as the Program Director in Social Psychology for the National Science Foundation, as a Liason Scientist for the Office of Naval Research, London, as NATO Senior Scientist, University of Southampton, and was a Fulbright Fellow to the Federal University-Rio Grande do Sul, porto Alegre, Brazil. Dr. Crano was the founder/director of the Center for Evaluation and Assessment, Michigan State University, and directed the Public Policy Resources Laboratory of Texas A & M University. Crano has written 10 books, more than 20 book chapters, and more than 200 scholarly articles and scientific presentations. He is the past president of the Society for Experimental Social Psychology, and is a Fellow of the American Psychological Association, the American Psychological Society, and the Society for Personality and Social Psychology.

Dr. Stewart I. Donaldson is Professor and Chair of Psychology, Director of the Institute of Organizational and Program Evaluation Research, and Dean of the School of Behavioral and Organizational Sciences, Claremont Graduate University. He has taught numerous courses and published widely on the topic of evaluation in workplaces, schools, communities, and human service organizations. Dr. Donaldson has developed one of the largest graduate training programs in evaluation at Claremont Graduate University. He has served as Co-Chair of the Theory-Driven Evaluation and Program Theory topical interest group of the American Evaluation Association (AEA), is on the Editorial Boards of the *American Journal of Evaluation* and *New Directions for Evaluation*, and is or has been principal investigator on numerous evaluation grants and contracts. Dr. Donaldson was a 1996 recipient of the AEA's Marcia Guttentag Early Career Achievement Award, in recognition of his work on theory and method and for accomplishments in teaching and practice of evaluation. In 2001, he was honored with Western Psychological Association's Outstanding Research Award, an early career achievement award given to a scientist younger than 40 working in the Western United States or Canada.

Dr. David M. Fetterman is a member of the faculty and the Director of the MA Policy Analysis and Evaluation Program in the School of Education at Stanford University. He was formerly Professor and Research Director at the California Institute of Integral Studies; Principal Research Scientist at the American Institutes for Research; and a Senior Associate and Project Director at RMC Research Corporation. He received his Ph.D. from Stanford University in educational and medical anthropology. He has conducted fieldwork in both Israel (including living on a kibbutz) and the United States (primarily in inner-cities across the country). Dr. Fetterman works in the fields of educational evaluation, ethnography, policy analysis, and focuses on programs for dropouts and gifted and talented education.

Dr. Bianca L. Guzmán is a community psychologist with research interests in women's reproductive health issues. As the co-founder and current Director of Research of CHOICES, a community-based non-profit organization serving ethnic teens in the Los Angeles area, Dr. Guzmán has implemented numerous programs to increase instances of safe sexual behavior and healthy parenting skills among adolescents. She has been a postdoctoral-fellow at the National Institute of Health, and has a long-standing history of grantsmanship with national, state, and local funding agencies. She is an active member in The Society for Community

Action and Research (Division 27 of the American Psychological Association), and was recently co-editor of a special issue of *The Community Psychologist* focusing on women's health issues.

Dr. Yvonna S. Lincoln is Ruth Harrington Chair of Educational Leadership and University Distinguished Professor of Higher Education at Texas A&M University. She is the co-author of *Effective Evaluation* (1981), *Naturalistic Inquiry* (1985), and *Fourth Generation Evaluation* (1989); the editor of *Organizational Theory and Inquiry* (1985), and the co-editor of several other books, including the *Handbook of Qualitative Research*, 1st and 2nd Editions (1994; 2000), and the 4-volume set, *The American Tradition in Qualitative Research* (2001). She is also the author of more than 200 journal articles, book chapters, and conference papers. Her major interests lie in program evaluation in higher education and in qualitative research methods. She is the current co-editor of the bimonthly journal, *Qualitative Inquiry*, and has pioneered work in constructivist evaluation models, and qualitative research and evaluation work which promotes more democratic forms of stakeholder participation, wider social inclusion, and utilization-oriented evaluation practices.

Dr. Melvin M. Mark is Professor of Psychology and Senior Scientist at the Institute for Policy Research and Evaluation at Penn State. He is currently Editor of the *American Journal of Evaluation*. His written work in evaluation involves such topics as the role of stakeholders, systematic values inquiry, mixed methods, quasi-experimental design, and the development of a realist theory of evaluation. He has been involved in evaluations in a number of areas, including prevention programs for at-risk youth, federal personnel policies, technology assistance programs for small manufacturers, and higher education. His latest book (with Gary Henry and George Julnes) is *Evaluation: An Integrated Framework for Understanding, Guiding, and Improving Policies and Programs* (Jossey-Bass, 2000).

Dr. Donna M. Mertens is a Professor in the Department of Educational Foundations and Research at Gallaudet University. She teaches research methods, program evaluation, and educational psychology to deaf and hearing students at the graduate and undergraduate levels. She has conducted research and evaluation studies on topics such as improvement of special education services in international settings, enhancing the education experiences of students with disabilities, preventing sexual abuse in residential schools for deaf students, and improving court access for deaf and hard of hearing people. Her publications are numerous, including: co-editor and contributing author of *Research and Inequality* (with C. Truman and B. Humphries, 2000), author of *Research Methods in Education and Psychology: Integrating Diversity with Quantitative and Qualitative Approaches* (1998), co-author (with John McLaughlin) of *Research Methods in Special Education* (1995), and editor of *Creative Ideas for Teaching Evaluation* (1989). In her work, she integrates the viewpoints of people with disabilities, ethnic/racial minorities, and feminists in order to be inclusive of groups traditionally not represented in the research and evaluation process. As Past-President of the American Evaluation Association (AEA), Dr. Mertens continues to serve on the AEA Board. She is currently providing leadership on two critical on-going issues: First: AEA, through the topical interest group for International and Cross-Cultural Evaluations, recently received a grant to help build an international community of evaluators. She will continue working as AEA's representative on that initiative. Second, she established a priority for increasing diversity in evaluation and AEA. She is serving as the chair of the oversight committee for AEA's Building Diversity in the Profession of Evaluation Initiative, an effort designed to increase diversity in the profession of evaluation and in AEA.

Dr. Michael Scriven is Professor of Psychology at Claremont Graduate University. He is a past president of the American Evaluation Association and the American Educational Research Association. He taught previously at Swarthmore and Berkeley, Minnesota and Indiana, the Universities of San Francisco and Western Australia, in departments of mathematics, philosophy, psychology, and education. He was appointed as a Whitehead Fellow at Harvard, a Fellow at the Center for Advanced Study in the Behavioral Sciences at Stanford, and a Fellow of the Academy of the Social Sciences in Australia. He was awarded the President's Prize of the Evaluation Network, AEA's Lazarsfeld Prize, and is author of 300+ publications in 11 fields, including *The Evaluation Thesaurus* (4th Ed, Sage, 1991), and *Critical Thinking: Its Definition and Assessment* (EdgePress, 1997).

Dr. Edith P. Thomas is the National Program Leader for Nutrition and Food Security in the Families, 4-H and Nutrition Unit of the Cooperative State Research, Education, and Extension Service, U.S. Department of Agriculture, Washington, D.C. She provides national program leadership in determining nutrition education needs and developing program models and evaluation processes for families throughout the life-cycle stages. Dr. Thomas conducts nationwide assessments to report impact data relative to community-based nutrition education programs delivered through the

Land Grant Universities. Dr. Thomas recommends and provides guidance for additional research needs to strengthen extension educational programs relative to nutrition and food security issues. She was the primary author for *A Citizen's Guide to Food Recovery* (U.S. Department of Agriculture, 1998). Dr. Thomas has received a number of awards, including the Founders' Day Award from Fontbonne College, St. Louis, Missouri and the Secretary of Agriculture Team Honor Award for Outstanding Customer Service, June 2000. She is the Immediate Past Chair of the Awards Committee, American Evaluation Association and serves on the Board of Advisory Editors, *New Directions for Evaluation*.

Dr. Joseph S. Wholey is Professor of Public Administration at the University of Southern California and Senior Advisor for Performance and Accountability at the U. S. General Accounting Office. His work focuses on the use of strategic planning, performance measurement, and program evaluation to improve performance, strengthen accountability, and support decision making in public and nonprofit organizations. Before joining the University of Southern California, he served as Deputy Assistant Secretary for Planning and Evaluation at the U. S. Department of Health and Human Services and as Director of Program Evaluation Studies at the Urban Institute. Dr. Wholey is a fellow of the National Academy of Public Administration, the senior author or editor of eight books, and author of many journal articles, book chapters, and reports.

AUTHOR INDEX

A

Agar, M., 100, 102, 103
Aiken, L. S., 118
Alcoff, L., 93
Au, J., 128

B

Bakan, D., 79
Ballweber, C. A., x
Banks, J. A., 93, 169
Baumgardner, M. H., 187
Berger, D., x
Best, S., 77
Bickman, L. B., 122, 125, 127, 131
Binet, A. 153
Birckmayer, J. D., 116, 128
Birman, D. 168
Bledsoe, K., ix
Bloland, H. G., 77, 80
Bronfenbrenner, U., 174
Brunswick, E., 85
Burns, B. J., 125

C

Campbell, D. T., 11, 12, 145, 146, 147,
    148, 151, 152, 153, 154, 155, 159,
    187, 188, 192, 199, 200
Campbell, H., ix
Campbell, R. M., 171
Casad, B. J., 179
Cervantes, A., ix
Chambers, J. M., 189
Chelimsky, E., 93, 198
Chen, H. T., 113 - 115, 117, 130, 132 -
    136, 137, 186
Cook, T. D., 11, 15, 111, 113, 130, 131,
    187, 192, 195, 198
Cordray, D. S., 11
Costanzo, M., x
Cousins, J. B., 195

Craft, M., x
Crano, W. D., 131, 151, 152
Cronbach, L. J., 187, 195
Crosse, S., 112

D

Dagenais, C., 118
Datta, L. E., 197
De Koning, K., 93
Dello Stritto, M. E., 179
Denzin, N. K., 77
DeStefano, L., 94
Donaldson, S. I., 47, 111, 113-117,
    119, 121, 122, 125 - 128, 130- 137,
    145, 146, 183, 186, 187, 192
Downey, M., 51
Droitcour, J., 198
Drucker, P. F., 53
Dugan, M., 72
Dunkel, J., 112
Dwyer, J. H., 127

E

Erlebacher, A. E., 146, 159

F

Feria, A., 179
Festinger, L., 194
Fetterman, D. M., 63, 64, 68, 72, 188,
    190, 192
Fine, M., 93
Fischer, M. M. J., 86
Fishman, D. B., 86
Fiske, D. W., 152
Fitzpatrick, J., 114, 115, 131, 135, 146,
    190
Flaherty, M. P., 97
Flay, B. R., 126
Foxhall, K., 146

SUBJECT INDEX

A

Accountability, 6, 7, 43, 44 - 46, 48, 50, 53, 57, 58, 59, 72, 83, 164, 165, 173, 201
Action theory, 117, 134
AIDS/HIV, 5, 110, 117, 169
Alleged program theory, 22
American Evaluation Association's (AEA) Guiding Principles, 164
Applied psychology, ii, 3, 75, 167
Applied research, 48, 56, 153
Applied social science, ii, 6, 19, 21, 28, 30, 35
At-risk youth, 98

B

Baseline, 43, 68, 69, 113
Between-group non-equivalence design, 147
Bias, 15, 27, 94, 95, 96, 146, 189, 191, 194, 198
Black box evaluation, 81, 113, 131
Brainstorming, 71, 72
Building capacity, 57, 74

C

Coach, 7, 8, 64, 70, 71, 73
Collaboration, 10, 45, 52, 72, 74, 132
Community based programs, 83, 110, 111, 159
Community-based evaluations, 161
Community-devised methods, 85
Comparison group, 147, 148, 149
Compensatory criteria, 39, 40
Compensatory programs, 146 -148, 150
Conceptual theory, 117, 134
Construct validity, 12, 145, 151, 152, 153, 154

Constructivist, 78, 80, 83, 85, 173, 191
Contingency approach, 10, 113, 115
Continuous quality improvement, 136
Control group, 29, 41, 55, 97, 102, 146, 147
Critical friend, 68, 70
Cultural competency, ix, 13, 167, 169, 170, 171, 177, 180
Cultural sensitivity, 13, 104, 168, 177
Culture, 9, 13, 51 - 53, 55, 63, 74, 77, 78, 85, 94, 98, 101, 102, 167 - 169, 171 - 173, 175 - 177, 179

D

Deaf, 100, 101, 103
Democratic, 20, 44, 65, 67, 73, 82, 85, 86, 94
Design sensitivity, 10, 113, 133, 134, 137
Dialogue, 67 - 69
Disabilities, 9, 93, 94, 98, 101, 105
Diversity, 98, 100, 101, 103
Dose-response, 119, 125, 134

E

Ecological contexts, 174
Education programs, 83, 100, 111, 169
Effectiveness evaluation, 45, 48, 49, 50, 72, 135, 137, 162, 186, 192, 198
Efficacy evaluation, 112, 136, 146
Emancipatory, 93, 94, 96, 97, 98
Embracing diversity, 14, 15
Empowerment evaluation, ix, 7, 8, 13, 14, 63 - 68, 70 - 75, 160, 164, 188, 189
Ethical concerns, 97, 161
Ethical theory, 161
Ethnography, 63
Eurocentric research, 78, 84
Evaluability assessment, 22, 115, 133

V

W